INDUSTRIAL SAFETY MANAGEMENT

INDUSTRIAL SAFETY MANAGEMENT

Nasser Elahi

Publications

KALPAZ PUBLICATIONS

DELHI-110052

Industrial Safety Management

Rs. 750

ISBN: 81-7835-503-5

Published in 2006 in India by
Kalpaz Publications
C-30, Satyawati Nagar, Delhi-110052
E-mail : kalpaz@hotmail.com

Laser Typesetting at : Shiva Infosystem, Delhi
Printed at : Salasar Imaging System, Delhi

Contents

Acknowledgements

'The Relationship of Human Factors and Safety Norms with Involvement in Industrial Accidents', is a reflection of my heart felt concern towards the human miseries erupting as a result of industrial hazards inflicting revocable or irrevocable injuries or sometimes causing even the death of the innocent individuals without a fault of their own. Such industrial hazards affect not only the particular organization or its employees but also their families, sometimes the general public and so the society in general. In the wider sense it hits the country economically. In order to explore the various causes of accidents in the domain of my research work and to suggest remedial measures to mitigate the agony of the individuals, I have taken up this upheaval task as a challenge in the interest and benefit of the individuals, the society, the organization and ultimately my country, Iran. Since the industrialization is a universal phenomenon, so my study will directly benefit the entire humanity.

The process of learning about the various aspects of this universal phenomenon started 20 years back and I learned about many things through my experience as a teacher as well as a professional. I got deeply involved with the subject when I practically started collecting information from the NISOC, Iran and the ONGC, India since 1997-98. Ultimately in the year 2000, I got myself registered for this Ph.D. degree in the Faculty of Management Studies, University of Delhi, Delhi, under the supervision of Prof. S.P. Gupta, the Head and Dean of the Faculty. I express my deep and heart felt thanks to Professor S.P. Gupta for providing me an opportunity to work under his able guidance throughout my research for an humanitarian cause. I gained knowledge to enrich my research work from the valuable discussions with my various friends and colleagues specially, Prof. H. Shokrkon, Department of Psychology, Jandi Shapor University, Ahwaz, Iran, Prof. N.K. Chadha, Department of Psychology, University of Delhi, India, Prof. S. Aliul H. Rizvi, Department of Mechanical Engineering, Jamia Millia Islamia, India and Prof. Nisar Ahmad, Head, Department of Commerce and Business Studies, Jamia Millia Islamia, India. For me they were constant source of inspiration and enlightenment and shared my concern all through. I am highly thankful to all of them.

My research would have remained deficient had the top brass, the Managers, the Executives, etc. at the National Iranian South Oil Company (NISOC) and Oil and Natural Gas Corporation Ltd. (ONGC) not given me an opportunity to carry out the required study in their respective organizations. I am thankful to all the members of these organizations.

Since the results of my study are based on the responses of my questionnaire, I am thankful to all the managerial staff at NISOC for participating as subjects in my study and their help in arranging meeting for educating the workers and inspiring them to respond to the questionnaire with all patience and peace of mind. My sincere thanks are due to all the workers who participated in the questionnaire session after performing their eight hour long duty at the dangerous situations to which they were associated and that too in the holy month of 'Ramzan' even before having their 'Iftar'.

I also express my thanks to all the members of staff including the learned Faculty members at the Faculty of Management Studies, University of Delhi, for their valuable discussions and moral support and cooperation.

I would like to express sincere gratitude to my friend Prof. A.K. Singh, Prof. S.D. Sharma and Mr. Madhukar Tewari, B.Sc., for the help received in editing of this dissertation. Without there help it would not have been possible to submit my thesis well in time, and last, but not the least, I express my deepest thankful and gratitude to my wife for her moral support and constant and timely inspiration whenever my confidence shattered. I also express my love to my sons, Amin and Eman, who were source immense strength and moral support throughout the conclusion, and for their patience while they missed me because of my preoccupations with the research work. I would also like to express my thank and gratitude to my mother, who helped me in her own special way at the various stages, and with moral support and blessings.

Nasser Elahi

Abstract

The present study investigates, examines and evaluates the industrial safety under practice in the contemporary Iranian Industrial setups with special reference to Iranian Oil Industries. It deals with the process of formulation and implementation of safety plans and measures in oil industries. In the last decade Iran has experienced large scale Industrial expansion and many heavy industries have come into existence due to the technological advancements. The establishment of heavy industries and the large scale use of sophisticated technologies, are not only charged the nature of risks but also have increased the magnitude of harzards of accidents. The changing nature of occupational accidents and different types of industrial hazards and ailments demand a redical rethinking in all the aspects related to safety norms. Industrial setup have become common for most of the citizens of the country. Citizens life is gradually getting dependent on industries where they work. To avoid human causalities through major or minor accidents or through different kinds of poisonous and hazardous elements through appropriate and required levels of safety measures have become the major concern for industries and for skilled and unskilled human security. The study tries to investigate the reasons behind most of the accidents and take out some common factors responsible for different kinds of accidents. It further suggests some recommendations and leads that can be the part of the safety norms of Iranian Oil Industries in particular and Industries is general.

List of Abbrevation

AC	Aghajari Oil and Gas Producing Company
Acc.	Accident
Acc. Inv.	Accident Involvement
EAI	Extend of Accident Involvement
ALARP	A Level-As Low As Reasonably Practicable
AMA	Adareh Markazi Ahwaz (Tashclat Markazi Ahwaz)
ANSI/UL	American National Standards Institute/Underwriters Laboratories
AOGC	Aghjari Oil and Gas Producing Company
APM	Ahvaz Pipe Mill
API	American Petroleum Institute
ASME	American Society of Mechanical Engineers
ASTM	American Society for Testing and Materials
AWS	American Welding Society
BIP	Bandar Imam Petrochemical Co.
BIS	Bureau of Indian Standards
BMCT	Bennett Mechanical Comprehension Tests
BPD	Barrels Per Day
BOE	Barrels of Equivalent
BS	British Standards Institution
BSI	British Standards Institute
Buld	Building
CBM	Coal Bed Methane
COC	Caspian Oil Co.
CRBC	Central Region Business Center
DAYs L	Days Lost
DIA	Directorate of International Affairs (Marketing and Export)
DII	Disabling Injury Index
DMR	German Standards
DGMS	Directorate General of Mines Safety
EMS	Environmental Management Systems
EJMA	Expansion Joint Manufacturers Association

Engg	Engineering
E and P	Exploration and Production
Er	Error
ERBC	Eastern Region Business Center
ESA	External Safety Audit
ESC	Exploration Services Co.
EAI	Extend of Accident Involvement
Ext of Acc. Inv.	Extend of Accident Involvement
F	Fatal
FF	F Test
FIT	Flannagan Industrial Test Form-A (Mechanics)
Fr.	Frequency Rate
Frqu	Frequency
Gc	Gachsaran Oil and Gas Producing Company
GOGC	Gachsaran Oil and Gas Producing Company
HMO	Home Office (Fire Department) Fire
HP	Heavy Products: Fuel oil, bitumen, furfural extract, stack wax and mulch
I/O	Industrial/ Organization
IO and GPT	Institute of Oil and Gas Production Technology
IADC	International Association of Drilling Contractors
IDT	Institute of Drilling Technology (IDT), Dehradun.
IDT	Institute of Drilling Technology
IEE	Institution of Electrical Engineers
IEEE	Institute of Electrical and Electronic Engineers
IEOT	Institute of Engineering and Ocean Technology
IMD	Institute of Management Development
IMO	International Maritime Organization
INBIGS	Institute of BioTechnology and GeoTechonics Studies
IO & GPT	Institute of Oil and Gas Production Technology.
IOOC	Iranian Offshore Oil Co.
IP	Institute of Petroleum
IPS	Iranian Petroleum Standards
IPSEM	Institute of Petroleum Safety and Environment Management
IRS	Institute of Reservior Studies
IS	International Standards
ISO	International Organization for Standardization
ISPEM	Institute of Petroleum Safety and Environment Management

KOGPC	Karron Oil and Gas Producing Company
KDMIPE	Keshava Deva Malvija Institute of Petroleum Exploration
KMO	Bartlett's Test of Spercity-Klpan Meir
Ld. Fac.	Loading Factor
LPG	Light Products Gasoline
MC	Marun Oil and Gas Producing Company
MOGC	Marun Oil and Gas Producing Company
MD	Middle Distillates: Kerosene, gas oil, heavy jet fuel, base oil, lubricating oil
MI	Minor
MIS.C	Masjid-I-Suleyman Oil and Gas Producing Company
MIS.OGC	Masjid-I-Suleyman Oil and Gas Producing Company
MRBC	Mumbai Region Business Center
MSS	Manufacturers Standardization Society
MVT	Mines Vocational Training
NACE	National Association of Corrosion Engineers
NEMA	National Electrical Manufacturers Association
NF	NON-FATAL
NFC	National Fires Codes
NFPA	National Fire Protection Association
NIDC	National Iranian Drilling Co.
NIGC	National Iranian Gas Co.
NICOC	National Iranian Central Oil Co.
NIOC	National Iranian Oil Co.
NISOC	National Iranian South Oil Co.
NIORDC	National Iranian Oil Refining and Distribution Company
NITC	National Iranian Tanker Co.
NRBC	Northern Region Business Center
NPC	National Petrochemical Co.
OISD	Oil Industry Safety Directors
OMR	Oil Mines Regulations
ONGC	Oil and Natural Gas Cooperation Limited
OPEC	Organization of Petrolleum Exporting Countries
Org	Organization
PFP	Practical Fire Protection GW Underdown
PME	Periodical Medical Examination
POGC	Pars Oil and Gas Co.
PPE	Personal Protective Equipment
Prcnt	Percentage
QAS	Quality Assurance Systems
QRA	Risk Analysis

RPC	Razi Petrochemical Co.
RR	Relative Risk
SR	Severity Rate
SFELC	Standard Foam Equipment and Liquid Concentrate 1989
Sig.	Significant
SIS	Standardizing Commission I Sverige
SMC	Sulfur Mono Chloride
SR	Severity Rate
S.N.	Safety Norms
SPSS	Special Programme for Social Science
SRBC	Southern Region Business Center
SRV	Experience
SS	S Test
Std.	Standard
Deviation	Standard Deviation
Std. Er.	Standard Error
SS	S Test
Tech. Edu.	Technical Education
TOT	Total
TT	T Test
UMD	Understanding of Mechanical Dynamic
UL	Underwriters Laboratories
Varb	Variable

List of Tables, Charts and Figures

Charts and Figures

1
Introduction

Need, Significance and Scope of Research Study

The twenty-first century has been recognized as the age of common man. Sine dubio, there has been as increasing appreciation of the importance of human needs both industrially and socially. Complex and competitive nature of industrial life, new products, new methods, new machines, new control techniques all are posing a tough challenge to the traditional approach to manpower placement and management. After the World War II, there was tremendous growth of industrial in the developing world world have been growing by leaps and bounds leading and education in the developing world have been grwoing by leaps and bounds leading to frequent occurrence of occupational accidents causing more industrial hazards.

Since the last few decades while the industry is amazingly prospering towards modern technology, it entailed complicated production techniques inherently associated with many dangers. In the event of an accident the tragedy may cause serious major irrevocable damage. It has been observed that industrialization and complexity of industrial activities have raised the serious problem of occupational accidents in the form of industrial hazards or ailments. The heavy and large industries like mining, steel, petrochemicals, pharmaceuticals, dyes and paints, pneumatic, pesticide, beverage, power generation, textiles, food processing, chemicals, ceramics, shipping, railways, roadways, aviation, nuclear energy, etc., are always exposed to major accidents. Such industries employ a huge number of manpower ranging from a few thousand to millions. And so, even the intensity of the accident is small, a large number of employees get involved without a fault of their own.

The previous studies reveal that so many factors are responsible for major industrial accidents including the most frequently occurring phenomena, the negligence. One or the other factor has always been found to cause an accident. So, the heavy industries are always prone to have major accidents. This accident proneness nature of heavy industries does not tend us to conclude that we should not have such industries. While taking a positive view of the scenario we find that development and industrialization, have made emphatic contributions to health including personal and social wealth. It has vastly improved health and education services, transportation, communication and various other amenities. Unquestionably, on the global scale longevity has improved and people are healthier than they were centuries and even decades ago. On the other hand, industrialization has had adverse health consequences not only for workforces but for the general population as well. These effects have been caused either directly by exposure to industrial hazards and harmful agents or indirectly through environmental degradation locally and globally. The environmental health hazards, like occupational health hazards, may be biological, chemical, physical, biomechanical or psychosocial in nature. They include traditional hazards of poor sanitation and shelter, as well as agricultural and industrial contamination of air, water, food and land. Such hazards have caused detrimental health impacts, ranging from catastrophic direct effects like the recent cholera epidemic in Latin America and the chemical poisoning outbreak in Bhopal India (Bhopal, India 1985, had Environmental Hazard in Methylisocyanate, as Acute Lung Disease, which caused 2,000 deaths and 200,000 poisoned), to chronic effects (like Love Canal tragedy in USA). Environmental health impacts thus include the indirect effects of industrial disruption of the adequate food and housing, as well as the degradation of the global systems on which the health of the planet depends. (Stellman, 1998: pp. 53.2).

- In this study the main emphasis is on the occurrence of accidental hazard. So, the term *accident* needs an explanation since the researchers have used it in wider sense.
- By definition all the following must be regarded as constituting an *accident*: (1) All errors or slip 'near accidents' which result in an injury; (2) all unplanned events resulting in minor injury; (3) all unplanned events resulting in major or lost time injuries which incapacitate; and (4) all unplanned events resulting in death.

- Other scholars are of the view that all accidents are incidents but all incidents are not accidents. All injuries result from accidents but all accidents do not result in injury. An accident is an unexpected, unplanned event in a sequence of events that occurs through a combination of causes; it results in physical harm (injury or disease) to an individual, damage to property, a near miss,·a loss or any combination of these effects. (L. Banlor in Ridley, 1995, p. 125).
- Further, an accident is an incident, which occurs as the effect of string factors; or an accident is an incident, which invariably results from a completed sequence of factors culminating in the accident itself. Accident is a casualty or unforeseen event, usually characterized by suddenness and external force or violence. Or it is applied most frequently to an unfortunate happening that causes death or personal injury or damage to or loss of property, or an accident is an occurrence that could not have been prevented by the exercise of ordinary care. (Encyclopaedia Americana, 1993: p. 80).

So, from the views expressed above, it is clear that accidents, when they occur, cause disaster howsoever big or small it may be. Now, let us have a look at other forms of disasters like flood, fire, earthquake, etc. occurring around the world.

Over the past few decades, disaster data on a global level reveal a distinct pattern with two main features: an increase over time of the number of people affected, and a geographical correlation (International Federation of Red Cross and Red Crescent Societies (IFRCRCS, 1993) reports the number of events for individual disaster types. This figure reveals the significance fact that the item 'Accidents' includes all sudden human-made events, and is second only to 'Flood' in frequency. 'Storm' is in third place, followed by 'Earthquake' and 'Fire'. So, this fact leads us to conclude that accidents are the most disastrous *human-made events* occurring most frequently and killing largest number of people all over the world (Fig. 2), injuring thousands and rendering millions homeless over the years.

Now, let us have a look at the most serious disaster in the past. Bhopal (India) represents, probably, the worst chemical industrial disaster ever (Das 1985a, 1985b; Friedrich Naumann Foundation 1987, Tachakra 1987). In this devastating event gas leak caused a deadly cloud to spread over the city of Bhopal, in central India, leaving thousands dead and hundreds of thousands injured within a span of a few hours.

Figure 1.1 = 1967-91: Total number of event for each type of disaster

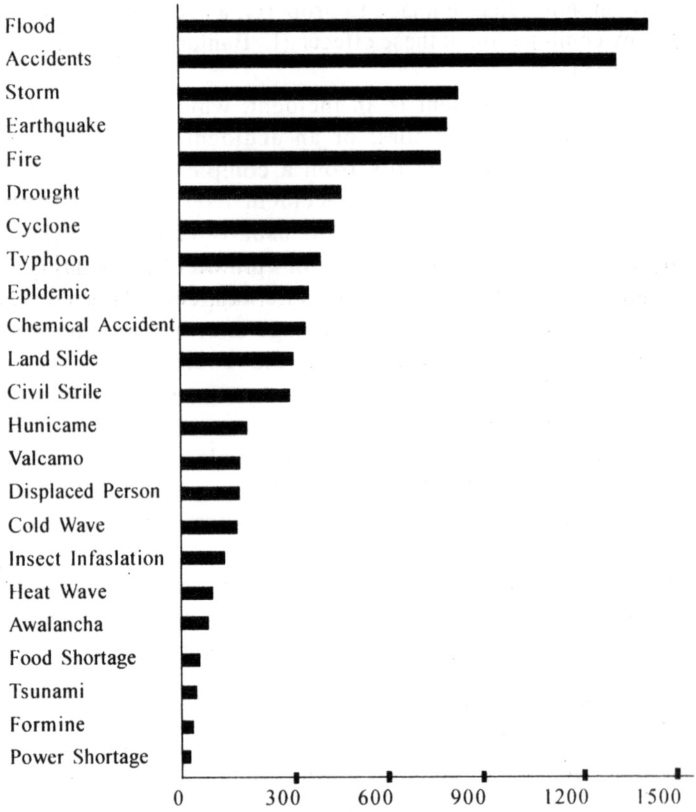

Fig.1: The Number of Events for Individual Disaster Types.

The other significant fact, which is a matter of great concern, is that the disaster affects every country of the world, but it is the poorest countries where people most frequently lose their lives. Fig. 2 shows the countries most severely affected by major disasters in 1991. Position of India and Iran in this figure.

Figure 1.2 Number of people dead from major disasters in 1991: Top 20 countries

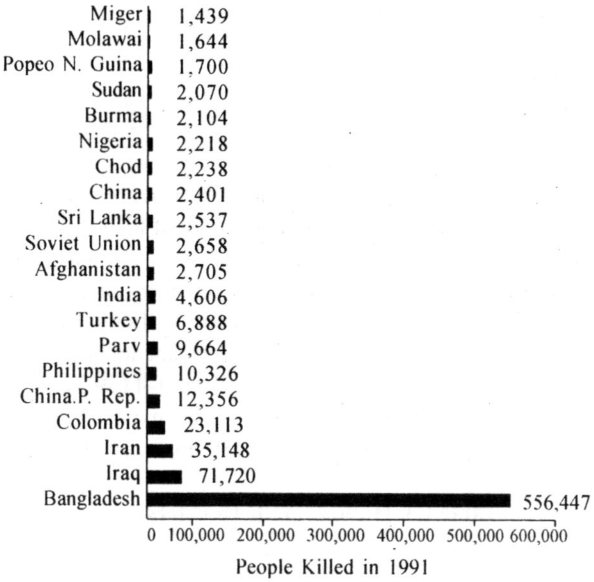

Fig. 2: The Countries Most Severely Affected by Major Disasters in 1991

Table 1.1: Non-Natural Accident (Technological Accidents)

	Accident	*Technological accident*	*Fire*	*Total*
Killed	3,419	603	3,300	7,321
Injured	1,596	5,564	699	7,859
Affected	17,153	52,704	32,771	102,629

Source: Walker 1995.

The data in Table (1-2 & 1-3 (39.7 & 39-9)) reveals the fact that Asian countries are the most affected regions in the world with major accidents.

Table 1.2: The grouped disaster (Non-Natural Accident)

	Africa	*America*	*Asia*	*Europe*	*Ocean*	*Total*
Accident	213	321	679	274	18	1,502
Technological accident	24	97	97	88	4	310
Fire	37	115	236	166	29	583

Source: Walkr, 1995.

Although agencies measure the severity of disaster by the number of people killed, it is becoming increasingly important also to look at the number *affected.* Across the world, *almost a thousand times more people are affected by disaster than are killed* and, for many of these people, survival after the disaster is becoming increasingly difficult, leaving them more vulnerable to future shocks. This point is relevant not only for natural disasters, but also for *human-made* disasters (Table 1-4 (39.3), especially in the case of chemical accidents whose effects on exposed people may become apparent after years or even decades (Stellman, 1998: pp. 39.2-3).

Table 1.3: Human-made Disasters

	Africa	*America*	*Asia*	*Europe*	*Ocean*	*Total*
Killed	16,172	3,765	2,204	739	18	22.898
Injured	236	1,030	5,601	483	476	7.826
Affected	3,694	48,825	41,630	7,870	670	102.629
Homeless	2,384	1,722	6,275	7,664	24	18,069

Taking into consideration the multidimensional view of the accidents, we are concerned with unexpected events that cause a negative effect on productivity or other aspects of performance (Cf. Meister, 1987). The negative effects could be due to workers' injury, loss of time, damage to equipment, or loss of material. Whatever their forms, accidents are costly to organizations, with annual estimated losses in the tens of billions of dollars. (Mackeven, 1995: p. 454).

According to International Labour Office statistics, 120 million occupational accidents occur annually at workplaces worldwide. Of these, 210,000 are fatal accidents. Every day, more than 500 men or women do not come home because they were killed by accidents at work. These are dramatic numbers, which nonetheless draw fairly little public attention. Considering the fact that accidents are taking a considerable economic toll from nations, companies and individuals, accidents do not get much publicity. (Stellman, 1998: p. 56.2).

In Iran, in 1982, there have been, in total, 14074 cases of occupational accidents in plants and factories, which has caused the loss of more than 300 thousand workdays. Furthermore, during this year, more than 53 million Tomans have been paid to workers as unemployment benefit while on sick leave, and more than 8 million Tomans paid as compensation for deficient limbs, a total of 61 million Tomans. The Organization's expenses on pensions paid to the lost workers' relatives show a 2 million Tomans increase in 1984. According to Adareh Cole Bazrasi Vazarat Car and Omoreh Ajtehmaeh, a total of 2179 occupational accidents were reported in 1986. (Zahedi, 1369: p. 166).

So, from the above stated facts, figures and tables, it is quite evident that an industrial accident is a human made event and its severity can be judged by the frequency of its occurrence which is several times more than natural disasters, universality of the phenomena affecting the poor countries the most, resulting in a loss of large number of human lives, affecting innocent people far beyond the place of their occurrence and leaving behind shocked family, relatives and in general the society, because of the irreparable loss and the question of survival for the affected.

Really the losses due to industrial accidents are phenomenal and call for immediate attention of the scientists, engineers, doctors, psychologists, social thinkers, industrialists, managers, etc. to address the situation for the salvation of human sufferings.

The phenomenon of industrial accidents is as old as the industry itself. Many researchers have tried to look into the causes of these industrial accidents to mitigate the agony caused by disasters and to reduce the frequency of their occurrence. They have studied the problem in their own perspectives and provided viable solutions. Some of the previous studies and their outcome is being discussed here to have an over all view of the situation.

In the twentieth and twenty-first centuries, the worst non-natural disasters in human suffering and death have been caused by wars, transport and industrial activities. At first, industrial disasters mainly affected people engaged in specific occupations, but later, particularly after the Second World War, with the rapid growth and expansion of the chemical industry and the use of nuclear power, these occurrences led to serious dangers even to the people outside work areas, and to the general environment. A common feature is that they usually are uncontrolled events involving fires, explosions or releases of toxic substances that result either in the death and injury of large number of people inside or outside the plant causing extensive property and environmental damage, or both. Fires occur in industry more frequently than explosions and toxic releases, although the consequences in terms of loss of life are generally less. Better prevention and preparedness might be the explanation. Chlorine and ammonia are the toxic chemicals most commonly used in major hazardous quantities, and both have a history of major accidents. The release of flammable or toxic materials in the atmosphere may also lead to fires. (Stellman, 1998: pp. 39.2-3).

The other researcher is of the view that different psycho-physiological qualities may affect the liability to accidents of individuals working in similar environmental situations. The more important of these can be listed as: Health, Age and Experience, Alcohol and Fatigue.

It is a well-known fact that many physical defects can place individuals at a disadvantage in certain situations. Defect of the senses, height, strength, neuro-muscular co-ordination, rapidity of reaction, etc. may predispose individuals to accidents in occupations which make heavy demands upon these factors.

Some of the accident factors could be due to lack of safety equipment, lack of tools, wrong tools or damaged tools, equipments and machines, lack of discipline and the mechanical malfunctioning of machines and apparatuses. There are also the non-observance of the safety rules and regulations, personal difficulties, lack of medical service, lack of safety training, and lack of experience. Still other dangers result from workers themselves from tendencies to engage in risk or dangerous work behavior or from fatigue and stress. The two main criteria used are length of time on the job and accident rate. This very high labour turnover is not characteristic of normal times although turnover is sufficiently large to be a problem. (Brown, 1948: p. 478)

Despite this worrying situation, international awareness of the magnitude of the problem remains surpassingly modest. The inadequate dissemination of knowledge and information hampers action, especially in developing countries. It also limits the capacity to design and implement effective policies and programmes. To reduce the human suffering and financial loss associated with these risks, there is a need for increased and sustained action to protect occupational health and safety, and the environment. (Alli, 2001: pp. 9-11)

The chemical and petrochemical industries have shown leadership in this area worldwide. As a result of major catastrophes, such as Bhopal and Chernobyl, the use of the new predicative techniques has increased. Remarkable progress has been made since the mid-'70s in the area of safety. Many governments have also been leaders in making safety analysis mandatory. Sweden, Finland, Japan and Federal Republic of Germany have all reduced fatal occupational accidents by 60 to 70 per cent during this time. Many other countries show similar progress. Now, the challenge is to transfer our knowledge from research into practical applications and further improve our preventive efforts.

One of the new steps in safety management is the notion of *safety culture*. It may be a difficult concept, since culture is not a visible entity. It is an abstract concept prevailing within an organization or society. There are no direct ways of adjusting it. Safety culture is, however, a crucial concept for understanding the possibilities of prevention. (Stellman, 1998: p.56.2)

According to U.S. Bureau of the Census, (1993), workplaces have improved since safety legislation has been enacted in 1970, the death rate from accidents in the U.S. workplace was 18 deaths per 100,000 workers, but in 1990 the rate was only 9 deaths per 100,000 workers. Similarly the rate of disabling injuries fell 18 per cent during that period. (Mackeven, 1995: p.460)

However, an understanding of the 'cause and effect' relation of the accident-causing factors is required before continuous improvement of safety processes can be undertaken.

In this research factors responsible for the occurrence of accidents have been divided into two categories: 1. Non-Human Factors (Direct Factors) or Technological (visible) Factors including safety norms such as (Safety Rules and Discipline, Worker's Safety Delegate, Safety Equipment, Safety Personnel Equipment, Safety Committees, Safety Officials etc.), 2. Human Factors (Indirect Factors) or Invisible Factors including Individual Characteristics and Cognitive Ability, such as: Employee's Age, Job Experience, Understanding of Mechanical Dynamics, sociopath attitudes and post behaviors, delinquent and law breaking, marital and strife, disregard for other people, immaturity, emphasis on exaggerated masculinity (for males) hostility and angers irresponsibility, superficial social relationships, self-centredness, alcoholism, aggressive attitudes, physical violence, impassivity, and authority problem. A worker high on this 'neurotic-anxious' factor would tend to be anxious, tension-ridden, panicky, unduly sensitive to criticism, indecisive, unable to concentrate, easily fatigued, depressed, emotionally labile, easily intimidated, and with feelings of inadequacy. Overall, *it appears that these Factors including (Safety Norms, Individual Characteristics and Cognitive Ability), have close relationship with Industrial Accident*, so an in-depth study is required to be made before recalling any conclusion. The researcher's aim is to study some of the related compilations of their characteristics including (Safety Norms, Employee Age, Job Experience and Understanding of Mechanical Dynamics), with accident involvement on NIOCs' employees.

Iran is the first nation in the Middle East and the second in the world (after Mexico), to have nationalized its oil industry (in 1951). In addition, Iran is also one of the founding member countries of the OPEC. It helped to set up the OPEC in 1960 with the prime objective of safeguarding the interests of oil producing nations. And today Iran is commonly viewed as the stronghold of the Middle East's petroleum industry. It is not only instrumental in augmenting and galvanizing the nation's economy, but also contributing considerably to future development of other nations in fulfilling their requirements for obtaining this valuable commodity. Iran is a pioneering country in Oil Industry. The drilling for oil wells first started in the west of Iran in 1901 and then in the south of Iran (NIOC). National Iranian Oil Company in Iran is one of the largest Iranian Industries and the only Iranian Oil Industry, with approximately 18,000 personnel.

A tremendous investment in Oil Industry after 1970, and a rapid growth of this industry in developing countries caused the owners and managers of large companies to pay more attention to safety issues and maintain the growth of production, particularly with respect to the causes of increase in accidents vis-à-vis the rate of growth of production. Of course, statistical figures of accident in developed and industrial countries are not less than those in developing countries.

This study has sought to minimize the accidents by developing a composite measure of accident behaviour. The purpose of this research was to construct and test a causal model of accident process.

This study proposes several causal parameters regarding accident risks: (1) Greater exposure to risk will lead to higher accident rates. (2) Cognitive ability will causally affect the accident risk rating of employees' jobs, because more mentally alert and capable workers are generally assigned jobs with greater skill requirements, responsibility, and accident potential. (3) Likewise, employees with high emotional stability would be assigned demanding jobs. (4) Because many individuals are promoted to higher skill jobs on the basis of greater experience; tenure should cause placement in higher risk positions. (5) Similarly, the older employee is to hold a job with greater responsibility and skill requirements. (6) Working in higher risk jobs is stressful (Manuso, 1983). Stress often leads to situation problems, which prompt one to become involved in counselling (Beeh and Newman, 1978). In fact, it has been estimated that as much as 75 per cent of all machinery accidents could have been prevented if proper precautions had been taken.

Industries in Iran and India do not have long history. However, the present rapid growth and diversification of industries has been possible only due to the planned process of industrial development during the last two decades. This quick process of drafting workers with an agrarian background into the industrial environment, under conditions of tension, high speed, intricate and revolving machines full of hazards, have brought to the fore the invention of welfare of the people as a major objective of national economic advancement. Since hazardous situation is present everywhere i.e. homes, roads, industries etc., and NISOC is not an exception to it. So long as these hazards are controllable and manageable, no incident/ accident occurs. The loss of control over these hazards either due to personal factor or environmental factor results into disequilibria of man, machine and environment. This causes release of energy from the system in uncontrollable manner and hits the person, machine, equipment, property or all. The severity of damage/loss depends upon the intensity of energy. The typical research design has been:

1. together data from previous 6 years 'accidents' record within NIOC's employees. In this research the subjects, should have minimum 5 years continuous experience in production and maintenance related jobs in NIOC.
2. the main data will be collated information from employees record and complete questionnaires.
3. to divide measurements of individual characteristics on all subjects.
4. in this study, partial correlation could be used to assess the relationship between Industrial Accidents and independent variables such as, Personality Characteristics, Individual, Characteristics and Cognitive Ability.

In this research, the Human Factors including Safety Norms, Individual Characteristics and Cognitive Ability and their relationship with Industrial Accident have been studied. The researcher's aim is to study some of the related compilations of these characteristics (including Safety Norms, Employee Age, Job Experience and Understanding of Mechanical Dynamics), with accident involvement on NIOC's employees. Because it is believed that these factors have relationship with accident involvement in NIOC's employees.

The Safety Norms, Employee Age, Job Experience and Cognitive Ability, Understanding of Mechanical Dynamics (Mechanical Perception and Understanding), have independent causal effects on the accident criterion, in NIOC's even when the effects of accident risk and involvement in counselling were controlled. (The present study takes this research a step further by proposing and testing a causal model of the accident process. The proposed accident model is presented as a pitch diagram in Fig. 3.)

This model shows that:

1. Safety Norms have relationship with Accident Involvement on NIOC.
2. Understanding of Mechanical Dynamics (UMD) has relationship with Accident Involvement.

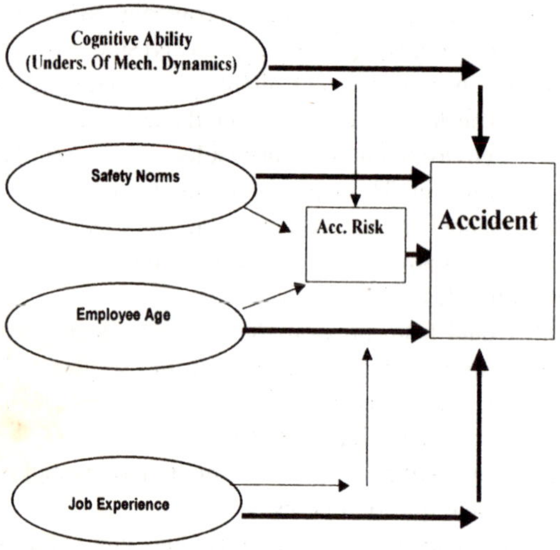

Fig. 3. Accident Model Diagram.

3. Employee Age has relationship with Accident Involvement.
4. Job Experience has relationship with Accident Involvement.
5. Accident Risk has relationship with Safety Norms, Employee Age, JobExperience and Understanding of Mechanical Dynamics and on the other hand they have relationship with Accident Involvement. To conclude, greater exposure to risk will lead to higher accident rate and involvement.
   - 5.1 Accident Risks have relationship with Safety Norms
   - 5.2 Accident Risks have relationship with Employee Age
   - 5.3 Accident Risks have relationship with Job Experience
   - 5.4 Accident Risks have relationship with Understanding of Mechanical Dynamics
   - 5.5 Accident Risks have relationship with Accident Involvement

The linear combination of Safety Norms, Employee Age, Job Experience and Understanding of Mechanical Dynamics is related to accident involvement in NIOC's employees. The predicative variable of Safety Norms, Employee Age, Job Experience and Understanding of Mechanical Dynamics is related to accident involvement.

So, generally the researcher believes that the independent variables, such as, Safety Norms, Individual, Characteristics and Cognitive ability, have relationship with Accident Involvement.

The proposed accident model is presented as a pitch diagram in Fig. 3. The variables included are Safety Norms, the understanding of Mechanical Dynamics, Employee Age, Job Experience, involvement in accident risk and accident involvement. As the diagram in Fig. (3) shows, there is no relationship among the four original variables. Each of these four original variables had direct relation with 'accident involvement' and indirect relation with intermediary variables of 'accident risk'. It has been assumed that there is relation between intermediary variable of 'accident risk' and variable basis of 'accident involvement'.

The study revealed that:

1. Safety Norms are related positively with Accident Involvement.
2. Understanding of Mechanical Dynamics, is related positively with Accident Involvement.
3. Employee Age is related positively with Accident Involvement.
4. Job Experience is related positively with Accident Involvement.
5. Accident Risks are related negatively with Accident Involvement, and greater exposure to risk will lead to higher accident risk and involvement.

In order to make the research systematic and practical the entire study was carried out in two stages. First stage was to standardize the questionnaire and make it more comprehensible. For the response, 60 victim employees were interviewed randomly (Open Ended) as a random sample and 120 victim employees were practically given the written self-devised inventory to complete the query.

After formulating the idea about the accident variables through the study and the responses of the victims, I prepared a questionnaire to test the accident variables in the sample. This stratified random sample included 600 employees (365 non-victim and 235 victims) to whom the standard tests of BMCT (S & T) of Bennett and FIT of Flanagan were given. The employees were selected randomly from NISOC.

The outcome of the research has been divided into seven chapters. Chapter I is introductory chapter and it gives the historical background of the industry and industrial accidents mentioning the various kinds of accidents, natural as well as human-made. The magnitude and the amount of devastation caused by the human-made accidents have also been discussed with adequate reference to the previous researches.

The nature of accidents, hypothesis, major divisions of the study, basic definitions of the terms have also been discussed along with chapter wise classification of the entire study. In the end what the researcher hopes from the results of the study has also been added.

The second chapter presents the demography of the NIOC of Iran and ONGC of India. Both of these organizations' companies (NISOC and ONGC) have been studied with respect to manpower, maximum number of accidents, the personnel lost, the working days lost, the number of road accidents, the number of fire accidents, the place of occurrence of the accidents (Derrick Floor), etc. The study has also been made regarding causes of occurrence of accidents, such as, Strike against or by Objects or Slip and Fall of person, the part of body injured (Upper Limb), whether the accident was fatal, non-fatal, whether it was mine or non-mine accident, the time of occurrence of accident, i.e., during which hours of duty the accident occurred (10.00-12.00 o'clock) and the specific years in which maximum number of accident occurred in an individual company.

Chapter three presents the standard of safety norms, which are being used in NISOC of Iran and ONGC of India. The implementation and impact of their safety rules, regulations, measures and polices, has been studied of these two organizations. Also, the norms followed by other safety organizations for education, training, training evaluation and personal safety protective equipment has also been discussed.

Chapter four deals with the review of previous literature on the subject. The study of this literature forms the basis of this research work. The basic theories of accident proneness, perception of risk, accident prevention, safety norms, human factors specially, cognitive ability, experience and age as individual characteristics have been discussed, in this chapter.

The fifth Chapter has been devoted to the main issues involved in the study of safety of values, sampling features, explanation of the means and methods used to test the hypotheses. This chapter deals with the methodology of the present investigation. An attempt has been made to present a summary review of the statement of the problem, its rationale and objectives, the samples, tools and techniques used, process of data collection, sample testing and statistical treatment of data.

Further, the model of hypotheses evolved for the study to ascertain the relationship between value congruency, bio-data variables and employee commitment has also been discussed. This relationship is ascertained in the present chapter by resorting to the bivariate analysis of the data collected from the sample respondents.

It is important to mention here that during the course of study two new aspects (factors), that is, *"Lack of attention to the humanitarian aspects in the organization (NISOC), in relation to safety aspects"* and

"Carelessness from management side towards general personnel's problems", have came to light which are responsible to cause an accident to a large extent. These aspects have been discussed and analyzed in detail in this chapter. For the statistical analysis, statistical techniques, such as, Descriptive Statistics (Mean, Standard Deviation, etc.) and Inferential Statistics (Factor Analysis, Reliability, Correlation, etc.) have been used to get the desired results.

In Chapter six, the results of the study have been thoroughly discussed in the light of the research findings of the previous studies carried out by researchers from time to time. The chapter ends up by highlighting the practical implications of the study for the industrial safety in general and the sample NISOC organization in particular.

To determine the central tendencies and dispersion of the distribution of the scores obtained on the variables, study of skewness and kurtosis were tested for both the groups, that is Group I (victim) and Group II (non-victim), in NISOC for all variables.

The 't-test' is applied to compare the mean responses of different variables on both the groups and it shows good reliability. This consisted Factor Analysis for shortening the questionnaire for main factors.

In order to understand the relationship between different variables selected in the present study, correlation were computed separately for the two groups.

To study the extent of Accident Involvement in NISOC, as dependent variables and the rest of the variables as independent variables, stepwise Multiple Regression has been used in different ways for different factors.

Before shortening the questionnaire for Reliability, tools, such as, Spearman Brown, Guttman, Split-half, and Alpha-Grombach have been used. The normalised beta coefficient suggested that the relative contribution was significantly above 1 per cent level.

Owing to the formalities involved, people from all the departments of NISOC could not be taken as a sample for the study. The sample may not be truly random. The sample was taken on the basis of non-probability incidental sampling technique, which is characterized by collecting data from the available individuals of the population.

Since this study deals with confidential matters of the company, it is perhaps impossible to avoid altogether all sampling errors. Hesitation to put down factors on papers in such organizations (in fact it is everywhere) is a part of 'human nature'. People hesitated to give their identify in the questionnaires. So, the researcher didn't ask respondents to give their name in the questionnaire.

Moreover, the length of the questionnaire was too big to welcome anyone to complete it peacefully with interest. So, the investigator really encouraged them by constant persuasion. Comprehensibility of the questionnaire and responding it carefully was not frequent but this fact made the sample limited.

The last chapter that is Chapter seven, deals with the suggestions and recommendations based on this research work to be implemented in all the industries prone to have major accidents specifically the petrochemical industry. I hope, when these measures are adopted and a *safety culture* is developed among the organizations, managers and workers, we can minimize the accident rate to have accident proof industry in the world while reducing human agony due to accidents.

2
The Organisations Studies Demographic Profile and Industrial Accidents in N.I.O.C. (NISOC)

Brief History

According to NIOC's catalogues and brochures, the following information has been compiled.

A number of exploration wells drilled in the southern Iran and its western boarder regions, laid the foundations of the national Oil Industry at the onset of 20th century, and after 7 years of relentless efforts, the first well drilled in Naftoon area of Masjid-e-Suleiman, toward oil at the depth of 360 metres on 26th May 1908.

The operation, for the first time, was a proof of the availability of oil of considerable quantity in Iran, which as an initiator of oil operations in the Middle East region, joined the rank of the few world oil producing countries.

A number of other wells were also drilled in Masjid-e-Suleiman; and the Masjid-e-Suleiman-Abadan pipeline was constructed, and the Abadan Refinery with a daily capacity of 2400 barrels went on stream in 1912 as the first oil refinery in the Middle East.

Booming oil industry and trade in Iran, resulted in the collection of geological information in the region, and ultimately new onshore and offshore oil reserves were discovered and the relevant fields were connected to the production network. Production units were installed in the oil-rich regions of the country and huge crude export terminals were built in Persion Gulf.

Pipeline networks transported oil, gas and petroleum products to production units, export terminals, oil and gas refineries, and petrochemical complexes. Oil production and export gained greater momentum and rose beyond the 6-million b/d level. Because of the growing domestic need for petroleum products, several other refineries were also constructed throughout the country. Installation of huge petrochemical plants, centralisation of activities related with oil, gas and petrochemical industries, establishment of the petroleum university, expansion of R and D centres, with special focus on exploration are some of the major steps taken in this direction. Four decades after its birth, the oil industry in Iran was nationalised as a result of the religious and political leader's campaigns and the all-out support of the nation.

Nationalisation of Iran's oil industry is considered a major economic and political event of the second half of the 20th century, especially for the oil producing countries of the Middle East. Although the relevant nationalisation law did not enter into force because of the 1953 *coup d'etat*, the victory of the Islamic Revolution opened the way for its implementation, and after a quarter century of delays, Iran's oil industry was fully freed from foreign domination.

In the course of 8 years of imposed war with Iraq, Iran's oil industry which played a key role in the nation's economy, suffered immense attacks and damages because of the proximity of the oil producing regions and installations to the frontlines. During those years of sacred defence and economic sanctions, Iranian oil industry's experts carried out operations of epic proportion and magnitude. Maintaining the flow of petroleum exports and the required fuel for domestic consumption. But the results of cumbersome efforts also left behind hundreds of martyrs and disabled in operational units.

Based on the sublime goals of the Islamic system, Iran's oil industry is pursuing independence in planning and decision making, non-reliance, and endeavours for self-sufficiency as the most top items on its agenda. In the international oil politics arena, this approach is most evident, especially in Iran's membership in the Organization of Petroleum Exporting Countries (OPEC). Besides, the technical capabilities of the petroleum industry's experts have enabled them to provide their technical and advisory services to other countries. The petroleum industry of Iran is fully gratified and honoured for being run by domestic experts and talented manpower, which makes Iran's position among the oil producers of the world very unique and exclusive.

Organization Structure and Human Resources

- National Iranian Oil Company
- National Iranian Oil Refining and Distribution Co.
- National Iranian Gas Co.
- National Petrochemical Co.
- Human Resources
- Training Provided by NIOC and NIORDC

New, advanced technologies have slowed and even reversed the depletion of oilfields. In the upstream section, technology is helping to reduce costs and risks and in downstream operations, new catalysts increase productivity and facilitate more environment-friendly products.

In today's competitive markets and complex circumstances, costs should be reduced to the minimum extent possible. During 1998-99, the organisational structure of NIOC and other affiliated companies were improved. This improvement, on the one hand, makes it possible to decentralize authority that was formerly the preserve of directorates and, on the other hand, activities can be monitored by employing suitable methods.

Constant upgrading of organisational structures makes it possible to reduce costs and encourages improvement in scientific and technological skills.

With regard to the broad scope of Iranian Oil Industry, it is recognised that activities should be decentralised more to achieve higher productivity. Following changes were made to the organisational structures of the affiliated companies :

National Iranian Oil Company

In the new organisational structure, the National Iranian Oil Company comprises seven subsidiary companies as follows :

1. National Iranian South Oil Co.
2. Iranian Offshore Oil Co.
3. Pars Oil and Gas Co.
4. Caspian Oil Co.
5. Exploration Services Co.
6. National Iranian Central Oil Co.
7. General Services and Oil Industry Health Care Co.

During 1998-99, 27 specialised companies were registered to be in line with NIOC's organisational restructuring.

National Iranian Oil Refining and Distribution Co.

Due to the changing circumstances in downstream sector, the National Iranian Oil Refining and Distribution Co. has improved its organisational chart such that each refinery will henceforth act as an independent firm. These refineries are:

1. Tehran Oil Refining Co.
2. Bandar Abbas Oil Refining Co.

3. Kermanshah Oil Refining Co.
4. Shiraz Oil Refining Co.
5. Shazand (Arak) Oil Refining Co.
6. Tabriz Oil Refining Co.
7. Abadan Oil Refining Co.
8. Isfahan Oil Refining Co.
9. Lavan Oil Refining Co.

Meanwhile, nine companies have been registered in order to achieve higher productivity in downstream operations. After the stabilisation of these companies, their managing directors, in the light of defined authority and responsibilities, are expected to increase productivity and strive hard to achieve the objectives set by the Petroleum Ministry.

National Iranian Gas Co.

In order to meet the country's objectives in the gas sector with regard to the expansion of gas supply system, 38 companies were registered as affiliates to NIGC.

National Petrochemical Co.

The main companies affiliated to NPC may be listed as follows :

1. Bandar Imam Petrochemical Co.
2. Arak Petrochemical Co.
3. Shiraz Petrochemical Co.
4. Tabriz Petrochemical Co.
5. Isfahan Petrochemical Co.
6. Razi Petrochemical Co.
7. Khorasan Petrochemical Co.
8. Kharg Petrochemical Co.
9. Petrochemical Commercial Co.

During 1998-99, 25 companies were registered to facilitate related operations.

Human Resources

The National Iranian Oil Company and other subsidiary companies benefit from the services of their qualified, well-trained and experienced workforce. NIOC does not act as other major oil companies with regard to services. Service companies usually provide logging and drilling services to majors, but NIOC has its own staff to carry out such works.

Table 2.1: Employees Statistics (NIOC)

Company	*Staff*	*Labour*	*Total*
National Iranian Oil Co.	40,107	5,225	45,332
National Iranian Oil Refining and Distribution Co.	26,807	7,792	34,599
National Iranian Gas Co.	15,553	1,583	17,136
National Petrochemical Co.	14,919	2,616	17,535
Grand Total	97,386	17,216	114,602

Training Provided by NIOC and NIORDC

NIOC Training Centre is one of the biggest training centres in the Middle East. As per NIOC policy, all applicants should have minimum qualifications designated for specific jobs. In addition, the people who apply for jobs are interviewed to comply with NIOC requirements before the suitable applicants are absorbed. Apart from offering on-the-job training, it is the company's policy to identify the training needs of its personnel at all levels and provide them with the necessary training. The table below illustrates to what extent, NIOC has seriously provided training facilities to its employees:

Table 2.2: Courses Provided by NIOC Training Centre

Subject	*Numbers*	*Tehran*	*Other Areas*	*Participants*
Engineering/Technical Courses	1,791	159	1,591	25,547
Management and Supervision	1,032	180	852	19,939
English Language	265	128	137	4,194
Computer Science	362	94	268	5,065
Total	3,450	561	2,848	54,745

Table 2.3: Training Provided by NPC Training Center (NIOC)

Subject	*Technical*	*Non-Technical*	*English*	*Computer*	*Technical Seminars*	*Total*
Man-Hours	264,507	195,045	63,760	63,392	48,674	635,378

National Iranian Oil Company

(A) Exploratory Activities

- National Iranian Drilling Co.
- National Iranian South Oil Co.
- Iranian Offshore Oil Company
- National Iranian Tanker Co.
- Ahvaz Pipe Mill (APM)

(B) Directorate of International Affairs (Marketing and Export)

- Other Affiliated Companies
- Important Projects Under Way
- National Iranian South Oil Co.
- Iranian Offshore Oil Co.
- National Iranian Tanker Co.

The National Iranian Oil Company (NIOC) produces crude oil from onshore and offshore fields to meet the energy requirements of industrial and other sectors. It secures the country's foreign currency needs as well. Its subsidiary companies are:

- National Iranian Drilling Co.
- National Iranian South Oil Co.
- Iranian Offshore Oil Co.
- National Iranian Tanker Co.
- Ahvaz Pipe Mill.

In addition, NIOC has other departments or organisations which do not operate as firms due to the nature of their responsibilities, such as the Directorate of Exploration, Directorate of Corporate Planning and Directorate of International Affairs.

Exploratory Activities

A vast plan, covering an area of 730,000 sq. km onshore and 195,000 sq.km offshore, was implemented for the exploration of oil and gas during 1991-92. Its main objective was to replenish oil and gas reserves. Totally, eight projects were earmarked under this plan, of which four were onshore projects, two Caspian Sea projects and two Persian Gulf projects. In 1998-99, these projects showed good progress with the drilling of exploratory wells such as Gordan-2, Kilor Karim-4, Changouleh-2, Shanoul- 2, Nir-Kabir 2, Zireh-2 and Tarakemeh-1.

Table 2.4: Oil and Gas Exploration in 1998-99 (NIOC)

Project		*Unit*	*Projected*	*Performed*
Onshore Exploratory		Rig-Month	72	72
		Meter	27,000	14,426
Geophysics	Seismic Survey	km	4,000	4,876
Activities (Onshore)	Gravimetry Magnetometry	Station	4,800	4,225
Geology	Group-Month	Group-Month	22	16.7
	Stratigraphy	Meter	26,000	32,874
	Tectonic	sq. km	18,000	14,931
	Rock Sampling	No	5,200	5,555
Road and Cellar Construction	Road	km	51	58
	Cellar	No	6	4.2
Seismic Survey (Persian Gulf)		km	9,000	6,700

(I) National Iranian Drilling Co.

National Iranian Drilling Company (NIDC) became operational with six drilling rigs in 1979. The number has now increased to 46, three of which are active in offshore regions. After the company's potentials were established, a marketing unit was formed in 1991. This unit is presently active in Central Asian and Persian Gulf states, apart from Libya.

Table 2.5: NIDC Operations During 1998-99 (NIOC)

Description	*Unit*	*1998-99*
Drilling Activities	Meter	300,000
Wells Drilled / Repaired	No.	133
Acidizing of Wells	No.	138
Logging	No.	265
Horizontal and Directional Drilling	No.	33

Other noteworthy NIDC activities may be summarised as follows :

- In 1998-99, it received the ordered equipment and six groups were equipped to provide drilling services to interested companies. Earlier, production companies had to wait for a long time to receive the services of foreign companies. Now NIDC fulfills the request of domestic companies while foreign companies are no longer active in the field.

- The company's clients were satisfied with the quality of services, which is assured by its qualified personnel.
- Based on a contract, NIDC provides logging services to Halliburton Products and Services Ltd. (HPSL), in Persian Gulf. The company has earned $4 million in 1998-99 from this source.

(II) National Iranian South Oil Co. (NISOC)

National Iranian South Oil Co. (NISOC) produces crude oil from onshore fields It supplies:

- Domestic refineries (except Lavan Refinery, which is fed by Iranian Offshore Oil Company)
- Kharg Island for export Meanwhile, NISOC is also responsible for supplying of gas, which comes from three sources, i.e., associated gas, dome gas and gas produced from independent wells. These gases are used as follows:
- Delivered to gas refining installations as feedstock
- Re-injected in oilfields for increasing the pressure of wells
- Delivered to Bandar Imam Petrochemical Co (BIPC) and Razi Petrochemical Company (RPC) as feedstock.

At present, the production capacity of this company is 3.7 million barrels per day, but is expected to increase in the coming years in the light of projects planned and/or activities being carried out now. Following are highlights of NISOCs activities in 1998-99 :

- Production of crude oil from 1,041 running wells
- Loading tankers at Kharg Terminal (821 tankers)
- Lean gas delivered to National Iranian Gas Co reached 146 million cubic metres per day
- Gas injection in seven oilfields equal to 67.5 MMCM/d
- Delivery of gas and gas-liquids to petrochemical companies: During 1988-99, 73,000 barrels of gas-liquids were delivered to BIPC Bandar Imam Petrochemical Co.
- Supply of sour gas to Razi Petrochemical Co from Jurassic formation equal to 4 MMCM/d

Table 2-6: NISOC Gas Production in 1998-99

Description	*Quantity*
Rich Gas (MMCM/d)*	267
Lean Gas (MMCM/d)	196

*MMCM/d = million cubic metres per day.

National Iranian South Oil Co. NISOC Today

Upon the victory of the Islamic Revolution and dispossession of foreign contractors, all exploration, drilling and production operations were taken over by the Iranian personnel. All strategic supporting facilities were transferred from Abadan to Ahwaz.

More than 85 per cent of the gas and gas liquids required by internal refineries and National Iranian Gas Company (NIGC) as well as provision of hydrocarboric inputs of petrochemical complexes are supplied by National Iranian South Oil Company (NISOC).

The organization within the years 1989 to 1999 about 3585 k.m. pipeline (4", 6", 8",10", 12", 16", 20", 36" and 42") have been crude oil and gas.

Present Situation

With due attention to the Petroleum Ministry's plans and policies as to implementing changes in organization structure to increase efficiency and effectiveness of the organization and to specify the actual production and service expenses of each oil sectors and to develop the oil industry management skill with a view to enhancing the industry quantitatively and qualitatively on a basis of competition. However, the oil fields organization was restructured and following five subsidiary companies were established:

1. Karoon Oil and Gas Producing Company - Ahwaz Headquarters.
2. Marun Oil and Gas Producing Company-Ramhormoz Headquarters.
3. Aghajari Oil and Gas Producing Company-Aghajari Headquarters.
4. Gachsaran Oil and Gas Producing Company-Gachsaran Headquarters.
5. Masjid-E-Suleyman Oil and Gas Producing Company-Masjid-E-Suleyman Headquarter.

Responsibilities and Reporting Relationship of the Subdiary Companies with the Holding Company (NISOC)

Considering the overall policies of the Ministry of Petroleum as to restructuring the organisation and establishing economic firms to work economically on the ground of exploration, production, refinery and oil product distribution, major objectives and responsibilities of the subsidiary companies have been outlined as follows:

1. Planning and implementing oil and gas production activities and operations according to NIOC policies.

2. Compiling and preparing technical and special procedures.
3. Oil fields studies and reservoir preservation.
4. Close supervision and control over implementation of oil and gas and gas liquid production plans and projects.
5. Monitoring over activities and implementation of technical, financial and administrative procedures of the subsidiary oil and gas companies.
6. Allocation of financial resources based on the approved budget.
7. Manpower planning and personnel training development.
8. Rendering technical and specialized services to subsidiary companies.

Principles and Responsibilities of the Oil and Gas Producing Companies

1. Production based on reservoir preservation principles and in line with the relevant geographical limits.
2. Maintaining oil, gas and gas liquid production facilities.
3. Providing material and spare parts to meet production operation requirement.
4. Providing and regulating financial book keeping and implementation of industrial accounting to compute cost-price of crude oil and gas.
5. Manpower training and development.
6. Primary resource estimation based on oil and gas production rate.
7. Production operation safety in order to prevent damages to living environment and production installations.
8. Rendering services through service contractors.
9. Preparing activity reports for the holding company.

(III) Iranian Offshore Oil Company

Iranian Offshore Oil Company (IOOC) produces crude oil from offshore oilfields. Its production operations are conducted at the following zones :

- Kharg Island (Abouzar, Doroud, Forouzan and Soroush oilfields)
- Lavan Island (Resalat, Reshadat and Salman oilfields)
- Sirri Island (Sivand, Dena, Esfand, Alvand and Nosrat oilfields)
- Bahregan Area (Hendijan, Bahregansar and Norouz oilfields)

Presently, production from the Soroush oilfield has been stopped while that from a few fields, i.e., Resalat, Reshadat, Hendijan, Bahregansar and Norouz, is limited.

Table 2.7: IOOC Operations in 1998-99 (NIOC)

Tanker Loaded	189
Crude Oil Delivered to Lavan Refinery	10,699,741 barrels Crude Oil
Delivered to Bandar abbas Refinery	2,445,673 barrels
Associated Gas Produced	238 billion cubic feet
Sour Gas Delivered to Kharg Petrochemical Co.	47 billion cubic feet Acidizing
and Chemical Injection	60 wells

(IV) National Iranian Tanker Co.

National Iranian Tanker Company (NITC) plays an important role in the field of marine transportation of crude oil to international markets as well as transfer of oil products. The NITC fleet comprises 18 vessels with a tonnage of 3 million tons. There are 11 crude oil tankers and the rest transport oil products. In addition to tankers, there are 26 vessels, including tugboats, service vessels, passenger boats, oil tankers and fire extinguishing and exploration vessels. These vessels provide services to oil terminals and platforms.

Table 2.8: NITC Operations in 1998-99 (NIOC)

Description/No. of Vessels	*No. of Voyages*	*Distance (miles)*	*Tonnage*
Crude Oil Transportation (CIF Basis)/9 Vessels	116	1,020,404	32,041,212
Crude Oil Transportation (Contracted Directly)/5 Vessels	13	208,900	3,376,369
Crude Oil Transportation to Bandar Abbas Refinery/4 Vessels	318	539,120	10,785,024
Transportation of Crude Oil from Offshore Terminals/23 Vessels	85	46,200	5,652,082
Total	**532**	**1,814,624**	**51,854,687**

(V) Ahvaz Pipe Mill (APM):

Ahvaz Pipe Mill (APM) is affiliated to the National Iranian Oil Company and has nearly 30 years of experience in manufacturing oil and gas pipes with a capacity of up to 420,000 tons/year. APM operates three mills with the following specifications:

Mill No. 1 : The mill is able to manufacture pipes of diameters 6 inches to 16 inches (168.3-406.4 mm) and of thickness 0.172 inch to 0.375 inch. The type of steel used in this mill ranges from Grade A to X52. The manufacturing method is rolling and resistant-welding with high frequency (ERW).

Mill No. 3 : The mill applies the same method used for manufacturing pipes, in Mill No. 1. Diameters of pipes vary from 21.1 mm to 558.8 mm. Steel type ranges from Grade A to X60.

Mill No. 4 : The mill manufactures pipes of 24 inches to 56 inches diameters. This mill applies three-layer polyethylene coatings to pipes of diameters 2.375 inches to 56 inches, according to DIN 30670 standard.

Table 2.9: APM Performance in 1998-99/1997-98 (NIOC)

Description	Unit	1997-98	1998-99	(Decrease) Increase
Pipe Production	tons	236,055	1 75,933	(25.4%)
Polyethylene Coating	sq.m	1,322,586	1,359,667	3%

Directorate of International Affairs (Marketing and Export)

Directorate of International Affairs undertakes marketing and export of crude oil and oil products. The directorate also oversees cooperation with OPEC. Although NIOC's production capacity exceeds 4.3 million barrels per day, Iran has limited its production to 3.6 million barrels per day due to its commitment to the OPEC ceiling for member countries. In 1998-99, the maximum crude oil production of NIOC was approximately 3.62 million bpd, 2.34 million bpd of which were exported and the rest delivered to domestic refineries.

Other Affiliated Companies

In addition to these companies, NIOC benefits from the services of the following affiliated companies:

- Kala Naft (Tehran, London and Canada)
- Oil Engineering and Development Co.
- Material Transportation and Forwarding Co.
- Air Transportation Co.

Important Projects Under Way

(A) National Iranian South Oil Co.

- Gas injection in oilfields (phases I and II)
- Development of the North Pars offshore gas field
- Procurement and treatment of associated gas for Bangestan (Amak)
- Construction of production lines and well head installations for new wells

- Construction of crude oil export pipelines
- Construction of new gas and liquefied gas units
- Studies for saving energy.

(B) Iranian Offshore Oil Co.

- Development of Sirri oil fields "A" and "E".
- Renovation/rehabilitation of Norouz oil field installations.
- Renovation/rehabilitation of Abouzar oil field installations.
- Renovation/development of Soroush oil field.
- Water injection in Doroud oil field.

(C) National Iranian Tanker Co.

- Construction of 5 X 300,000 DWT tankers.
- Construction of five Suezmax tankers.
- Construction of five Aframax tankers.

National Iranian Oil Refining and Distribution Company

Types of Oil Products

- Light Products
- Middle Distillates
- Heavy Products

Performance of Refineries

National Iranian Oil Distribution Company

Supply and Export

- LPG
- Mogas
- Kerosene
- Gas Oil
- Fuel Oil

Directorate of Pipeline and Telecommunications

Directorate of Engineering and Construction of Refineries

Projects Under Way

Refining crude oil in Iran dates back to the first decade of this century when Abadan Refinery was built in the southwest of the country before it was damaged during the imposed war. Abadan Refinery was one of the biggest refineries in the world. After renovation, it is once again a prominent crude oil refinery in the region.

Experts trained at Abadan Refinery as chemical, process, mechanical and electrical engineers have participated in the construction of other refineries in the country. At present, the total capacity of domestic refineries is beyond 1. 5 million bpd Table 2-10 details domestic refineries, type of feedstock, nominal. capacity and the means by which they receive raw materials such as crude oil from production units.

Table 2.10: Specifications of Refineries (NIOC)

Refinery	*Type of Crude*	*Capacity (1000bpd)*	*Provided by*	*Tranportation Means*
Abadan	Heavy and Light	370	NISOC	Pipeline
Arak	Light	165	"	"
Isfahan	Light	335	"	"
Bandar Abbas	Heavy	232	From Kharg	Tanker
Tabriz	Light	105	NISOC	Pipeline
Tehran	Light	225	"	"
Kermanshah	Light	22	"	"
Shiraz	Heavy	50	"	"
Lavan	Light	30	IOOC	"

Types of Oil Products

Domestic refineries have the capability of producing nearly all kinds of oil products needed in the country. These products can be categorized as follows:

Light Products : LPG, motor gasoline, platformate and jet fuel.

Middle Distillates: Kerosene, gas oil, heavy jet fuel, base oil, lubricating oil and various kinds of solvents.

Heavy Products: Fuel oil, bitumen, furfural extract, stack wax and malch. Among domestic refineries, Tabriz Refinery is distinguished for its light products, Isfahan for middle distillates and Abadan for heavy oil products. The output of domestic refineries are as follows:

Light Products	18%
Middle Distillates	41.3%
Heavy Products	40.6%

Performance of Refineries

The volume of main oil products produced by refineries are illustrated in the following table:

Table 2.11: Production Capacity of Oil Products (NIOC)

Product		*Abadan*	*Arak*	*Isfahan*	*Bandar*	*Tabriz*	*Tehran*	*Shiraz*	*Kerman*	*Lavan*
LPG		1,720	807	2291	949	601	1,245	241	98	111
Mogas	Regular	5,828	3,468	6,552	6,423	2,011	4,761	1,464	621	886
	Premium	0	614	0	0	0	554	19	2	0
Kerosene		4,329	3,667	7,918	3,561	2,610	5,190	654	513	0
Gas Oil		14,195	7,608	14,537	8,598	4,580	10,419	2,299	633	1863
Fuel Oil		21,325	6,026	11,439	14,952	4,328	9,732	1,994	1,522	1,748

National Iranian Oil Distribution Company

If products to various industrial and commercial sectors: It transports products from domestic refineries by means of pipelines, road tankers, vessels and railroads. These products are stored in 33 locations, which are fully equipped to directly deliver products to consumers.

Supply and Export

LPG: During 1998-99, 9,223 cubic meters of LPG were supplied daily National Iranian Oil Distribution Co. received approximately 97 3 per cent of this quantity from domestic refineries and the rest was provided by petrochemical complexes.

Mogas: During the same period, 33,701 cubic meters/day of motor gasoline were supplied to consumers, of which 3,322 cubic meters/day were imported.

Kerosene: During 1998-99, 27,277 cubic meters of kerosene were supplied to consumers.

Gas Oil: The total quantity of gas oil supplied in 1998-99 was 59,777 cubic meters/day.

Fuel Oil: During the same period, 37,367 cubic meters/day of fuel oil were supplied to domestic consumers, including power plants. Meanwhile, 42,686 cubic meters of fuel oil were exported to international markets. The production volume of other products in domestic refineries indicates that these also possess export potentials.

Table 2.12: Production Type (NIOC)

Description	*LPG*	*Mogas*	*Kerosene*	*Gas Oil*	*Fuel Oil*
Supplied	9,223	33,701	27,277	59,777	37,367
Imported	0	3,322	0	0	0
Exported	0	0	0	0	42,686

Directorate of Pipeline and Telecommunications

The Directorate of Pipeline and Telecommunications organizes the transportation of crude oil from fields to refineries and delivers products from refineries to distribution networks. Making arrangements for performing such a huge task requires precise planning, high level of expertise and prompt maintenance work. This directorate carried out these activities successfully in 1998-99, particularly given the huge volume of crude oil/oil product transported, i.e. 4,100 million - tons/km.

Directorate of Engineering and Construction of Refineries

This directorate undertakes the following activities :

1. Enhancing production capacities of refineries by constructing new refineries or new processing units at existing refineries.
2. Process improvements for upgrading oil products and increasing productivity.

Important activities carried out by this directorate in 1998-99 can be listed as follows

- Cooperation with Oil Industry Research Center for the construction of an industrial unit for manufacturing ZDDP.
- Cooperation with Isfahan Refinery concerning engineering design of the unit for producing special solvents.
- Preliminary studies for the construction of a lubricating oil unit at Tabriz Refinery.
- Providing technical services to Lavan Refinery with regard to construction of an LPG unit.
- Offering technical services for the construction of a condense refining plant.
- Continuing supervision over the commissioning and construction of pumps on the 26-inch Bandar Abbas-Rafsanjan pipeline

This directorate has a key role in managing downstream projects to increase oil refining and distribution capacity to meet the increasing domestic demand for fuels.

Projects Under Way

Some of the most important projects under way in this regard are:

- Process improvement at Shiraz and Lavan refineries for upgrading purpose
- Increasing the production capacity of Isfahan Refinery
- Second Tehran-Tabriz crude oil transportation pipeline
- Miscellaneous projects for improving the distribution system, namely construction of pipelines/storage tanks
- Loss reduction and saving energy at refineries
- Developing new potentials for the transportation and distribution of oil products.

National Iranian Gas Company

Gas Treatment Units

- Natural Gas Consumption
- Production of Condensate and Sulfur
- Projects Under Way

In view of the country's huge gas reserves, the National Iranian Gas Company (NIGC) is obliged to play a key role in the coming decade with regard to the supplying energy to the industrial world. Natural gas, which is very environment-friendly as opposed to other fossil fuels, is expected to offer intense competition in oil markets as global concerns about environment protection increases. At present, natural gas is supplied throughout the country and NIGC has the potential of exporting gas to neighbouring countries and to Europe after the completion of the Iran-Turkey gas pipeline.

Gas Treatment Units: During 1998-99, 144.9 million cubic meters of gas have been treated at treatment plants and supplied to consumers.

Table 2.13: Performance of Gas Refineries in 1998-99 (NIOC)

Refinery	*Actual Performance*
Hashemi-Nejad Gas Refinery	23.8
Vali Asr Refinery	74.2
Bid Boland Refinery	32.8
Dalan Gas Treatment Complex	6.3
Sarajeh Treatment Plant	0.4
Sarkhoun Refinery	7.4
Total	**144.9**

Natural Gas Consumption: During 1998-99, NIGC focused on expanding its gas supply system. Determined efforts to establish pressure lines and new connections boosted the supply of natural gas to newsubscribers. At the end of 1998-99, 375,494 consumers in the household sector, 16,067 in commercial sector and 369 in industrial sector were connected to the gas supply network. Meanwhile, nearly 274 cities were covered by the natural gas distribution system, while pressure lines are being laid in 48 cities. During the same period, 150 MMCM/d of natural gas were supplied to consumers.

Production of Condensate and Sulfur: Natural gas produced from Khangiran gas field has a high sulfur content in the form of hydrogen sulfide. Meanwhile, most gases entering the gas treatment plant carry some liquid hydrocarbons (condensate), which are separated during treatment NIGC exports the excess sulfur and condensate after supplying the domestic demand.

Table 2.14: Sulfur and Condensate Production (NIOC)

Gas Treatment Plant	*Sulfur (1,000 Tons)*	*Condensate*
Hashemi-Nejad	196	141,000 cubic metres
Vali Asr	-	206,000 cubic metres
Sarkhoun	-	242,000 tons
Gavarzin	-	19,000 tons

Table 2.15: Major Projects under Groups 1 and 2 (NIOC)

Project	*Executive*	*Progress (End of Year)*
Khangiran Gas Treatment Plant	OIEC	83%
Liquid Stabilization Unit 700 Sarkhour Treatment Plant	OIEC	99%
Sarakhs-Neka Gas Line Compressor Station	Namvaran	100%
Gas lines S1 and S2 Compressor	DAILEM	100%
Underground Storage of Natural Gas	KBB NIDC	94%

Table 2.16: Execution Phase of Projects Project (NIOC)

Project	*Executive*	*Progress (End of Year)*
Distillation Unit for Khangiran Condensates	NIGC Personal	86%
Compressor Stations (Line 83)	"	12%
Construction of 2nd Phase of Khangiran Treatment Plant	Tehran Jonoub	8.5%
Construction of Unit 700 Sarkhoun Treatment Plant	Shina	17%
Compressor Station (Chaalvand)	NIGC Personnel+Jaminco	97%
Second Compressor Station (Sarakhs-Neka line)	Farabetone	99.7%
Construction of condensate storage	"	60%

National Petrochemical Company

- Production Activities
- Commercial Activities
- Directorate of Research and Development
- Production Increase
- Important Projects Under Way

Development of petrochemical industry in Iran has followed a particular strategy after the imposed war. This industry has generally focused on the following objectives :

- Directing the complexes toward production of final petrochemical products.
- Diversifying and increasing production to meet the demands of downstream chemical industries.

Although the total production of petrochemical complexes increased in 1998-99 in comparison with that of the previous year, the foreign currency income of N.P.C. decreased due to low crude oil prices and/or low economic growth rate in some parts of the world. During the past 2-3 years, the growth rate of this industry declined in comparison with the rate at the beginning of this decade. This is due to delays in the completion of some huge projects. The completion of projects under way will boost the production capacity of petrochemical complexes, which has been constant since last few years.

Production Activities

During 1998-99, 11.1 million tons of petrochemicals were produced, which is nearly 3 per cent more than the production recorded in the previous year. Some of the prominent indices in the petrochemical sector are as follows:

- Bandar Imam Petrochemical Co. (BIPC) ranks first among petrochemical complexes due to its diversified products and high production capacity.
- The production of Tabriz Petrochemical Co. doubled in comparison with the output in 1997-98.
- Petrochemical production in complexes has reached 80 per cent of their nominal capacity.

Table 2.17: Production Volume of Petrochemical Plants in 1998-99 (NIOC)

Petrochemical Complex/Plan	*Type of Products*	*Production Volume*
Shiraz Complex	Ammonia. Urea. Methanol. Nitric Acid Ammonium itrate. Arqon. Sodium Bicarbonate.Per-cholorine, Sodium Hypo-chlorate and Perchloric Acid	1,835
Bandal Emam Complex	Ethvlene. Propylene. Polvethviene. Polypropvlene. Propave. Pentane. CFO. PVC. VCM. EDC. Gasoline Mixture of Xvlenes. Svnthetic Rubber Sodium Hypro- chlorate, C4 Cuts and C5+	4,139
Kharg Complex Orumieh Plant	Propane, butane, Pentane and Sulfur Melemine Crystals and Ammonium Sulfate	457 9.3
Tabriz Complex	Ethvlene. Propylene. Light and Heavy Polvethviene. C4 Cuts, Styrene, Polystyrene, Toluene and Benzene	446.7
Korasan Complex	Urea and Ammonia	871
Arak Complex	Ethvlene. Propylene. C4 Cuts. Pvrolysis qasoline Butadiene 2-ethvl-hexanol. CFO. Ala chlore Butachlore, Isobutanol, MEG, TEG	912
Razi Plant	Ammonia. Urea Sulfuric Acid. Phosphoric Acid. Sulfur and Di-ammonium phosphate	2,228
Isfahan Complex	Benzene, Toluene, Ortho-Xylene and Para-Xylene	242

Commercial Activities

Petrochemical Commercial Company is entrusted with the task of marketing and exporting petrochemical products. Also supplies·the feedstock of downstream chemical industries.

Table 2.18: Domestic Sales and Exports in 1998-99 (NIOC)

Domestic Sales	
Quantity (1,000 .Tons)	7,375
Value (Billion Rials)	4,419
Exports	
Quantity (1,000 Tons)	3,621
Value (Million Dollars)	452

Directorate of Research and Development

Advanced technology, safety and cost reduction are among the most important issues in the petrochemical industry. Consequently, research and development activities are vital for NPC's management, which supports measures taken in this regard. Based on NPC's organizational chart, the Directorate of Research and Development reports to production management, but arrangements have been made to establish independent investigating groups in all complexes. At present, organizational procedures, regulations and instructions to be followed have been established. Projects/improvements implemented by the directorate are as follows : Recovery of 2-EH alcohol at Arak Petrochemical Co. and waste reduction :

- Using the heat content of hot ammonia at Razi Petrochemical Co.
- Production of sulfur monochloride (SMC) at Arak Petrochemical Co.

Production Increase

NPC Productivity Committee supervises petrochemical complexes to improve productivity indices. During 1998-99, many seminars on TQM, quality assurance systems, organizational behavior and improvement were arranged to help its personnel improve their knowledge and achieve higher productivity rates. The committee has defined productivity indices and all complexes are obliged to report related facts and figures. Table 7 presents indices for two petrochemical complexes, namely BIPC and RPC.

Table 2.19: Productivity Indices (NIOC)

Productivity		RPC
Production Yield	87%	70%
Production Continuity	83%	78%
Per Capita Production (tons)	45.7	81.4
Per Capita Production Value (Million Rials)	18.3	16.7
Training Provided (Man-Hours)	1.2	1.9
Value-Added Rate	75%	39%
Frequency of Accidents	0.99	0.6

Meanwhile, petrochemical complexes have started to implement Quality Assurance Systems (QAS) and Environmental Management Systems (EMS) according to the requirements of ISO 9000 and ISO 14000 series respectively.

Table 2.20: Status of QAS 8 EMS Implementation (NIOC)

Company	*ISO 9002*		*ISO 14001*
	Scope	*Status*	
BIPC	PVC, LD 1 and 2, Lab, NF	Certified	-
Arak	All Products	"	-
Khorasan	-	91.5%	-
Razi	-	79.1%	-
Shiraz	Ammonia, Urea, Argon and Methanol	Certified	-
Isfahan	BTX	"	Certified
Kharg	All Products	"	-
Orumieh	Training Courses Applied	-	-
Tabriz	Olefin, DPG, B-1 and Polyethylene	Certified	-

Important Projects Under Way

Following table illustrates the progress of projects under way in Iran's petrochemical industry:

Table 2.21: Progress of Projects in 1998-99 Description (NIOC)

Description	*Progress (%)*
Methanol (Kharg)	28
Para-Xylene	36.3
1st MTBE	15.3
6th and 7th Olefin Plants	2.1
1st MTBE	15.3
6th and 7th Olefin Plants	2.1
1st PTA/PET	6.8
3rd Aromatic Plant	5.1
Engineering Polymers	*
2nd PTA/PET	*

* Selection of licensor/concluding contracts/subcontractor evaluation.

Financial Statement

- Capital Requirements and Foreign Currency Incomes
- National Iranian Oil Company
- National Iranian Oil Refining and Distribution Company
- National Iranian Gas Company
- National Petrochemical Company
- Foreign Currency Incomes

Capital Requirements and Foreign Currency Incomes

Investment for expanding oil industry resources and capabilities helps to increase the production capacities of crude oil, oil products and natural gas. It also serves to realize NPC's plan to produce final products rather than primary and intermediate products. As in previous years, the oil industry's affiliated companies and directorates initiated various capital projects during 1998-99. These projects and the budgets allocated to them will be referred to in the following section.

National Iranian Oil Company

The budget allocated in 1998-99 to various capital projects, including offshore production, onshore production, exploration, special projects, training programmes and health care, amounted to 3,264 billion rials. Additionally, a foreign currency portion of $565 million has also been allocated to the above projects.

Table 2.22: NIOC Budget Allocation in 1998-99 (NIOC)

Unit	*Rial Portion (Billion Rials)*	*F.C. Portion (Million Dollars)*
Onshore Production	1,738	241
Offshore Production	785	143
Exploration	408	121
Independent Projects	303	60
Health Care	7.7	-
Central Training Programs	6. 1	-

National Iranian Oil Refining and Distribution Company

A budget of 1,729 billion rials and foreign currency portion of $354 million was allocated to the development projects of NIORDC in 1998-99.

Table 2.23: Funds Allocated to NIORDC Projects (NIOC)

Directorate/company	*Capital Requirement/Project*	*Credits Rial Portion*	*F.C Portion*
Refining Directorate	Process Improvement	528	145.5
Engineering and Construction of Refineries	Auxiliary Installations and Upgrading Product Quality	538	84.5
General Engineering and Construction Pipelines and Telecom	Manufacture of Pipelines and Storage Tanks and Gas Stations	388	77.1
Directorate of Pipeline and Telecommunication	Renovation and Reconstruction of Pipelines, Pumping Stations and Auxiliary Installations	31.3	100
Independent Projects	Kangan Natural Gas Project (Surface Installations) Aghar -Dalan Natural Gas (Subterranean Installations)	137	2
National Iranian Oil Distribution Co.	Construction of Storage Tanks for Petroleum Products	82	13.1

National Iranian Gas Company

Totally, 2,029 billion rials and a foreign currency portion of $200 million were allocated to NIGC for the completion of gas treatment projects, construction of compressor stations and expansion of gas supply networks and consumer connections. The amount was allocated for the following projects:

- Implementation of Phase II of Hashemi-Nejad Gas Treatment Plant.
- Completion of Sarkhoun Gas Treatment Plant.
- Upgrading the capacity of Vali Asr Gas Treatment Plant.
- Construction of underground natural gas storage facilities.
- Establishment of a compressor station.
- Laying gas pipelines.

National Petrochemical Company

The capital requirements of NPC in 1998-99 amounted to 3,087 billion rials. The projects covered by the above budget were as follows:

1. Kharg Methanol.
2. MTBE Production.
3. 6th Olefin Project.
4. PTA/PET Production.
5. Engineering Polymers.
6. Various projects for infrastructural facilities and installations such as 3rd Aromatic Project and Para-xylene Production Project (Bandar Imam Petrochemical Complex).
7. 7th Olefin Project.
8. Research projects.

Foreign Currency Incomes

The oil industry's foreign currency incomes during 1998-99 were derived from the following five sources :

1. Export of crude oil from Kharg, Sirri and Lavan oil loading terminals.
2. Exports of oil products produced by domestic refineries, notably Abadan, Lavan and Bandar Abbas refineries.
3. Export of petrochemicals produced after meeting domestic demand.
4. Export of sulfur produced by gas treatment plants.
5. Export of condensate produced from gas wells.

The following table shows the foreign currency incomes derived from the first three sources.

Table 2.24: Foreign Currency Incomes in 1998-99 (NIOC)

Export of Crude Oil	8,943
Export of Oil Products	1,137
Export of Petrochemicals	452
Total	10,532

Research and Higher Education

- Oil Industry Research Centre (1998-99)
- Research Divisions
- Projects Conducted at the Centre
- Oil Industry University

The oil industry should apply new technologies for both upstream and downstream activities in order to lower production costs and survive in the global competitive markets. A key parameter in operation, expansion and development of oil industry is to employ qualified engineers to help find appropriate solutions to technical problems facing the industry. Based on this concept, NIOC has established its own higher education and research centres.

Oil Industry Research Centre (1998-99)

The Oil Industry Research Centre is active in the following fields:

- Research.
- Technology and development.
- Ancillary services.

The research centre connects the oil industry to universities and harmonizes the industry's needs. The industry has its own problems and plans while the universities are interested in undertaking projects/studies and participating in troubleshooting. At present, this centre has seven research divisions and 130 laboratories.

Research Divisions

- Exploration and Production
- Refining
- Gas
- Industrial Protection and Environment
- Chemistry and Petrochemicals
- Polymer Science and Technology
- Improvement of Chemical Processes

Projects Conducted at the Centre

- Study and manufacture of additives to lubrication oils and inhibitors for oil fields
- Application of oil derivatives in agriculture
- Substitution of MTBE for TEL
- Research on bituminous coatings.
- Design of mathematical models for reservoirs.

- Study on thermodynamic properties of reservoir liquids.
- Research for finding suitable solutions to the problems of drilling mud.
- Oil recovery techniques.
- Geophysics/Geochemistry researches.

Oil Industry University

The concept of establishing an institute for training experts, managers, engineers and technicians for the oil industry dates back to 60 years ago. Abadan Institute of Technology (A.I.T) was established in 1938-39 for training of the personnel at various levels.

A large number of managers in the oil industry have graduated from AIT. Its credibility is well established and it has expanded to offer many 4-year courses, including those in the field of chemical/ reservoir/mechanical/ gas/ NDT and corrosion engineering.

As an internal regulation, the graduates of AIT (now Oil Industry University) are employed in the industry. The university can also offer MS and Ph.D courses even in special subjects, if deemed necessary.

Secondary Data

Oil and Natural Gas Corporation Company Data Glance

Established in 1956, today ONGC is India's permier and one of the word's largest Exploration and Production (E and P) Companies.

- One of the eleven Navrathans in the country.
- One among the top 25 oil companies of the world.
- Produces crude oil, natural gas and value added products like LPG, NGL, C2-C3.
- Made 285 hydrocarban finds within the country.
- Established over 6 Billion Tonnnes of in-place hydrocarbon reserves within the country.
- Oil and Gas Reserves of over 8 Billion Barrels of oil Equievalent (BOE)(1.499).
- Produced 584 Million Tonnes of oil and 277 BCM of natural gas upto 1999-2000.
- Contributtes about 85 per cent of domestic oil and gas production.
- Largest producer of LPG in India accounting for over 1/3rd of the total LPG production.
- Complete expertise in Geological and Geophysical studies,

Reservior management, production operations and related technical and technological services.

- Since the offshore strike in 1914, commissioned 28 process platforms, 131 well platforms and 3200 kms, of sub-sea pipelines.
- Offering R and D and consultancy services worldwide through eight Research and Training Centers on aspects of E and Pactivities.
- Market capitalisation of around US $4.43 Billion on 31st March 2000.
- Annual revenue of US $ 4.61 Billion (prov.) during the year 1999-2000.
- Earned a net profit of US $ 831.6 Million (prov.) during the year 1999-2000.
- Eighteen (18) major projects completed at the cost of US $ 4.5 Billion during the last seven years. Eight (8) major projects in hand.
- Successful record of international ventures in Iran, Tanzania and Iraq.
- Discovered 58 BCM of gas overseas in Vietnam.
- Development activities undertaken in Vietnam.
- Operating prestigious drilling contracts in Oman and Bangladesh, which were obtained in the face of stiff global competition.
- 40000 accomplished employees supported by state-of-the-art infrastructure, technology and facilities.
- Continued and Reinforced exploratory thrust on potential sectors of producing.
- Maximize recovery from established field.
- Frontier basin exploration.
- Deep water area.
- Central onland basin.
- Sub-trepan sectors.
- Exploration activities in north-eastern and northern mountain belts.
- Utilization of other subsurface energy options from various sources, e.g., Coal Bed Methance (CBM) and Gas Hydrates.
- Equity oil from overseas ventures

Intfrastructure and Facilities

Shore

• Production Installation	225
• Pipeline Network (kms.)	7900
• Major Onshore Terminals (including CFU), LPG, Gas Sweetening Plant, Storage Tanks	2
• Drilling Rigs	75
• Workover Rigs	66
• Seismic Units	33
• Logging Units	35

Off Shore

• Well Platforms	131
• Well-cuprocess Platforms	5
• Process Platforms	28
• Drilling/ Jack-up Rings	18
• Pipeline Network (kms.)	3200
• Offshore Suppls Vessels	32

ONGC Institutes Integrated Services (OIIS)

Eight R and D Training Institutes functioning under OLLS offer consultancy/ services covering nearly all aspects of E and P activities.

- Keshava Deva Malvija Institute of Petroleum Exploration (KDMIPE), Dehradun.
- Institute of Drilling Technology (IDT), Dehradum.
- Institute of Reservior Studies (IRS), Ahmedabad.
- Institute of Oil and Gas Production Technology (IO and GPT), Panvel.
- Institute of Management Development (IMD), Dehradun.
- Institute of Engineering and Ocean Technology (IEOT), Mumbai.
- Institute of Petroleum Safety and Environment Management (IPSEM), Goa.
- Institute of BioTechnology and GeoTechonics Studies (INBIGS), Jorhat.

A Comparative Analysis of Standard Safety Norms in N.I.S.O.C. of India

Table 2-25: Manpower Statistics in NISOC (1996-200)

Year Org	*1996*	*1997*	*1998*	*1999*	*2000*
AMA	9068	8330	7412	6726	7127
KOGC	3065	1567	2800	2952	2052
MOGC	721	768	758	779	1237
OTHER	25328	22018	24301	20364	18379
Total	94690	22037	24201	20363	18359

Table 2-26: Manpower in NISOC 2000

Manpower in 2000	
Tehran Year	5
Isfahan	6
Masjid-I-Suleyman	916
Adareh Markazi Awaz (Tashclat Markazi Ahwaz)	7127
Naheeh Ahwaz (KARRON)	2052
Marun	1237
Adareh Markazi Aghari	344
Naheeh Aghajari	3463
Adareh Markazi Gachsaran	131
Naheeh Gachsaran	3048

Manpower Statistics in NISOC 1996-2000

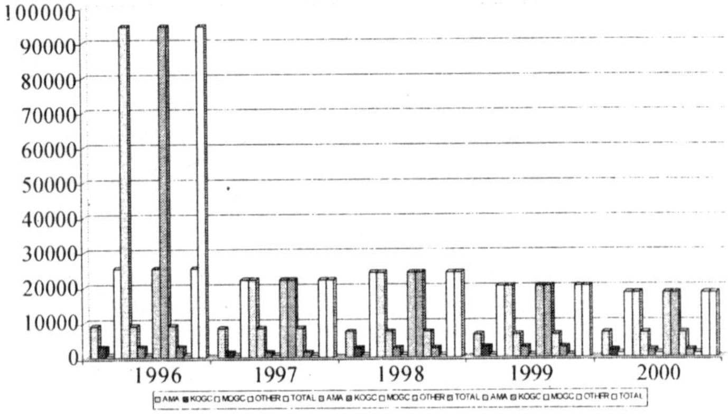

Manpower Statistics in NISOC 2000

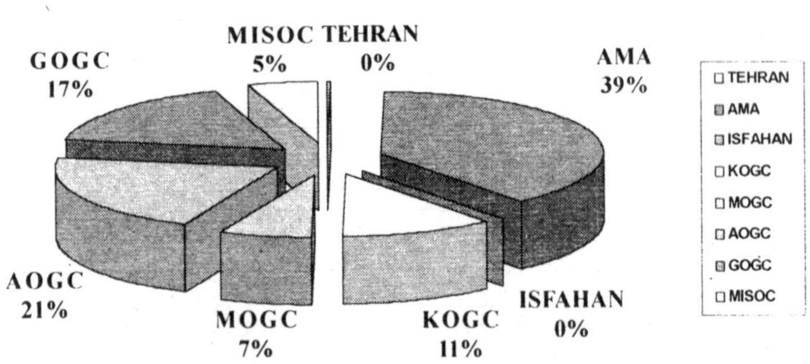

Fire Accident Statistics in NISOC 1996-2000

Region	1996					1997					1998				
	Departmental			City	Tot.	Departmental			City	Tot.	Departmental			City	Tot.
	Ind.Ins	Rs.Col.	Rel.Ins	Ins.		Ind.Ins	Rs.Col.	Rel.Ins	Ins.		Ind.Ins	Rs.Col.	Rel.Ins	Ins.	
Ahwaz					81					96	15	24	13	50	102
Aghjari					84					37	8	13	5	58	84
Gachsaran					81					43	9	12	5	34	60
Masjid-I-Suleyman					23					21	3	16	1	35	55
Khrag					4					6	3	5	0	0	8
Total					284					211	38	70	24	177	309

Legend : Ind. Ins = Industrial Rs. Col = Residential Colom Tot = Total
City Inst. = Instalation Out of Industrial Area and Privot Properties
Rel. Ins = Related to Industrial Installation
AHWAZ=Before 2000 Was (AMA+KOGC+MOGC)
Before 1998 There was not Supart Statistical Figure Information Departmental Area)

Accident Statistics in NISOC Since 1996-2000

1999								2000								From 1996 to 2000		
F	NF	MI	Tot	Days L.	Freq	S	Dii	F	NF	MI	Tot	Days L.	Freq	S	Dii	Total	%	Days L.
1	69	8	78	8908	480	3.76	1.804	0	62	10	72	1021	47	2.86	0.13	253	25	34287
3	80	14	97	24893	2584	8.61	22.248	0	24	6	30	487	119	5.85	0.7	156+	15	33059+
												7632	3242	2.97	9.63	47+	5	7632+
2	14	6	22	15318	1557	1.62	2,522	1	6	3	10	271	35	2.55	0.09	79+	8	23841
0	18	13	31	106	13	2.17	0.028	0	20	14	34	15160	2213	3.36	7.44	134	13	23351+
0	1	2	3	14	6	0.42	0.002	2	21	15	38	7	4	1.06	0.004	102	10	7780
0	11	9	20	99	28	2.55	0.071	0	2	3	5					63	6	490+
6	191	54	251	49338	945	3.77	3.562	3	135	51	189	24578	550	3.09	1.70	1029	100	176588

Legend : F=Fatal (Persons Killed) NF=Non Fatal (Persons with Major Injured)
MI=Major Injury (Persons with Minor Injured) Freq=Frequency Rate
S=Severity Rate DII = Disabling Injuf Days L.=Days Lost Tot=Total
Ahwaz=Before 2000 was (AMA+KOGC+MOGC) Days CHG=Days Charged (Lost Days)

Accident Statistics in NISOC 2000

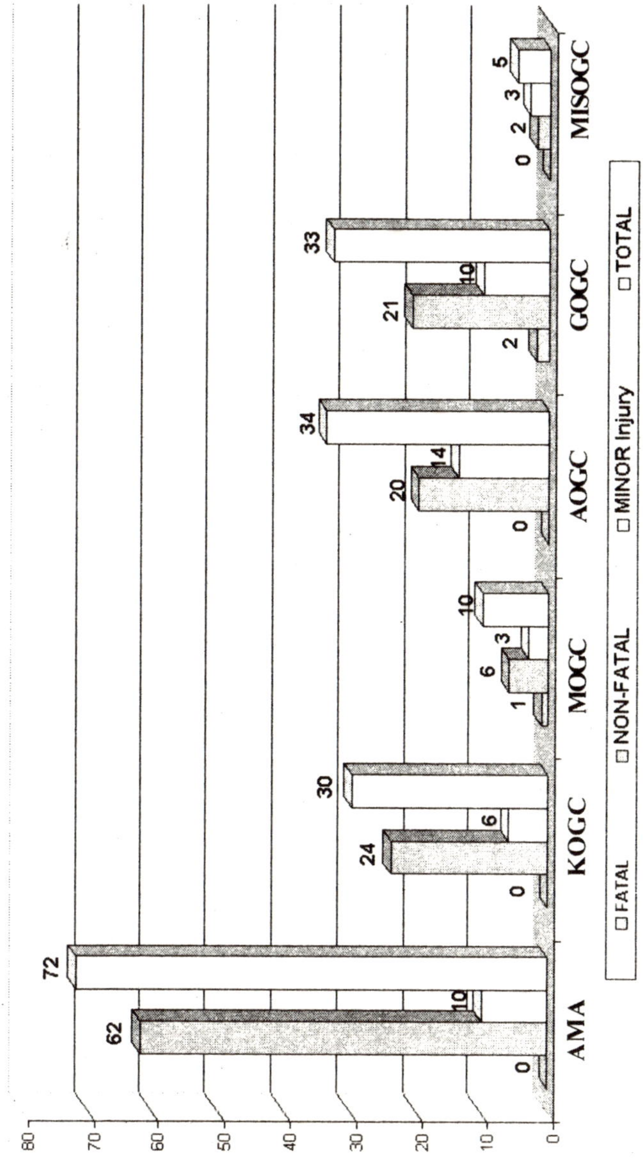

Accident Rate in NISOC 1996-2000

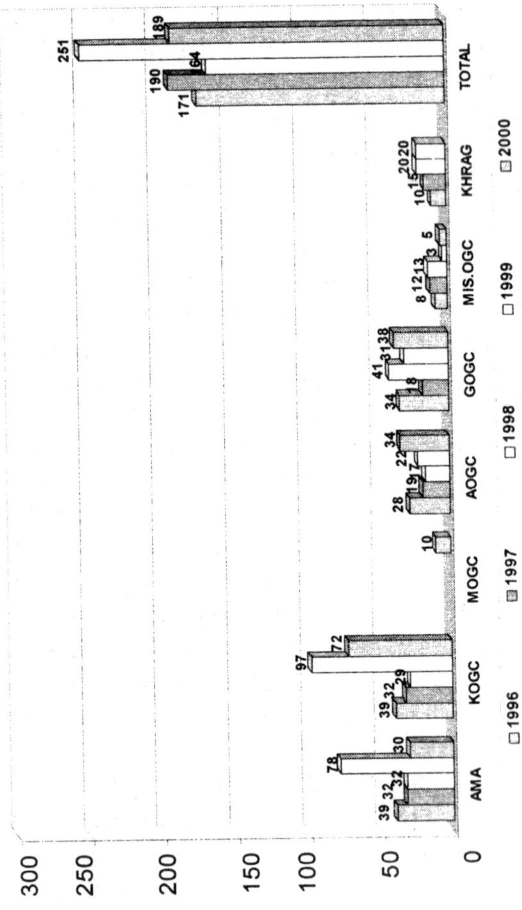

Region Wise Accident Status in NISOC 2000

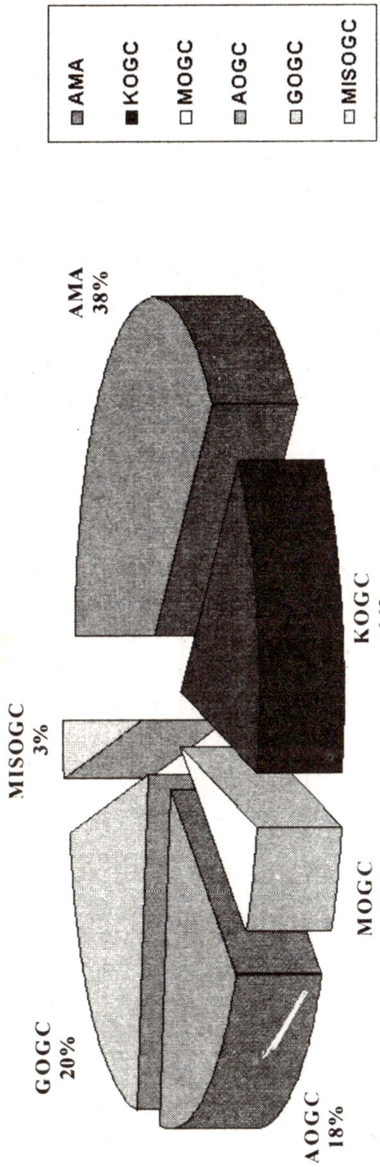

Road Accident Statistics in NISOC 1996-2000

	1996						1997					
Region	*Meter Work*	*Acc. No.*	*Fatal Emp*	*Un-Emp.*	*Injuried Emp*	*Un-Emp*	*Meter Work*	*Acc. No.*	*Fatal Emp*	*Un-Emp.*	*Injuried Emp*	*Un-emp*
Ahwaz/Ama		39										
KOGC.MOGC		39										
AOGC		28										
GOGC		34										
MISOGC		8										
KHRAG		10										
Total		507	5	2	33	26		570	7	2	69	22

Legend : Acc. No. Accident Number Emp.=Employment Un-Emp. Not Employment

Ahwaz=Before 2000 was (AMA+KOGC+MOGC)

Before 1998 there was not statistical data figure

Road Accident Statistics in NISOC 1996-2000

1998						1999					
Meter Work	Acc. No.	Fatal Emp	Fatal Unemp	Injuried Emp	Injuried Unemp	Meter Work	Acc. No.	Fatal Emp	Fatal Unemp	Injuried Emp	Injuried Unemp
64309654	426	2	3	29	13	64368836	365	1	4	10	8
18347807	33	2	1	4	0	19000612	36	2	0	13	1
18335653	12	0	1	5	2	26290370	12	0	0	1	0
3388387	20	0	1	1	3	2928906	12	0	0	0	1
3299989	11	0	0	3	1	2298086	0	0	0	0	1
1.08E+08	502	4	6	42	19	114886810	433	6	1	24	11

2000						From 1375 to 1379	
Meter Work	Acc. No.	Fatal Emp	Fatal Unemp	Injuried Emp	Injuried Unemp	Tot.	%Age
36437040	240	1	2	17	4	1070+	74
9434088	47	0	0	4	0	86+	6
16076184	36	0	1	8	2	133+	9
18853092	16	0	0	4	3	74+	5
3337680	15	0	0	0	2	55+	4
						21+	2
84138084	354	1	3	33	11	2366	100

Road Accident in NISOC from 1996 to 2000

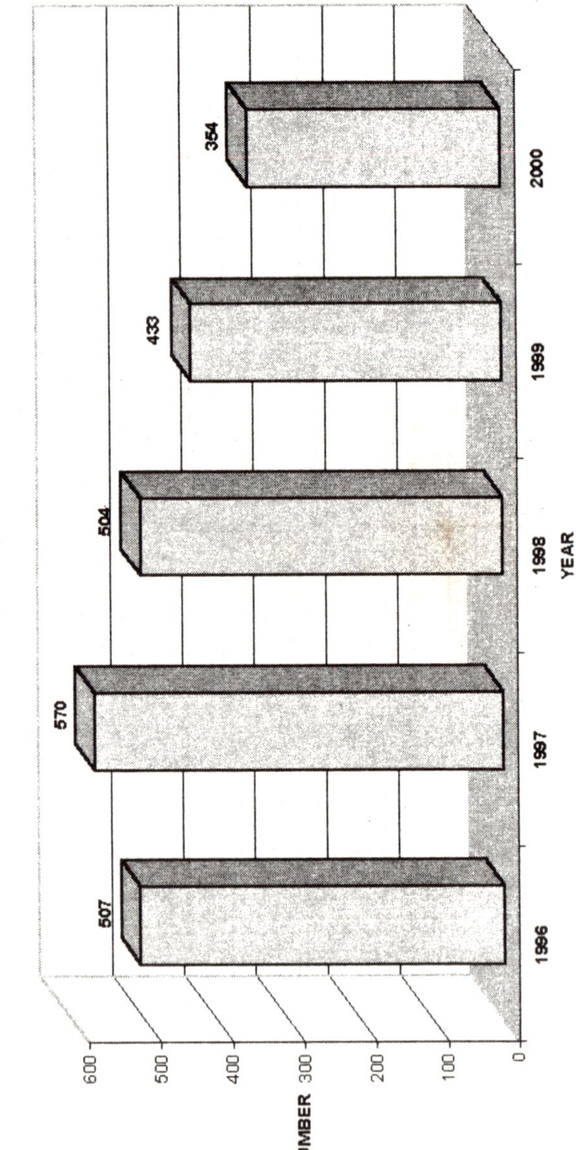

Road Accident Statiscs in NISOC from 1996 to 2000

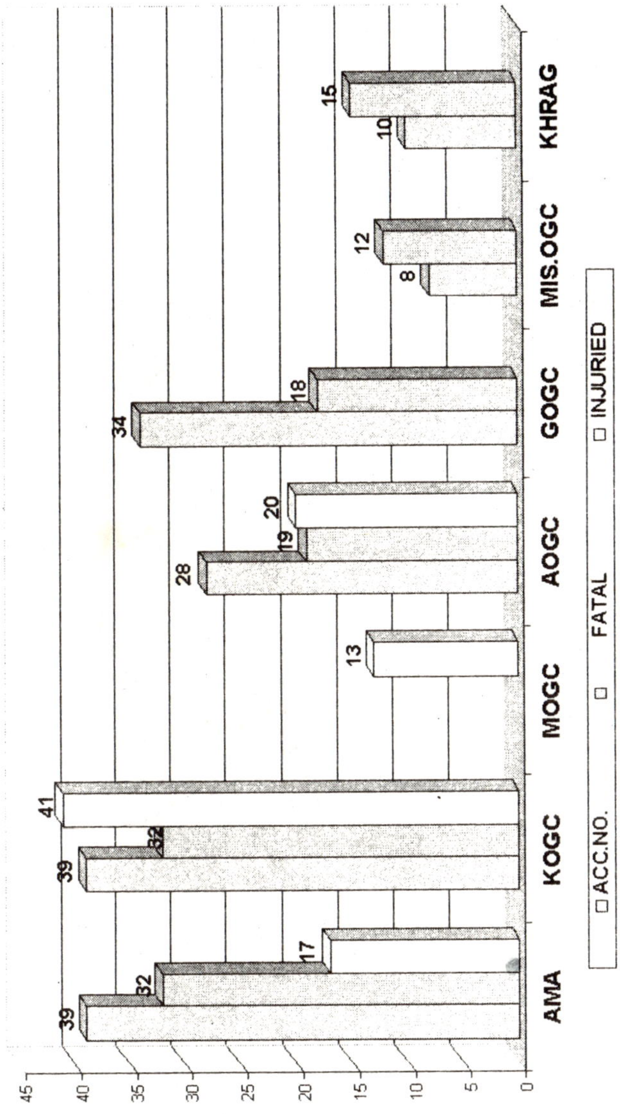

Region Wise Road Accident Status in NISOC 2000

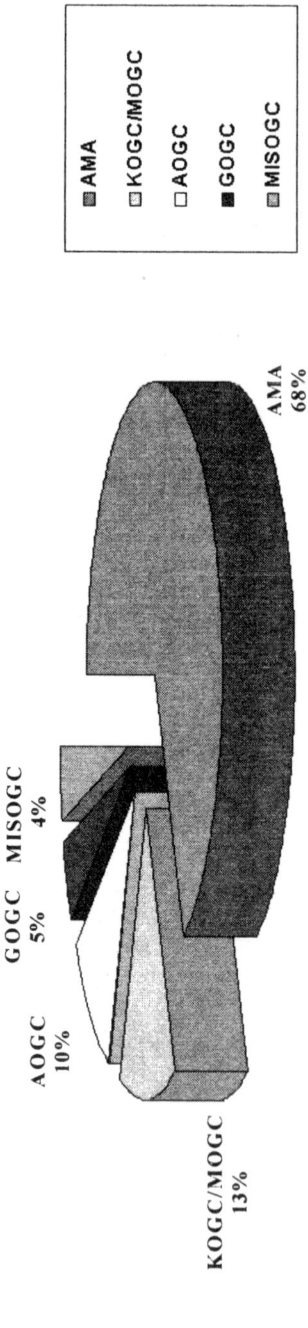

Fire Accident Statistics in NISOC 1996-2000

	1996					1997					1998				
	Departmental			City	Tot.	Departmental			City	Tot.	Departmental			City	Tot.
Region	Ind.Ins	Rs.Col.	Rel.Ins	Ins.		Ind.Ins	Rs.Col.	Rel.Ins	Ins.		Ind.Ins	Rs.Col.	Rel.Ins	Ins.	
Ahwaz					81					96	15	24	13	50	102
Aghjari					84					37	8	13	5	58	84
Gachsaran					81					43	9	12	5	34	60
Masjid-I-Suleyman					23					21	3	16	1	35	55
Khrag					4					6	3	5	0	0	8
Total					284					211	38	70	24	177	309

Legend : Ind. Ins = Industrial Rs. Col. = Residential Colom Tot = Total
City Inst. = Instalation out of Industrial Area and Privot Properties
Rel. Ins = Related to Industrial Instalation
AHWAZ=Before 2000 was (AMA+KOGC+MOGC)
Before 1998 There was not Supart Statistical Figure Information Departmental Area)

Fire Accident Statistics in NISOC 1996-2000

Region	1999 Departmental Ind.Ins	1999 Departmental Rs.Col.	1999 Rel.Ins	1999 City Ins.	1999 Tot.	2000 Departmental Ind.Ins	2000 Departmental Rs.Col.	2000 Rel.Ins	2000 City Ins.	2000 Tot.	From 1996 to 2000 Total	From 1996 to 2000 %
Ahwaz	12	20	30	30	92	6	9	19	15	49	420	32
Aghjari	11	8	10	85	114	2	20	16	12	50	369	28
Gachsaran	8	17	27	13	65	5	11	9	5	30	279	22
Masjid-I-Suleyman	2	26	2	12	42	3	19	6	13	41	182	14
Khrag	7	3	3	4	17					6	54	4
Total	40	74	72	144	330	16	59	50	45	170	1304	100

Legend :Ind. Ins = Industrial Rs. Col = Residential Colony Tot = Total
City Inst. = Installation Out of Industrial Area and Privot Properties
Rel. Ins = Related to Industrial Installation
AHWAZ=Before 2000 Was (AMA+KOGC+MOGC)
Before 1998 There was not Supart Statistical Figure Information Departmental Area)

Fire Accident in NISOC form 1996 to 2000

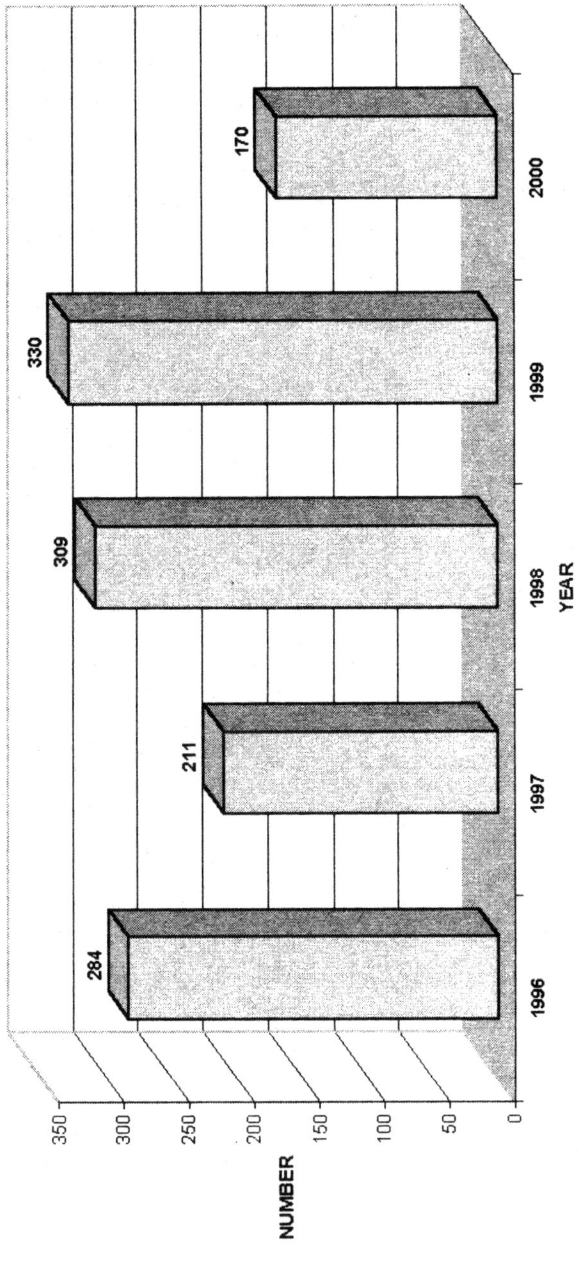

Region Wise Fire Accident Status in NISOC 2000

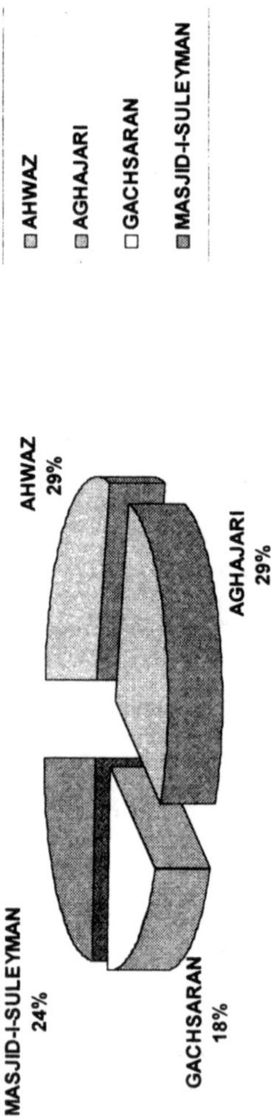

Days Lost Rate in NISOC 1996-2000

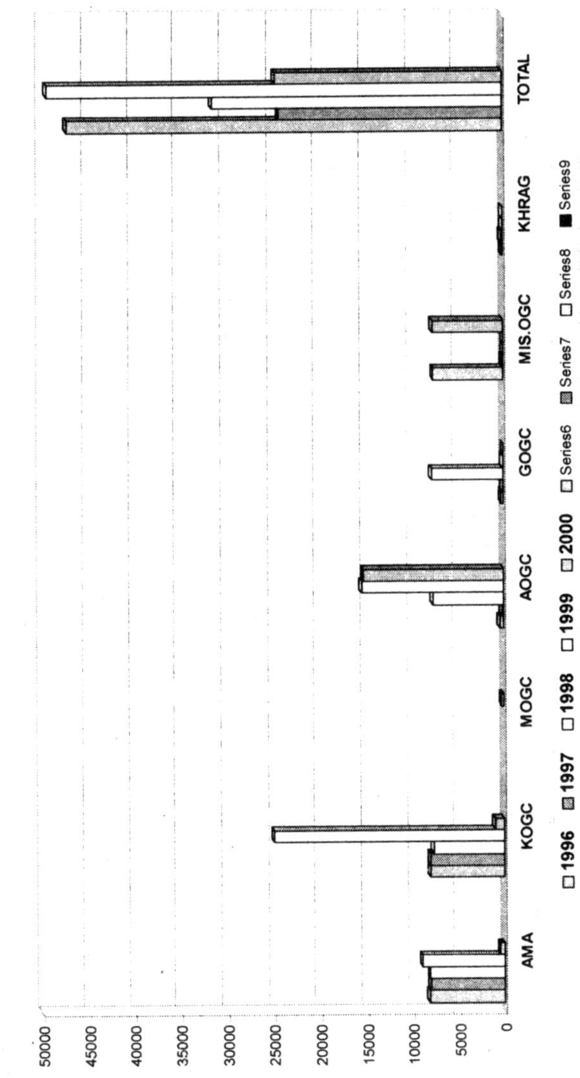

Table 2-27: Accident Rate in NISOC During 1996-2000

Year	*1996*	*1997*	*1998*	*1999*	*2000*
AMA	39	32	32	78	30
KOGC	39	32	29	97	72
MOGC	-	-	-	-	10
AOGC	28	19	17	22	34
GOGC	34	18	41	31	38
MIS.OGC	8	12	13	3	5
KHRAG	10	15	20	20	
Total	**171**	**190**	**164**	**251**	**189**

Table 2-28: Days Lost Rate in NISOC 1996-2000

Year	*1996*	*1997*	*1998*	*1999*	*2000*
AMA	8,150	8,031	8,077	8,908	487
KOGC	7,967	7,997	7,679	24,83	1021
MOGC	-	-	-	-	271
AOGC	420	175	7,657	15,318	15,160
GOGC	244	111	7,730	106	7
MIS.OGC	7,604	125	30	14	7,632
KHRAG	152	162	77	99	
Total	**47,133**	**24,156**	**31,283**	**49,338**	**24,578**

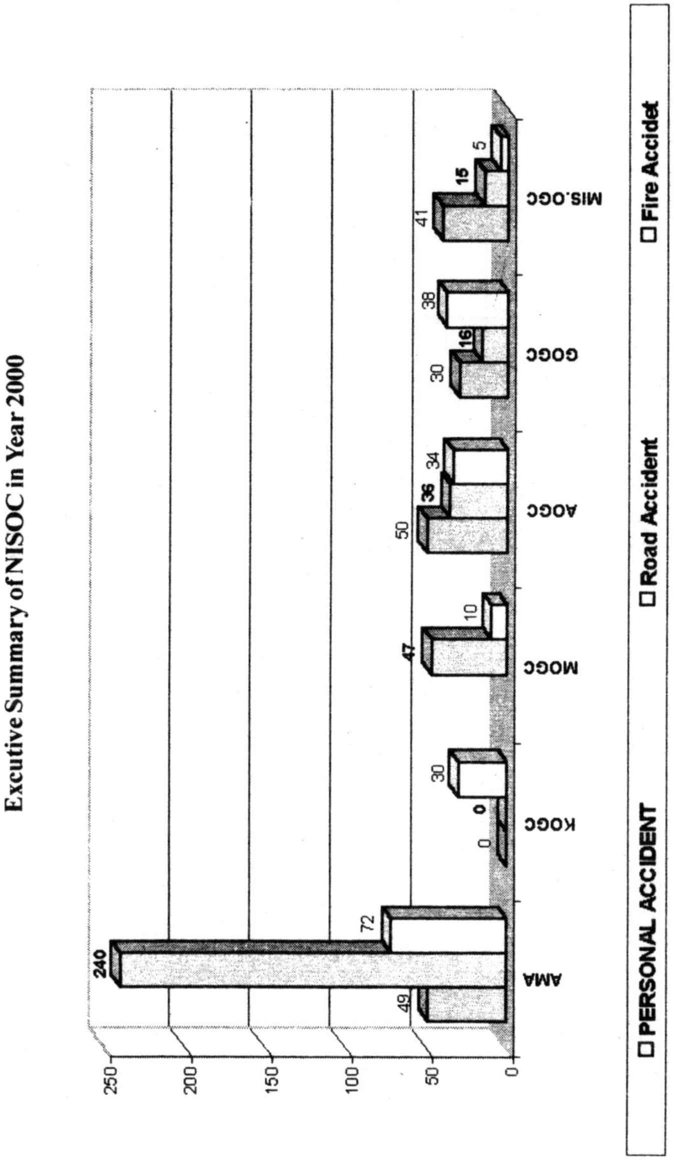
Excutive Summary of NISOC in Year 2000
0
50
100
150
200
250
AMA
KOGC
MOGC
AOGC
GOGC
MIS.OGC
49
240
72
0
0
30
47
10
50
36
34
30
16
38
41
15
5
PERSONAL ACCIDENT
Road Accident
Fire Accidet

Accident Rates in NISOC 2000

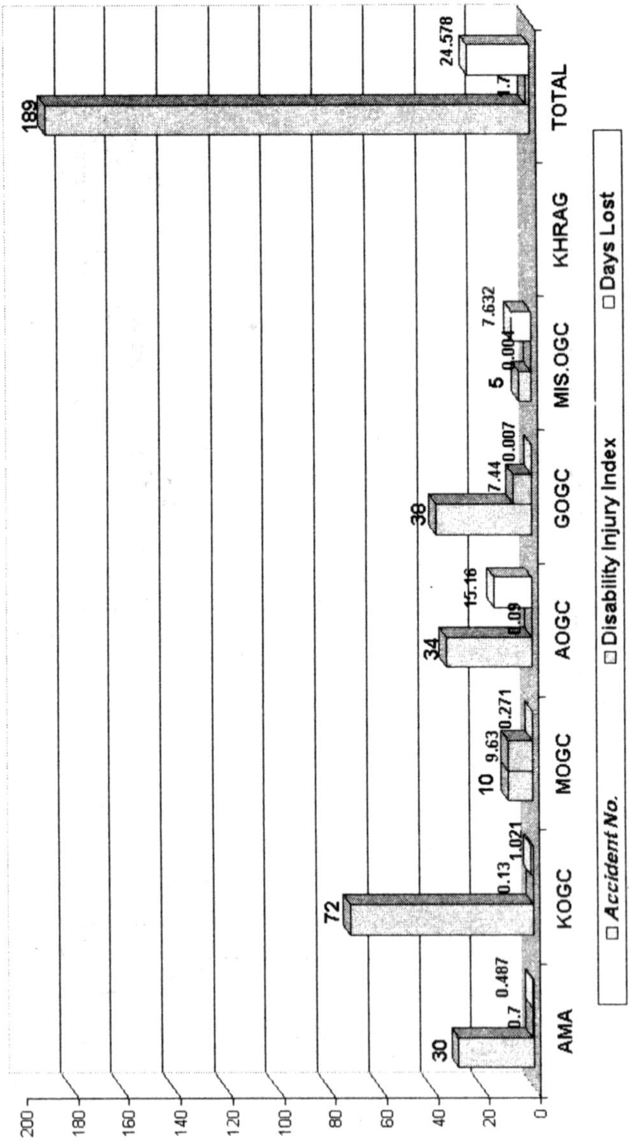

Personal Accident Statistics in AMA 1996-2000

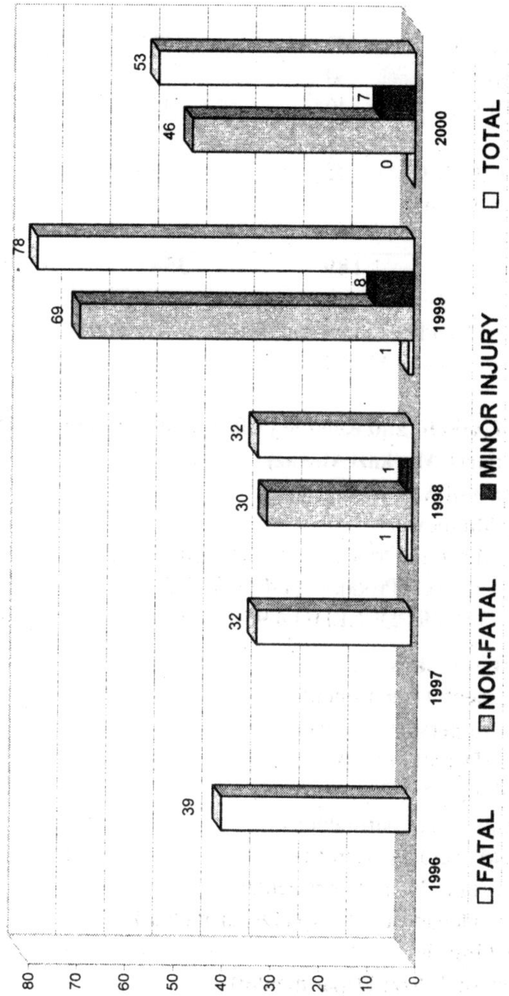

Table 2-29: Executive Summary of NISOC for the year 2000

Region	*No of the Mine Accidents*	*No. Road Accidents*	*No. Fire Accidents*
Ahwaz (AMA)	72	240	49
Karoon (KOGC)	30		
Marun (MOGC)	10	47	
Aghjari	34	36	50
Gachsaran (GOGC)	38	16	30
Masjid-I-Suleyman (MISOGC)	5	15	41
Total	**189**	**354**	**170**

The data of Road Accident and Fire Accident of KOGC and MOGC included in Ahwaz(AMA)

Details of NISOC and Related Offices and Companies of NISOC
AMA (Adareh Markazi Ahwaz)

Details of AMA 2000

- Manpower : 7127
- Meterage Drilled (1.4.99-31.3.2000) : MTS.
- Crude Oil Produced (1.4.99-31.3.2000) : MMT
- GAS PRODUCED (1.4.98-31.3.99) : MMm3

Accident Statistics

Total accidents (Departmental) (Number of persons involved)	:	72
Fatalities (Departmental)	:	00
Non fatal Injuries (Departmental)	:	62
Minor Injuries (Departmental)	:	10
Total road accidents reported (Departmental+Non-Departmental)	:	240
Fatalities (Departmental+Non Departmental)	:	01
Non-fatal Injuries (Departmental+Non-Departmental)	:	21
Total fire Accidents reported (Departmental+Non-Departmental	:	49

Accident Rate

Accident rate per thousand NISOC Employee	:	
Accident rate per million man-hours	:	3.18

Statistics Fire Accident AMA 1996-2000

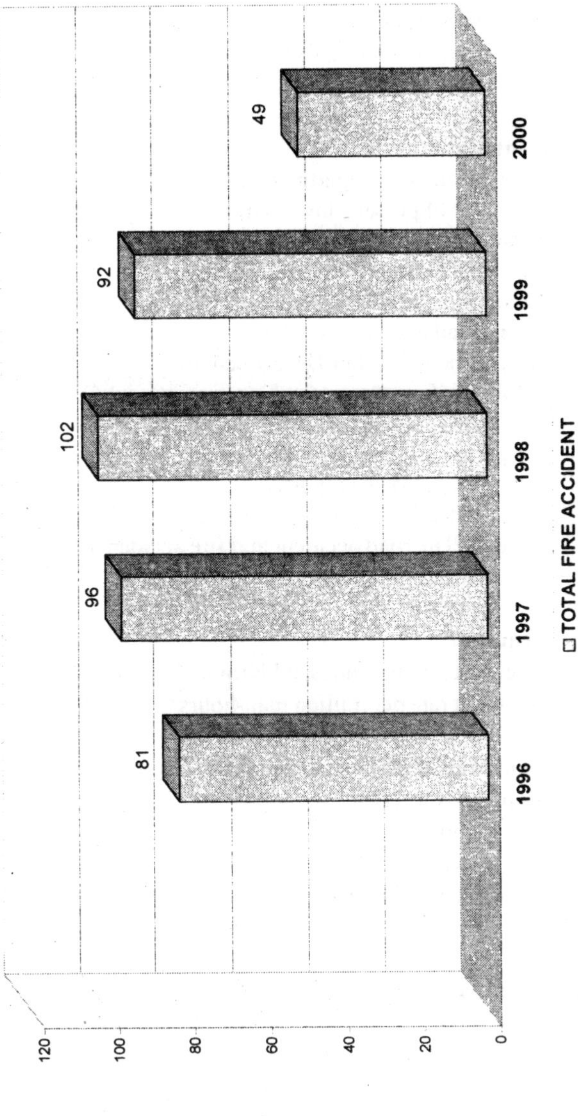

Details of KOGC (Karoon Oil and Gas Producing Company)

Details of KOGC 2000

• Manpower	:	2052
• Meterage Drilled (1.4.98-31.3.99)	:	MTS.
• Crude Oil Produced (1.4.98-31.3.99)	:	MMT
• Gas Produced (1.4.98- 31.3.99)	:	MMm3

Accident Statistics

Total accidents (Departmental) (Number of persons involved)	:	30
Fatalities (Departmental)	:	00
Non fatal Injuries (Departmental)	:	24
Minor Injuries (Departmental)	:	06
Total road accidents reported (Departmental + Non-Departmental)	:	-
Fatalities (Departmental + Non-Departmental)	:	-
Non fatal Injuries (Departmental + Non-Departmental)	:	-
Total fire accidents reported (Departmental + Non-Departmental)	:	-

Legend: The road accident and fire accident of KOGC is accounted in the AMA (Ahwaz).

Accident Rate

Accident rate per thousand NISOC Employee	:	
Accident rate per million man-hours	:	7.68

Details of MOGC (Marun Oil and Gas Producing Company)

Details of MOGC 2000

• Manpower	:	1237
• Meterage Drilled (1.4.98-31.3.99)	:	MTS.
• Crude Oil Produced (1.4.98-31.3.99)	:	MMT
• Gas Produced (1.4.98- 31.3.99)	:	MMm3

Accident Statistics

Total Accidents (Departmental)	:	10
(Number of persons involved) Fatalities (Departmental)	:	01
Non fatal Injuries (Departmental)	:	06
Minor Injuries (Departmental)	:	03
Total road accidents reported		

(Departmental + Non-Departmental) : 47
Fatalities (Departmental + Non-Departmental) : 00
Non fatal Injuries (Departmental + Non-Departmental) : 04
Total fire accidents reported
(Departmental + Non-Departmental) : 00

Accident Rate

Accident rate per thousand NISOC Employee :
Accident rate per million man-hours : 1.28

Details of AOGC (Aghjari Oil and Gas Producing Comapny):

Details of AOGC 2000

- Manpower : 3707
- Meterage Drilled (1.4.98-31.3.99) : MTS.
- Crude Oil Produced (1.4.98-31.3.99) : MMT
- Gas Produced (1.4.98- 31.3.99) : MMm3

Accident Statistics

Total accidents (Departmental) : 34
(Number of persons involved) Fatalities (Departmental): 00
Non fatal Injuries (Departmental) : 20
Minor Injuries (Departmental) : 14
Total road accidents reported
(Departmental + Non-Departmental) : 36
Fatalities (Departmental + Non-Departmental) : 01
Non fatal Injuries (Departmental + Non-Departmental) : 10
Total fire accidents reported
(Departmental + Non-Departmental) : 50

Accident Rate:

Accident rate per thousand NISOC Employee :
Accident rate per million man-hours : 2.87

Details of GOGC (Gachsaran Oil and Gas Producing Company):

Details of GOGC 2000

- Manpower : 3179
- Meterage Drilled (1.4.98-31.3.99) : MTS.
- Crude Oil Produced (1.4.98-31.3.99) : MMT
- Gas Produced (1.4.98- 31.3.99) : MMm3

Accident Statistics

Total accidents (Departmental)	:	38
(Number of persons involved)		
Fatalities (Departmental)	:	02
Non fatal Injuries (Departmental)	:	21
Minor Injuries (Departmental)	:	15
Total road accidents reported		
(Departmental + Non-Departmental)	:	16
Fatalities (Departmental + Non-Departmental)	:	00
Non fatal Injuries (Departmental + Non-Departmental)	:	07
Total fire accidents reported		
(Departmental + Non-Departmental)	:	30

Accident Rate

Accident rate per thousand NISOC Employee	:	1.73
Accident rate per million man-hours	:	0.78

Details of MISOGC (Masjid-I-Suleyman Oil and Gas Producing Company):

Details of MISOGC

- Manpower : 916
- Meterage Drilled (1.4.98-31.3.99) : MTS.
- Crude Oil Produced (1.4.98-31.3.99) :
- Gas Produced (1.4.98- 31.3.99) : MMm3

Accident Statistics

Total accidents (Departmental)	:	05
(Number of persons involved) Fatalities (Departmental)	:	00
Non fatal Injuries (Departmental)	:	02
Minor Injuries (Departmental)	:	03
Total road accidents reported		
(Departmental + Non-Departmental)	:	15
Fatalities (Departmental + Non-Departmental)	:	00
Non fatal Injuries (Departmental + Non-Departmental)	:	02
Total fire accidents reported		
(Departmental + Non-Departmental)	:	41

Accident By Place of Work in NISOC 1996-2000

Year	*1996*							*1997*						
Description	*AMA*	*KC*	*MC*	*AC*	*GC*	*MIS.c*	*Tot*	*AMA*	*KC*	*MC*	*AC*	*GC*	*MIS:c*	*Tot*
Derrick Floor	11	7	4	0	47	16	75	15	3	0	48	10	14	90
HSD/Water Tank	0	1	0	0	1	0	2	1	2	0	3	0	0	6
Pipe Rack	0	0	0	1	1	0	2	0	0	0	0	0	1	1
Monkey Board	0	0	1	0	1	0	2	2	0	0	3	0	2	7
Pump House	0	2	1	0	5	0	3	0	2	1	0	5	0	3
Cementing Unit	1	0	1	0	3	0	5	0	0	0	1	1	0	2
Cat Walk	0	0	0	0	0	0	0	0	0	0	0	0	0	0
Engine House	2	2	2	0	8	10	24	0	0	0	11	2	3	16
Mud Tank/Channel	2	1	0	0	3	0	6	0	2	0	2	1	0	5
Rig-Deck Area	0	0	0	0	15	16	31	1	0	0	17	6	0	24
Rig-Other Area	7	16	4	1	57	5	80	4	1	0	10	3	2	20
Platform	0	0	1	0	14	10	25	0	0	1	13	1	0	15
Rig Building	1	0	0	0	1	0	2	2	0	0	2	0	3	7
Uran/Hazira	0	0	0	0	2	6	8	0	0	0	6	0	0	6
OBG/Wo Rig/CGF/CTI	0	3	0	0	3	0	6	7	1	0	9	11	5	33
TBG/Workshop	1	0	1	0	2	0	4	0	0	0	4	0	2	6
Road Others	10	0	2	0	24	0	36	0	1	0	7	0	5	12
No Detail	0	13	0	0	13	4	30	12	1	0	17	0	1	31
Total	35	45	17	2	200	67	366	44	11	1	155	36	38	285

Accident by Place of Work in NISOC 1996-2000

1998							1999							2000							From 1975 to 2000	
AMA	*KC*	*MC*	*AC*	*GC*	*MIS.c*	*Tot*	*AMA*	*KC*	*MC*	*AC*	*GC*	*MIS.c*	*Tot*	*AMA*	*KC*	*MC*	*AC*	*GC*	*MIS.c*	*Tot*	*Tot.*	*%Age*
15	3	0	48	10	14	90	3	43	12	8	16	0	82	39							373	29
1	2	0	3	0	0	6	0	1	0	0	0	0	1	0							10	1
0	0	0	0	0	1	1	0	2	0	0	0	1	3	2							13	1
2	0	0	3	0	2	7	0	2	0	1	3	0	6	4							32	2
0	2	1	0	5	0	3	0	4	1	1	1	0	7	3							31	2
0	0	0	1	1	0	2	0	2	1	0	0	0	3	1							16	2
0	0	0	0	0	0	0	0	4	0	2	3	0	7	6							21	2
0	0	0	11	2	3	16	0	8	2	0	2	0	12	4							72	2
0	2	0	2	1	0	5	0	5	1	0	0	0	6	1							21	2
1	0	0	17	6	0	24	0	13	9	0	0	0	22	9							109	8
4	1	0	10	3	2	20	2	22	9	5	6	0	38	23							168	11
0	0	1	13	1	0	15	0	10	5	0	0	0	15	5							72	5
2	0	0	2	0	3	7	0	4	0	0	0	0	4	0							20	1
0	0	0	6	0	0	6	0	5	9	0	0	0	14	9							42	3
7	1	0	9	11	5	33	0	12	0	4	10	0	26	14							112	8
0	0	0	4	0	2	6	0	11	0	2	2	0	15	4							55	3
0	1	0	7	0	5	12	0	18	4	5	4	0	31	13							121	9
12	1	0	17	0	1	31	1	1	6	4	4	0	16	14							94	6
44	11	1	155	36	38	285	6	##	59	32	51	1	316	151							1273	100

Legend : Data Represents Number of Persons
AMA=Adareh Markazi KC=Karoon Oil & Producing Company Tot=Total
MC=Marun Oil and Gas Producing AC=Aghajuri Oil & Gas Producing
GC=Gachsaran Oil and Gas Producing MIS. C=Masjid-I-Suleyman Oil and Gas Producing

Cause of Accident in NISOC 1996-2000

Year	*1996*				*1997*				*1998*			
Description	*F*	*NF*	*MI*	*Days L.*	*F*	*NF*	*MI*	*Days L*	*F*	*NF*	*MI*	*Days L.*
Road or other Cause	42	3	9	45615	2	24	13	15351	3	14	12	22679
Str. Against or by object	0	32	20	362	0	39	18	470	0	22	8	234
Slip & Fall of Person	0	36	15	445	0	23	5	399	0	24	6	397
Material Handling	0	10	6	156	0	6	4	64	0	10	7	96
Fall of Person	0	13	4	172	0	21	4	255	0	12	5	176
Caught in Between	0	15	3		0	11	1	104	0	8	3	105
Slip & Fall of Object	0	5	3	28	0	0	0	0	0	3	0	16
Burning	0	8	3	29	1	5	4	7529	0	2	0	14
Exposure to harmful sub	0	0	1	0		0	0	0	0	3	2	27
Electricity					0	0	2	0	1	2	1	7511
No Detail	0	4	0	48	0	2	5	14	0	4	12	28
Total	6	165	64	47133	3	131	56	24156	4	104	56	31283

Cause of Accident in NISOC 1996-2000

1999				*2000*				*From 1975 to 2000*		
F	NF	MI	Days L.	F	NF	MI	Days L.	*Tot.*	*%*	*Days. L*
5	18	8	37820	1	31	13	7909	198	19	129364
0	48	13	592	0	32	13	477	245	24	2135
0	27	13	346	0	23	6	416	178	17	2003
0	12	2	89	0	5	1	80	63	6	485
0	7	3	59	0	22	9	407	100	10	1069
0	4	0	27	0	7	2	123	54	5	459
1	61	4	10230	0	3	1	32	81	8	10306
0	4	0	68	0	6	1	60	34	3	7700
0	0	7	0	1	2	3	7509	19	2	7536
0	0	0	0	1	4	2	7565	9	1	7769
0	10	4	107					48	1	7762
6	191	54	49338	3	135	51	24578	1029	100	17588

Legend : Data Represents Number of Persons
KC=Karoon Oil and Producing Company
MC=Marun Oil and Gas Producing AC=Aghajuri Oil and Gas Producing
GC=Gachsaran Oil and Gas Producing MIS.C=Masjid-I-Suleyman Oil and Gas Producing

Time Analysis of Accident in NISOC 1996-2000

From 1975 to 2000

Year/Time	1996	1997	1998	1999	2000	Age	%
0000-0200	6	4	3	10	7	30	1
2000-4000	11	2	2	6	10	31	1
4000-6000	3	8	3	8	11	33	2
6000-8000	24	23	31	44	27	149	9
8000-10000	48	40	28	39	62	217	13
1000-1200	60	40	82	67	64	313	19
1200-1400	24	22	24	85	39	194	12
1400-1600	37	43	17	44	58	199	12
1600-1800	30	36	31	42	46	185	11
1800-2000	15	25	13	35	35	123	7
2000-2200	8	10	25	20	31	94	6
2200-2400	9	7	3	9	9	37	2
Time Not Indicated	1	10	19	28	26	84	5
Total	276	264	281	436	425	1689	100

Legend : Data Represents Number of Persons Tot=Total
AMA=Adareh Markazi KC=Karoon Oil & Producing Company
MC=Marun Oil and Gas Producing AC=Aghajuri Oil and Gas Producing
GC=Gachsaran Oil and Gas Producing MIS.C=Masjid-I-Suleyman Oil and Gas Producing

Accidents Time Table NISOC 2000

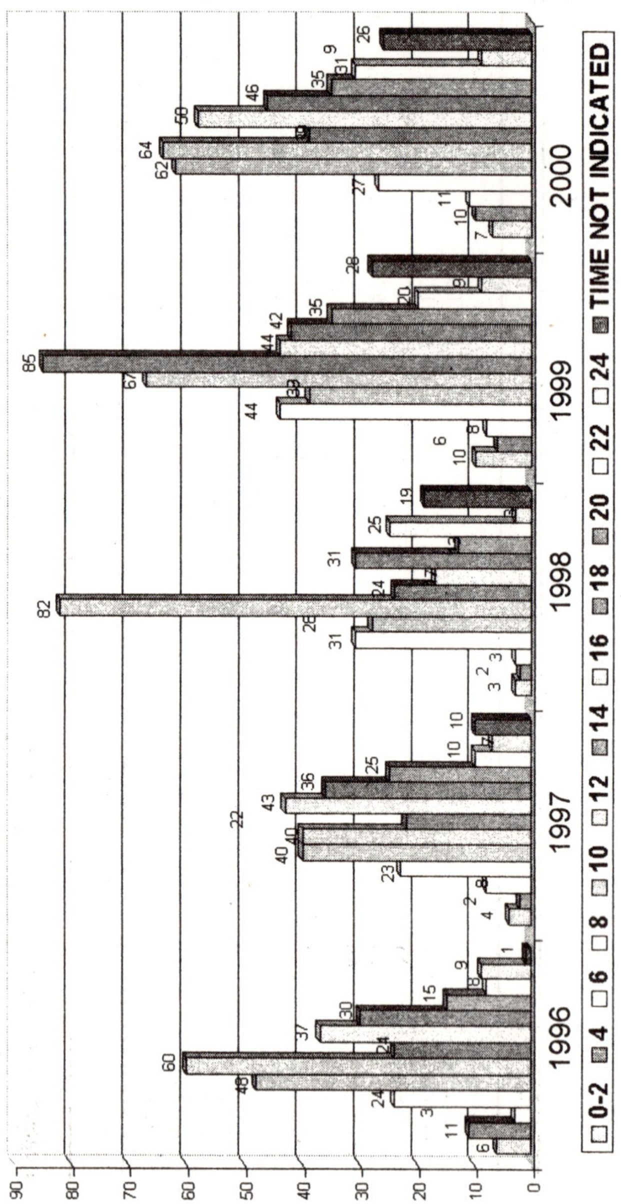

Accident by Part of Body Affected in NISOC 1996-2000

Year	*1996*				*1997*				*1998*			
Part of Body	*F*	*NF*	*MI*	*Days L.*	*F*	*NF*	*MI*	*Days L.*	*F*	*NF*	*MI*	*Days L.*
Head	2	7	6	15051	1	4	3	7530	0	2	4	16
Eye	0	6	6	30	0	4	5	38	0	4	2	18
Face	0	10	6	59	0	6	11	40	0	5	9	33
Body	0	11	7	161	2	12	8	15251	4	13	6	30116
Lumber/Back	0	7	7	77	0	5	3	54	0	3	7	70
Several Part	4	33	6	30340	0	19	6	283	0	10	3	61
Arm/Elbow	0	2	0	28	0	1	0	7	0	4	1	72
Hand	0	17	8	241	0	16	6	183	0	13	6	233
H.Fingers	0	27	11	333	0	24	9	258	0	16	7	216
Knee/Thigh	0	11	4	358	0	14	2	265	0	11	7	103
Foot/Ankle	0	29	3	364	0	24	1	322	0	18	3	286
Foot/Toe	0	5	0	91	0	2	2	25	0	5	1	59
Total	6	165	64	47133	3	131	56	24156	4	104	56	31283

Legend : Data Represents Number of Person Days L. = Days Lost
F=Fatal NF=Non-Fatal Days CHG = Days Charged (Lost Days)
MI=Minor Injury (Persons with Minor Injured)

Accident by Part of Body Affected in NISOC 1996-2000

1999				*2000*				*Total of 5 Years From 1975 to 2000*		
F	*NF*	*MI*	*Days L.*	*F*	*NF*	*MI*	*Days L.*			
0	3	5	32	30	2	3	40	42	4	22669
0	4	4	82	0	4	1	34	40	4	202
0	9	8	77	0	6	5	49	75	7	258
0	12	9	30184	0	14	6	7711	109	11	83423
1	6	4	7554	0	9	1	106	53	5	7861
1	67	10	10279	2	28	11	15348	200	19	56311
0	2	0	12	0	2	0	17	12	1	136
0	25	3	296	0	13	5	240	112	11	1193
0	26	7	365	0	17	10	245	154	5	1417
0	8	0	65	0	7	2	101	66	6	892
0	18	3	304	0	28	6	579	133	14	185
0	11	1	88	0	5	1	108	33	3	371
6	191	54	49338	3	135	51	24578	1029	100	17588

Legend : Data Represents Number of Person Days L. = Days Lost
F=Fatal NF=Non-Fatal Days CHG = Days Charged (Lost Days)
MI=Minor Injury (Persons with Minor Injured)

Accident Analysis in NISOC 2000

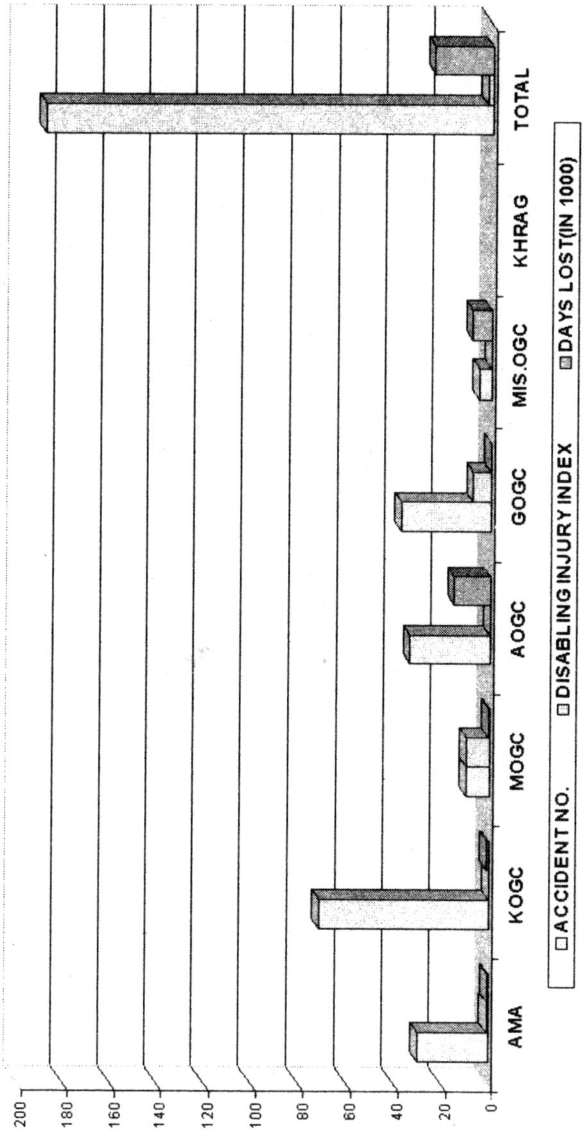

Observation and Analysis in NISOC

- Analysis reveals that during the last 5 years (1996-2000) there has been 1989 number of accidents occurred at various Installations of NISOC including Non mine accidents. It has been observed that in mine area the main cause of accidents has been slip and fall of person, whereas striking against or struck by object is the next most prevalent type of accident.
- This reflects slippery working places and poor house keeping is the main reasons behind occurrence of accidents due to slip and fall of persons.
- Careless and casual approach in dealing with the material and lack of coordination among the working crew could be the reason for occurrence of accident due to striking against/ striking by objects.
- Accident data reveals that out of 1989 accidents, maxiumum number of accidents occurred at derrick floor of drilling rigs alone.
- This can be attributed to the fact that most of the manual operations are being carried out at Derrick floor and require constant vigil. Moreover handling of tools and material is also very frequent as per the job requirement, which could also be one of the reasons for occurrence of more accident at derrick floor.
- In non-mine area most of the fatal accidents have occurred on roads where mainly hired vehicles as contractor were involved.
- The reason for high frequency of fatal accidents on roads is due to the negligence on the part of the contractual drives and old car using. Inadequate driving experiences and frequents change of drivers of contractual vehicles. Long working hours, inadequate rest could also be the reasons for occurrence of road accidents where contractual vehicles are involved.
- Time analysis of accidents reveals maximum numbers accidents occurred during the daytime (from 10:00 AM to 16:00 PM). Whereas the maximum frequency of accident have been observed between 10:00 AM to 12:00 AM.
- The reason could be attributed to the fact that many other operations like logging, hydro fracturing, perforation etc. are carried out during the daytime only. Moreover, personnel bid to accelerate the slack working during the change over shift and lunch break. Pre-lunch and post-lunch effects could also be the reasons for high frequency of accidents during this period.
- On comparing the accidents statistics of various regions of NISOC

during the period 1996-2000, it has been observed that there is a remarkable increase in occurrence of accidents during the calendar year 1998 as compared to same period in 1997. Also most of the accidents occurred during the year 2000 are minor in nature.

- Drilling Business Group is the most affected group in occurrence of accidents and most of the accidents occurred at drilling rigs.
- The reason is that particularly on drilling rigs most of the operation is manual and the working crew, sometimes has to work in hostile conditions. Moreover, involvement of mud and various chemicals at Drilling Rigs also contribute in soiling of the working area especially in rainy season thereby making Drilling Rigs more prone to accidents.
- Accident analysis also reveals that in most of the accidents, "Several parts of Body" is the most affected part of the body. Next most affected part body is "upper limb".

  Since most of the manual jobs at NISOC installations involve maximum use of hands, thereby increasing the probability of injuries at upper limbs. Non-usage of Personal Protective Equipment/ Improper usage or shortage of PPE could be the reason for occurrence of such Accidents.
- On comparing "Accident frequency Rate" of various regions of NISOC, it has been observed that "Accident rate per million working hours" is maximum in AMA.
- During the year 2000, maximum number of accident have taken place at Drilling Rigs and Derrick floor has been the most prone area.
- "Slip and fall of person" has been observed the main cause in occurrence of accidents whereas "Striking against or struck by object" is next most prevalent type of accident.
- Time analysis of accidents reveals that although maximum number of accidents has taken place during the time 10.00 hrs. To 16.00 hrs in 1998 but on comparing the accident statistics of last five-year (1996-2000), data reveals that maximum accidents prone time is 10.00 hrs-12.00 hrs.
- "Rate of accident per thousand employees" has been observed maximum in AMA, in terms of "Accident rate per million man hours".
- As per above, "Accident analysis Report- 1998" is being circulated to various Regions/ Projects of NISOC with a request that Recommendations suggested at this report kindly be implement to deter the occurrence of accidents in future.

Mine Area

Accident-Prone Area Derrick Floor

Time During which maximum number of Accidents took place: 10:00 AM TO 12:00 AM

Cause of Majority of Accidents: Slip and Fall of Person, Striking Against or Striking by object

Part of Body Most Affected Several Part of Body

Non-mine Area

Accident Prone Area: Road Accidents During Transportation of Personnel

Accident Statics in ONGC from 1993 to 1998

Details of NISOC and Related Offices and Companies of ONGC

Details of ONGC

- Manpower : 41,677
- Meterage Drilled (1.4.98-31.3.99) :587425 MTS.
- Crude Oil Produced (1.4.98-31.3.99) :26.5926 MMT
- Gas Produced (1.4.98- 31.3.99) :18443.87 MMm3

Accident Statistics

Total accidents reported (Departmental + Non-Departmental) (Number of persons involved) : 151

Fatalities (Departmental + Non-Departmental) : 011

Non fatal Injuries (Departmental + Non-Departmental) : 140

Fatalities (Departmental) : 001

Non fatal Injuries (Departmental) : 122

Total accidents (Departmental) : 123

Accident Rate

Accident rate per thousand ONGC Employee : 2.95

Accident rate per million man-hours : 1.34

Table 2-01: Total accident statistics in ONGC from 1993 till 2000

Chart 2-02: Total accident statistics in ONGC from 1993 till 2000

Chart 2-03: Region Wise Accident Status in ONGC

Details of MRBC

- Manpower : 7,428
- Meterager Drilled (1.4.98-31.3.99) :144657 MTS.
- Crude Oil Produced (1.4.98-31.3.99) :18.2745 MMT
- Gas Produced (1.4.98- 31.3.99) :14080.55MMm3

Accident Statistics

Total accidents reported		
(Departmental + Non-Departmental)	:	59
(Number of persons involved)		
Fatalities		
(Departmental + Non-Departmental)	:	03
Non fatal Injuries		
(Departmental + Non-Departmental)	:	56
Fatalities (Departmental)	:	00
Non fatal Injuries (Departmental)	:	40
Total accidents (Departmental)	:	40

Region Wise Accident Status in ONGC

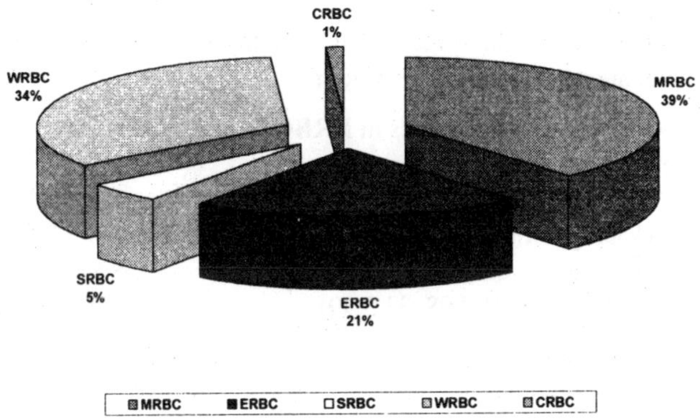

Accident Rate

Accident rate per thousand ONGC Employee	:	5.38
Accident rate per million man-hours	:	2.44

Chart 2-04 : Accident Statistics in MRBC from 1993 till 2000

DETAILS OF ERBC:

- Manpower : 10,290
- Meterage Drilled (1.4.98-31.3.99) : 66003 MTS.
- Crude Oil Produced (1.4.98-31.3.99) : 2.0390 MMT
- Gas Produced (1.4.98- 31.3.99) : 270.42 MMm3

Accident Statics

Total accidents reported (Departmental + Non-Departmental) (Number of persons involved)	:	32
Fatalities (Departmental + Non-Departmental)	:	03
Non fatal Injuries (Departmental + Non-Departmental)	:	29
Fatalities (Departmental)	:	00
Non fatal Injuries (Departmental)	:	29
Total Accidents (Departmental)	:	29

Accident Rate

Accident rate per thousand ONGC Employee	:	2.82
Accident rate per million man-hours	:	1.28

Chart 2-05 : Accident Statistics in ERBC from 1993 till 2000

Details of WRBC:

- Manpower : 13,682
- Meterage Drilled (1.4.98-31.3.99) : 249707 MTS.
- Crude Oil Produced (1.4.98-31.3.99) : 5.8281 MMT
- Gas Produced (1.4.98- 31.3.99) : 2550.20 MMm3

Accident Statistics

Total accidents reported (Departmental + Non-Departmental) (Number of persons involved)	:	51

Accident Statistics in MRBC from 1993 to 2000

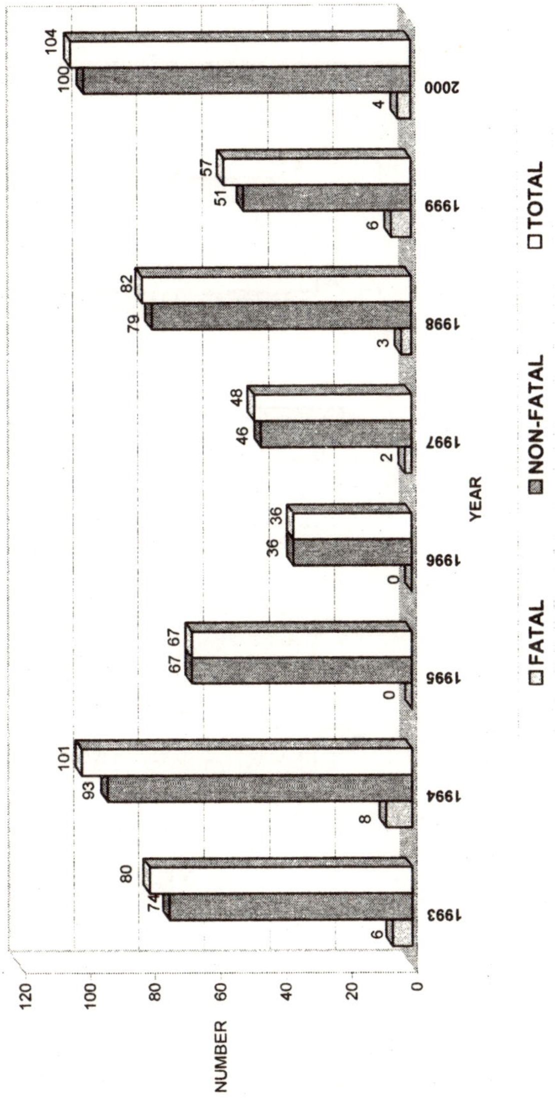

Accident Statistics in ERBC 1993-2000

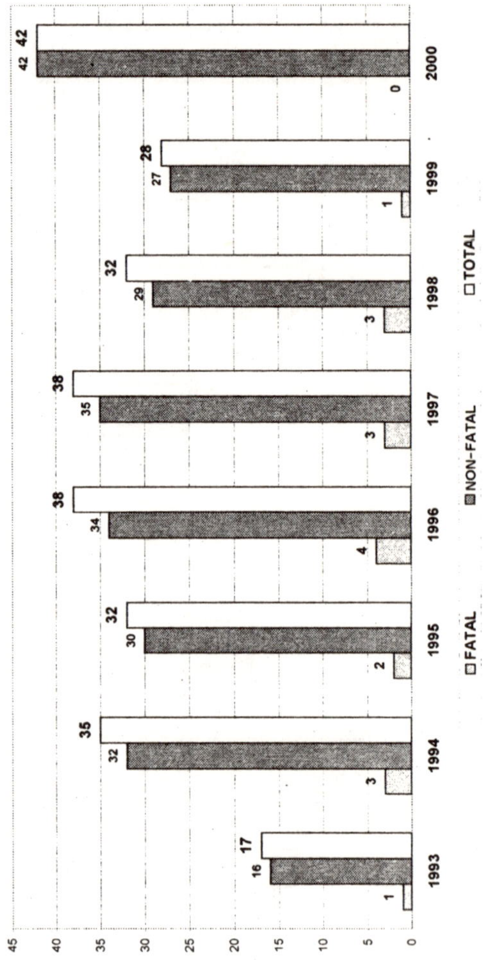

Fatalities (Departmental + Non-Departmental)	:	05
Non fatal Injuries (Departmental + Non-Departmental)	:	46
Fatalities (Departmental)	:	01
Non fatal Injuries (Departmental)	:	4
Total accidents (Departmental)	:	47

Accident Rate

Accident rate per thousand ONGC Employee	:	3.43
Accident rate per million man-hours	:	1.55

Chart 2-06 : Accident Statistics in WRBC from 1993 till 2000.

DETAILS OF SRBC:

- Manpower : 3,458
- Meterage Drilled (1.4.98-31.3.99) : 116696 MTS.
- Crude Oil Produced (1.4.98-31.3.99) : 0.4510 MMT
- GAS PRODUCED (1.4.98-31.3.99) : 1236.78 MMm3

Accident Statistics

Total accidents reported (Departmental + Non-Departmental) (Number of persons involved)	:	08
Fatalities (Departmental + Non-Departmental)	:	00
Non fatal Injuries (Departmental + Non-Departmental)	:	08
Fatalities (Departmental)	:	00
Non fatal Injuries (Departmental)	:	06
Total accidents (Departmental)	:	06

Accident Rate

Accident rate per thousand ONGC Employee	:	1.73
Accident rate per million man-hours	:	0.78

Chart 2-07 : Accident Statistics in SRBC from 1993 till 2000.

Accident Statistics in SRBC 1993-2000

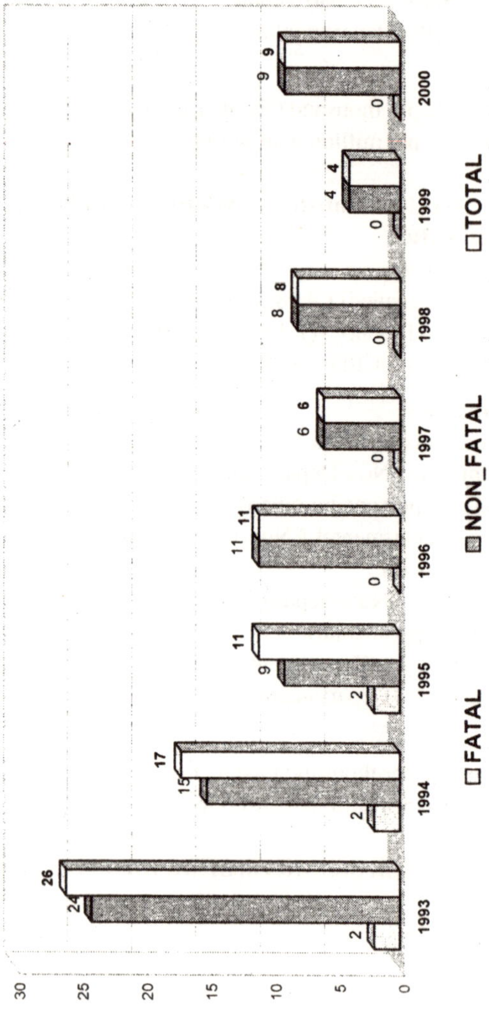

Details of CRBC

- Manpower : 2,324
- Meterage Drilled (1.4.98-31.3.99) :10362 MTS.
- Crude Oil Produced (1.4.98-31.3.99) : NIL
- Gas Produced (1.4.98- 31.3.99) :305.92 MMm3

Accident Statistics

Total accidents reported
(Departmental + Non-Departmental) : 01
(Number of persons involved)
Fatalities (Departmental + Non-Departmental) : 00
Non fatal Injuries
(Departmental + Non-Departmental) : 01
Fatalities (Departmental) : 00
Non fatal Injuries (Departmental) : 01
Total accidents (Departmental) : 01

Accident Rate

Accident rate per thousand ONGC Employee : 0.43
Accident rate per million man-hours : 0.0003

Chart 2-08 : Accident Statistics in CRBC from 1993 till 2000.

Chart 2-09 : Accident Statistics in NRBC from 1993 till 2000.

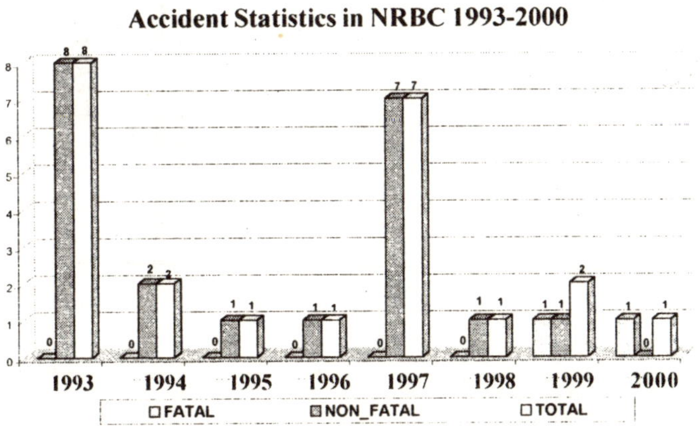

Accident Statistics in NRBC 1993-2000

Accident Enquiry

Fatal Accident

A special team duly constituted by Regional Director of the region and a representative from Corporate SEM will conduct enquiry into the fatal accident with a view to examine the possible causes of accident and to suggest remedial measures to prevent reoccurrence of similar accidents.

Non-fatal Accident

Inquiry will be conducted by a team of officers duly constituted by respective coordinator and remedial measures are widely circulated with a view to avoid reoccurrence of similar accidents.

Table 2.30: Accident Statistics in ONGC 1998

Region	*Departmental*		*Non-Departmetnal*		*Total*	*Grand*
MRBC	00	40	03	16	03 56	59
ERBC	00	29	03	00	03	29 32
WRBC	01	46	04	00	05 46	51
SRBC	00	06	00	02	00 08	46
CRBC	00	01	00	00	00 01	01
TOTAL	01	122	10	18	11 140	151

Table 2.31: Accident Rate in ONGC

Region	*Per Tthousand Employees*	*Per Million Man Hours*
MRBC	5.38	2.44
ERBC	2.82	1.28
WRBC	3.43	1.55
SRBC	1.73	0.78
CRBC	0.43	0.0003
ONGC	2.95	1.43

Accidents by Place of Work

Year	1993						1994						1995					
Description	*MR*	*ER*	*WR*	*SR*	*CR*	*Tot*	*MR*	*ER*	*WR*	*SR*	*CR*	*Tot*	*MR*	*ER*	*WR*	*SR*	*CR*	*Tot*
Derrick Floor	11	7	29	5	1	53	25	11	7	4	0	47	16	14	15	3	0	48
HSD/Water Tank	0	1	0	0	0	1	0	0	1	0	0	1	0	0	1	2	0	3
Pipe Rack	1	1	0	1	0	3	0	0	0	0	1	1	0	0	0	0	0	0
Monkey Board	3	0	1	3	0	7	0	0	0	1	0	1	0	1	2	0	0	3
Pump House	0	1	5	1	1	7	2	0	2	1	0	5	0	2	0	0	0	2
Cementing Unit	0	0	1	1	0	2	1	1	0	1	0	3	0	1	0	0	0	1
Cat Walk	0	0	0	0	1	1	0	0	0	0	0	0	0	0	0	0	0	0
Engine House	9	0	1	1	3	14	2	2	2	2	0	8	10	1	0	0	0	11
Mud Tank/Channel	2	0	2	2	0	6	0	2	1	0	0	3	0	0	0	2	0	2
Rig-Deck Area	13	0	0	1	0	14	15	0	0	0	0	15	16	0	1	0	0	17
Rig-Other Area	7	0	11	6	2	26	29	7	16	4	1	57	5	0	4	1	0	10
Platform	14	0	0	0	0	14	13	0	0	1	0	14	10	2	0	0	1	13
Rig Building	0	0	2	1	0	3	0	1	0	0	0	1	0	0	2	0	0	2
Uran/Hazira	3	0	0	0	0	3	3	2	0	0	0	2	6	0	0	0	0	6
OBG/Wo Rig/CGF/CTI	0	1	9	1	0	11	0	0	3	0	0	3	0	1	7	1	0	9
TBG/Workshop	11	3	0	0	0	14	0	1	0	1	0	2	0	4	0	0	0	4
Road Others	6	4	0	3	0	13	12	10	0	2	0	24	0	6	0	1	0	7
No Detail	0	0	17	0	0	17	0	0	13	0	0	13	4	0	12	1	0	17
Total	80	17	78	26	8	209	101	35	45	17	2	200	67	32	44	11	1	155

Legend :
MR : MRBC ER : ERBC WR : WRBC SR : SRBC CR : CRBC Tot : Total
Data Represents Number of Persons

Contd...

Accidents by Place of Work

1996						1997						*1998*						*93*	*98*
MR	*ER*	*WR*	*SR*	*CR*	*Tot*	MR	ER	WR	SR	CR	Tot	*MR*	*ER*	*WR*	*SR*	*CR*	*Tot*	*Tot.*	*%Age*
10	14	13	1	0	38	8	8	22	2	3	43	12	8	16	0	3	39	268	26.22
0	0	0	0	0	0	1	0	0	0	0	1	0	0	0	0	0	0	6	0.59
0	1	2	0	0	3	0	1	1	0	0	2	0	0	0	1	1	2	11	1.08
0	2	5	2	0	9	1	1	0	0	0	2	0	1	3	0	0	4	26	2.45
1	0	1	2	0	4	0	1	3	0	0	4	1	1	1	0	0	3	25	2.45
1	0	2	0	0	3	2	0	0	0	0	2	1	0	0	0	0	1	12	1.17
0	0	2	0	0	2	0	0	4	0	0	4	0	2	3	0	1	6	13	1.27
2	3	3	0	0	8	3	1	4	0	0	8	2	0	2	0	0	4	53	5.18
1	0	3	0	0	4	1	0	4	0	0	5	1	0	0	0	0	1	21	2.05
6	0	4	1	0	11	11	0	0	2	0	13	9	0	0	0	0	9	79	7.73
3	2	6	2	0	13	3	11	6	0	2	22	9	5	6	0	3	23	151	14.77
1	0	1	0	0	2	10	0	0	0	0	10	5	0	0	0	0	5	58	5.67
0	3	1	1	0	5	0	2	0	2	0	4	0	0	0	0	0	0	45	1.47
0	0	0	0	0	0	5	0	0	0	0	5	9	0	0	0	0	9	25	2.44
11	5	3	1	0	20	0	7	5	0	0	12	0	4	10	0	0	14	69	6.75
0	2	2	0	1	5	1	3	7	0	0	11	0	2	2	0	0	4	40	3.91
0	5	6	0	0	11	2	3	12	1	0	18	4	5	4	0	0	13	86	8.41
0	1	0	1	0	2	0	0	0	0	1	1	6	4	4	0	0	14	64	6.26
36	38	54	11	1	140	48	38	68	7	6	167	59	32	51	1	8	151	1022	

Legend :

MR : MRBC ER : ERBC WR : WRBC SR : SRBC CR : CRBC Tot : Total

Data Represents Number of Persons

Causes of Accidents

Year	1993						1994						1995					
Description	*MR*	*ER*	*WR*	*SR*	*CR*	*Tot*	*MR*	*ER*	*WR*	*SR*	*CR*	*Tot*	*MR*	*ER*	*WR*	*SR*	*CR*	*Tot*
Slip and Fall of Object	8	2	8	2	0	20	15	6	1	1	2	25	7	2	2	3	0	14
Slip and Fall of Person	19	1	22	6	0	48	28	2	7	4	0	41	16	10	9	2	0	37
Str. Against or by object	12	7	18	9	5	51	11	8	5	4	0	28	11	7	8	2	1	29
Caught in between	6	2	12	3	0	23	0	3	3	5	0	11	0	4	7	1	0	12
Road or other cause	19	3	4	2	1	29	17	10	12	1	0	40	13	4	11	0	0	28
Material Handling	15	0	0	2	0	17	20	3	17	0	0	40	11	2	7	1	0	21
Electricity	1	0	2	0	0	3	2	0	0	1	0	3	2	0	0	0	0	2
Exposure to harmful sub	0	0	1	0	0	1	0	0	0	0	0	0	0	0	0	0	0	0
Equipment Failure	0	0	0	0	0	0	3	0	0	0	0	3	3	0	0	0	9	3
Drowning	0	0	0	0	0	0	0	0	0	1	0	1	0	0	0	1	0	1
Blowout	0	0	0	0	0	0	0	0	0	0	0	0	0	0	0	1	0	1
No Detail	0	2	11	2	2	17	5	3	0	0	0	8	4	3	0	0	0	7
Total	80	17	78	26	8	209	101	35	45	17	2	200	200	67	32	44	.11	1

Legend :
MR : MRBC ER : ERBC WR : WRBC SR : SRBC CR : CRBC Tot : Total
Data
Represents Number of Persons

Contd...

Causes of Accidents

1996						1997						1998						93	98
MR	*ER*	*WR*	*SR*	*CR*	*Tot*	*MR*	*ER*	*WR*	*SR*	*CR*	*Tot*	*MR*	*ER*	*WR*	*SR*	*CR*	*Tot*	*Tot.*	%Age
4	2	3	0	0	9	7	3	3	1	1	15	7	2	5	2	1	17	100	9.78
12	10	12	1	0	35	10	11	15	0	2	38	16	9	15	1	0	41	240	23.48
4	8	18	7	1	38	0	8	18	1	2	29	5	4	13	2	0	24	199	19.47
8	1	7	1	0	17	0	6	9	2	0	17	5	2	6	2	0	15	95	9.29
0	4	6	0	0	10	4	4	2	0	0	10	0	4	3	0	0	7	124	12.13
3	1	6	0	0	10	14	1	10	0	1	26	7	3	0	0	0	10	124	12.13
0	3	0	0	0	3	2	0	4	0	1	7	0	0	1	0	0	1	19	1.85
0	1	1	1	0	3	0	0	0	0	0	0	2	0	0	0	0	2	6	0.59
1	0	1	0	0	2	5	5	1	0	0	11	6	2	0	1	0	9	28	2.74
0	0	0	0	0	0	0	0	0	0	0	0	1	0	0	0	0	1	3	0.29
0	2	0	0	0	2	0	0	0	1	0	1	2	0	0	0	0	2	6	5.59
4	6	0	1	0	11	6	0	6	1	0	13	8	6	8	0	0	32	78	7.63
36	38	54	11	1	140	48	38	68	6	7	167	59	32	51	8	1	151	1022	

Legend :
MR : MRBC ER : ERBC WR : WRBC SR : SRBC CR : CRBC Tot : Total
Data Represents Number of Persons

Accident by Part of Body

Year	1993						1994						1995					
Part of Body	*MR*	*ER*	*WR*	*SR*	*CR*	*Tot*	*MR*	*ER*	*WR*	*SR*	*CR*	*Tot*	*MR*	*ER*	*WR*	*SR*	*CR*	*Tot*
Fatal	6	1	7	2	0	16	8	3	11	2	0	24	0	2	8	2	0	12
Head	7	1	12	2	1	23	12	7	4	0	0	23	10	2	10	1	1	24
Trunk	5	0	9	2	0	16	8	0	14	0	0	22	1	1	4	2	0	8
Upper limb	21	8	29	8	3	69	39	9	8	8	2	66	31	6	14	3	0	54
Lower Limb	20	4	20	7	1	52	20	6	8	6	0	40	13	7	8	2	0	30
Other	2	3	1	3	0	9	3	2	0	1	0	6	6	14	0	0	0	20
No Detail	19	0	0	2	3	24	11	8	0	0	0	19	6	0	0	1	0	7
Total	80	17	78	26	8	209	101	35	45	17	2	200	67	32	44	11	1	155

Legend :
MR : MRBC ER : ERBC WR : WRBC SR : SRBC CR : CRBC Tot : Total

Contd...

Accidents by Part of Body

1996						*1997*						*1998*						*93*	*98*
MR	*ER*	*WR*	*SR*	*CR*	*Tot*	*MR*	*ER*	*WR*	*SR*	*CR*	*Tot*	*MR*	*ER*	*WR*	*SR*	*CR*	*Tot*	*Tot.*	*%Age*
0	4	6	0	0	10	2	3	7	0	0	12	3	3	5	0	0	11	85	8.32
5	3	10	2	0	20	11	2	11	1	1	26	5	2	8	2	0	17	133	13.01
4	3	5	1	0	13	4	5	2	0	2	13	8	0	2	0	0	10	82	8.02
17	8	20	7	0	52	19	12	34	3	1	69	23	9	14	4	0	50	360	35.22
10	7	11	0	1	29	8	10	13	0	1	32	13	2	16	2	1	34	217	21.23
0	7	2	0	0	9	4	4	1	0	1	10	4	7	3	0	0	14	68	6.65
0	6	0	1	0	7	0	2	0	2	1	5	3	9	3	0	0	15	77	7.53
36	38	54	11	1	140	48	38	68	6	7	167	59	32	51	8	1	151	1022	

Legend :

MR : MRBC ER : ERBC WR : WRBC SR : SRBC CR : CRBC Tot : Total

Observations and Analysis in ONGC

- Analysis reveals that during the last six years (1993-1998) there has been 1022 number of accidents occurred at various installations of ONGC including non mine accidents. It has been observed that in mine area the main cause of accidents has been slip and fall of person which accounts for 240 accidents (23.48%), whereas striking against or struck by an object is the next most prevalent type of accident which accounts for 19.47%.
  - This reflects slippery working places and poor house keeping is the main reasons behind occurrence of accidents due to slip and fall of persons.
  - Careless and casual approach in dealing with the material and lack of coordination among the working crew could be the reason for occurrence of accidents due to striking against/ striking by anobjects.
- Accident data reveals that out of 1022 accidents about 268 (26.22%) occurred at derrick floor of drilling rigs alone.
  - This can be attributed to the fact that most of the manual operations are being carried out at Derrick floor and require constant vigil. Moreover, handling of tools and material is also very frequent as per the job requirement, which could also be one of the reasons for occurrence of more accident at derrick floor.
- In non-mine area most of the fatal accidents have occurred on roads where mainly hired vehicles were involved.
  - The reason for high frequency of fatal accidents on roads is due to the negligence on the part of the contractual drive. Inadequate driving experiences and frequent change of drivers of contractual vehicles. Long working hours, inadequate rest could also be the reasons for occurrence of road accidents where contractual vehicles are involved.
- Time analysis of accidents reveals that about 62% accidents occurred during the daytime (from 0800 AM to o600PM). Whereas the maximum frequency of accidents have been observed between 10:00 AM to 12:00 AM.
  - The reason could be attributed to the fact that many other operations like logging, hydro- fracturing, perforation etc. are carried out during the daytime only. Moreover, personnel bid to accelerate the slack working during the change over shift and tea/ lunch break. Pre-lunch and post-lunch effects could also be the reasons for high frequency of accidents during this period.

- On comparing the accident statistics of various regions of ONGC during the period 1994-98, it has been observed that there is a remarkable reduction (9.6%) in occurrence of accidents during the calendar year 1998 as compared to same period in 1997. Also, most of the accidents occurred during the year 1998 are minor in nature.
- Drilling Business Group is the most affected group in occurrence of accidents and most of the accidents occurred at drilling rigs.
  - The reason is that particularly on drilling rigs most of the operation is manual and the working crew some times has to work in hostile conditions. Moreover involvement of mud and various chemicals at Drilling Rigs also contribute in soiling of the working area especially in rainy season thereby making Drilling Rigs more prone to accidents.
- Accident analysis also reveals that in most of the accidents, upper limb is the most affected part of the body, which accounts for 360 out of 1022 accidents (32.22%), occurred during the year 1994-1998. Next most affected part body is lower limb, which accounts for 21.23%.
  - Since most of the manual jobs at ONGC Installations involve maximum use of hands thereby increasing the probability of injuries at upper limbs. Non-usage of Personal Protective Equipment/Improper usage of PPE could be the reason for Occurrence of such Accidents.
- On comparing "Accident frequency Rate" of various regions of ONGC, it has been observed that " Accident rate per million working hours" is maximum in MRBC.
  - Although offshore operations are by and large similar to those onshore operations but the critical difference lies in problems created as a result of the marine environment, relative isolation and special working conditions thereby making offshore operations more prone to accidents. Since in MRBC, most of the fixed / mobile installations are situated in offshore hence high "Accident frequency rate" is observed in MRBC as compare to other regions of ONGC.

Mine Area

Accident-Prone Area	Derrick Floor
Accident-Prone Category	AEE (D), AE (D), and EE (D)
Time During Which Maximum Number of Accidents took place	10:00 AM TO 12:00 AM

Cause of Majority of Accidents	Slip and Fall of person Striking Against or Striking by Object
Business Group Most Affected Drill.	Business Group
Part of Body Most Affected	**Upper Limb**
Trend of Accidents in 1998 as	9.8% Reduction Education in compared to Accidents in 1997 Accidents

Recommendations

Based on the analysis, the following recommendations have been put forh to prevent occurrence of accidents as far as Mines are concerned:

- All personnel (Departmental as well as Contractual Employees) posted at installation/ work site should be imparted training (covering safety aspects related to their assigned duties) before inducting them on the particular job.
- Strict compliance of recommendations suggested by safety officers etc. during Internal / External Safety Audit of Installation.
- Case studies with remedial measures to prevent such accidents in future (related to their assigned duties) should be discussed in the safety meetings as well as on the job.
- Any operational abnormality observed should be brought to the knowledge of the Installation/site Incharge and to be rectified on top priority.
- Personnel should be encouraged and motivated by Installation / Site Incharge / Concerned officer to report "near-miss".
- Proper use of safety kit as safety shoes, hand gloves, helmet etc. must be ensured during working.
- Preventive / Periodic maintenance schedule of Safety Equipment/ System to be chalked out and religiously followed to ensure their reliability.
- Working place need to be kept spick and span, free slippery substances such as oil, mud, and obstruction before commencement of work.
- Better harmony, co-ordination and communication during work particularly in case of accident-prone area like Derrick floor, Pipe rack area etc. must be maintained.
- Properly trained, suitably experienced drivers (at least having five years driving experience in driving similar type of vehicles)

should be engaged in NISOC and ONGC as well as contract vehicles. Good condition of vehicle must be ensured. Art of defensive driving to be inculcated in drivers. Over exertion and fatigue leads to accident. So drivers must be given proper rest in intervals during continuous driving. The driver of a particular for the new driver to get accustomed and familiar with the vehicle.

- Every morning, before commencement of work, safety meetings should be held, chaired by Installation In charge /Site In charge to review potential safety problems and action plan to solve them. The details of safety meetings need to be recorded in hardbound register for record, reference and follow up.
- Safety Suggestion Scheme may be used as an avenue to receive suggestions from workers and safety.

  Committee should give them serious consideration. Accepted Suggestions with Committee's suggestion must be forwarded to Management for final decision. A communication should also be sent to the originator explaining reason for rejection, modification or acceptance. Once the suggestion has been accepted, the originator must be rewarded suitably.

3
Standard of Safety Norms

Safety Measure: Indian Scenario

According to T. K. Joshi, workers' health has been of interest to physicians in India for almost half a century. The Indian Association of Occupational Health was founded during 940s in the city of Jamshedpur, which has the country's best known and the oldest steel plant. However, multidisciplinary occupational health practice evolved during the 1970s and 1980s when the ILO sent a team which helped create a model occupational health centre in India. The industry and workplaces traditionally provided health care under the banner of First Aid Stations/Plant Medical Services. These outfits managed minor health problems and injuries at the worksite. Some companies have recently set up occupational health services, and hopefully more should follow suit. However, the university hospitals have so far ignored the speciality.

Occupational safety and health practice started off with injuries and accident reporting and prevention. There is a belief, not without reason, that injuries and accidents remain under reported. The 1990-91 incidence rates of injuries are higher in electricity (0.47 per 1,000 workers employed), basic metal (0.45), chemical (0.32) and non-metallic industries (0.27), and somewhat lower in wood and wood pulp industries (0.08) and machinery and equipment (0.09). The textile industry, employing more workers (1.2 million in 1991) had an incidence rate of 0.11 per 1,000 workers. Either regard to fatal injuries, the incidence rates in 1989 were 0.32 per 1,000 workers in coal mines and 0.23 in non-coal mines. In 1992, a total 20 fatal and 753 non-fatal accidents occurred in ports.

Figures are unavailable for occupational hazards as well as for the number of workers exposed to specific hazards. The statistics published by the Labour Bureau do not show these. The system of occupational health surveillance is yet to develop. The number of occupational diseases reported is abysmal. The number of diseases reported in 1978 was just 19, which climbed to 84 in 1982. There is no pattern or trend visible in the reported diseases. Benzene poisoning, halogen poisoning, silicosis and pneumoconiosis, byssinosis, chrome ulceration reported most frequently.

There is no comprehensive occupational health and safety legislation. The three principal acts are: The Factories Act, 1948; The Mines Act, 1952; and the Dock Workers Safety, Health and Welfare Act, 1986. A bill for construction workers' safety is planned. The Factories Act, first adopted in 1881, even today covers workers only in the registered factories. Thus, a large number of blue- as well as white-collar workers do not qualify for occupational safety and health benefits under any law. The inadequacy of law and poor enforcement are responsible for not a very satisfactory state of occupational health in the country.

When Delhi become a state in 1993, the Health Ministry came to be headed by a health professional who reaffirmed his commitment for improving public and preventive health care. A committee set up to study the issue of occupational and environmental health recommended setting up of an occupational and environmental medicine clinic in a prestigious teaching hospital in the city.

Dealing with the complex health problems arising out of environmental pollution and occupational hazards requires more aggressive involvement of the medical community. The teaching university hospital receives hundreds of patients a day, many of whom have exposure to hazardous materials at work and to the unhealthy urban environment. Detection of occupationally and environmentally induced health disorders requires inputs from many clinical specialists, imaging services, laboratories and so on. Owing to the advanced nature of disease, some clinics enjoy the sophistication of a teaching hospital, and following detection of the healthy disorder, treatment or rehabilitation of the victim as well as the suggested intervention to protect others can be more effective as teaching hospitals enjoy more authority and command more respect.

The clinic has expertise in the area of occupational medicine. It intends to collaborate with the labour department, which has an industrial hygiene laboratory developed with liberal assistance under as ILO scheme to strengthen occupational safety and health in India. This will make the task of hazard identification and hazard evaluation easier. Medical partitions will be advised about health assessment of the exposed groups at the point of entry and periodically, and regarding record keeping. The clinic will help sort out the complicated cases and ascertain work-relatedness. The clinic will offer expertise to industry and workers on health education and safe practices with regard to the use and handling of hazardous materials in the workplace. This should make primary prevention more easily achievable and will strengthen occupational health surveillance as envisaged under the ILO convention on Occupational Health Services (No. 161) (ILO 1985a).

The clinic is being developed in two phases. The first phase is focusing on identifying hazards and creating a database. This phase will also emphasize the creation of awareness and developing outreach strategies with regard to hazardous working environments. The second phase will focus on strengthening exposure monitoring, medical toxicological evaluation and ergonomic inputs. (Stellman, 1998: p.16.59-60)

Safety Measures in NISOC

Everyone who works at NISOC is responsible for protecting the environment, health and safety of their people and communities worldwide. Our commitment to HSE performance is an integral part of their business, and achieving cost-effective solution is essential to their long-term success.

The dedication to the causes of environmental hazards and safety in NISOC is amply demonstrated by the fact that a separate organization named Adareh Emani and Atashnashni (Safety Dept.) had been set up way back in 1900 to deal with these issues. The objectives of the institute are *inter alia* to upgrade and develop human resources with a view to minimizing the over all risk to human life, damage to property, process and environment. The main functions of this department are Training, Research and Development, Consultancy Services, Data Bank and information services and in an advisory capacity to evolve standards and procedures. The department offers training courses in basic and advanced training, safety and environment management, fire safety offshore survival and safety, coxswain boat handing, etc. The offshore survival and safety and coxswain programmes are practical training programs for offshore going personnel. It includes a certificate course in first aid and fire fighting.

NISOC's safety policy seeks to provide safe and healthy working conditions and enlist the active support of all staff in achieving these ends.

To promote standards of safety, health and welfare in accordance with the requirements of Directorate of Mines Safety and also other relevant statutory provisions as well as approved codes of practices are as follows:

- To maintain safe and healthy work places and safe systems and methods of work.
- To protect staff and others, including the public and employees of contractors, from foreseeable work hazards on NISOC's premises.
- To equip the staff with the information, instructions, training and supervision needed for safe working.
- To provide and maintain a safe and healthy working environment for staff with adequate facilities and arrangements for their welfare.

- To develop safety awareness amongst the staff.
- To make staff aware of their individual responsibility to make all reasonable care for the health and safety of themselves and others who may be affected by their acts of omissions at work, and to cooperate with management and other staff in matters of safety.
- To have required safety organization adequately manned for the purpose.
- To budget expenditure required for above purposes.

NISOC pays the highest priority in safety management system and ceaselessly strives for reducing the rate of accident. To keep it As Low As Reasonably Practicable (ALARP), NISOC has taken up the following steps to improve the safety level in all its work centres:

1. Code of Practices

1.1. International and National Code of Practices: This standard is intended to be used within and for Iranian Ministry of Petroleum (N.I.O.C., N.I.G.C., N.P.C. and other affiliated organizations and companies) and has been prepared on the basis of the recognized standards, scientific publications, technical documents, accumulated knowledge and experiences in petroleum industries at national and international levels. Iranian Petroleum Standards are prepared by Iranian Petroleum Standards Organization reviewed and amended by the relevant technical standard committees to incorporate acceptable comments made by oil, gas and petrochemical experts. Standards are finally approved by the "Standards High Council" of Iranian Ministry of Petroleum.

Iranian Petroleum Standards (IPS) are subject to revisions, amendment or with drawl, if required. Thus the latest edition of IPS shall be applicable. Any comment or recommendation submitted to the "Iranian Petroleum Standards Organization" will be evaluated in the relevant technical committee and will be considered in the next revision, upon approval. In addition to the above, NISOC also follows the relevant standards as under:

Iranian Petroleum Standards (IPS)

- National Fires Codes (NFC)
- National Fire Protection Association (NFPA)
- Practical Fire Protection GW UNDERDOWN
- Home Office (Fire Department) Fire (HMO)
- British Standards Institute (BSI)
- Underwriters Laboratories (UL)
- Standard Foam Equipment and Liquid Concentrate 1989
- American Petroleum Institute (API)

- American Society of Mechanical Engineers (ASME)
- American National Standards Institute (ANSI)
- Institute of Petroleum (IP)
- National Association of Corrosion Engineers (NACE)
- American Welding Society (AWS)
- American Society for Testing and Materials (ASTM)
- International Organisation for Standardisation (IOS)
- British Standards Institution (BS)
- Expansion Joint Manufacturers Association (EJMA)
- National Electrical Manufacturers Association (NEMA)
- German Standards (DIN)
- International Standards (IS)
- Manufacturers Standardisation Society (MSS)
- American National Standards Institute/Underwriters Laboratories (ANSI/UL)

1-2. Code of Driving Safety: NISOC has developed its own code on safety practices, which are based on the similar international codes. Implementation of this code is being monitored by the driving safety committee consisting of senior experienced managers.

2. Critical Facilities

2.1. Multi Telecommunication Network for Emergency Preparedness: A Multi Telecommunication network exists in NISOC, which is adequate to provide necessary communication requirement. A key during any emergency and its preparedness.

2.2. Fire Protection and Suppression: All the facilities at offshore are equipped with adequate fire detection, monitoring and suppression system, strictly adhering to the provisions of convention, inspected, maintained and tested to ensure their readiness at the time of any eventuality. NISOC strictly follows the guidelines contained in Fire Protection Systems Inspection, Test and Maintenance manual.

3. Safety Organisation and Management Systems

3.1 Safety Organisation: To plan, execute, monitor and control the safety and environment functions in NISOC.

3.2. Safety Policy: It is NISOC policy to seek and provide safe and healthy conditions and enlist the active support of all staff in achieving these ends.

3.3. Internal Controls: Regular audits and inspections are carried out on all the facilities with a predetermined frequency to ensure that all the safety systems are in place. The audit also ensures that safe practices are being followed. The observations made during the audits are implemented in specified time. The implementation status is monitored regularly at project, regional and corporate level.

3.4. Implementation of SMS based Communication: To have a systematic safety management online NISOC has introduced this system in all major Production Complexes and Drilling Rigs.

3.5. External Control

1. Re-certification of Offshore Facilities

(a) **Drilling Rigs:** Re-certification of drilling rigs is done as per the requirement of Merchant Shipping Act.

(b) **Production Installations:** Re-certification of the platforms has been initiated by international certifying agencies.

(c) **Ships and Vessels:** Re-certification of all the ships and vessels is carried out by surveyors of classifications societies as per the requirement of Merchant Shipping Act.

(d) **Reliability Assessment of Critical Equipment:** The reliability assessment of the critical equipment has been undertaken in the past through the internationally recognized companies.

2. Accident / Incident Analysis: Accidents at installations are reported to concerned agencies and enquiries are conducted to ascertain the causes, circumstances etc., and to suggest the remedial measures to avoid such recurrences. Recommendations suggested are followed religiously in a time bound manner.

3. Personnel Protective Equipment (PPE): In accordance with various statutory requirements, duly approved PPE required for personal safety and safeguard against Occupational Health Hazards are provided to working personnel and their usage is ensured.

4. Periodical Medical Examination: Each employee has to undergo a Periodical Medical Examination, whose periodicity depends on age bracket of the employee. The PME reports are critically analyzed and corrective actions are taken, wherever necessary.

5. Statutory and Development Training: At all the operational sites and offices in NISOC, more than adequate qualified and experienced manpower is available. This takes care of manpower, which is required during the whole year and also round the clock operations, which is vital for safety.

Conclusion

The E and P operations of NISOC at offshore / onshore are being carried out strictly adhering to the rules and regulations, both international as well as national, wherever applicable following the guidelines of best international practices and the path of continuous improvement through adoption of Safety Management System based on IPS with reference to benchmarking of its performance with Oil Majors.

Safety Measure in ONGC

Everyone who works at ONGC is responsible for protecting the environment, health and safety of their people and communities world-wide. The commitment to HSE performance is an integral part of their business, and achieving cost-effective solution is essential to their long-term success.

The dedication to the causes of environmental hazards and safety in ONGC is amply demonstrated by the fact that a separate institute named Institute of Petroleum Safety and Environment Management (IPSEM) had been set up way back in 1989 to deal with these issues. The objectives of the institute are committed to upgrade and develop human resources with a view to minimizing the over all risk to human life, damage to property, process and environment. The main functions of the institute are Training, Research and Development, Consultancy Services, Data Bank and information services and in advisory capacity to evolve standards and procedures. The institute offers training courses in basic and advanced training, safety and environment management, fire safety, offshore survival and safety, coxswain boat handling, etc. The offshore survival and safety and coxswain programmes are practical training programmes for offshore going personnel. It includes a certificate course in first aid and fire fighting.

ONGC's safety policy seeks to provide safe and healthy working conditions and enlist the active support of all staff in achieving these ends the main adjectives are:

- The promote standards of safety, health and welfare in accordance with the requirements of Directorate of Mines Safety and also other relevant statutory provisions as well as approved codes of practices.
- To maintain safe and healthy work places and safe systems and methods of work.
- To protect staff and others, including the public and employees of contractors, from foreseeable work hazards on ONGC's premises.
- To equip the staff with the information, instructions, training and supervision needed for safe working.
- To provide and maintain a safe and healthy working environment for staff with adequate facilities and arrangements for their welfare.

- To develop safety awareness amongst the staff.
- To make staff aware of their individual responsibility to make all reasonable care for the health and safety of themselves and other who may be affected by their acts of omissions at work, and to cooperate with management and other staff in matters of safety.
- To have required safety organization adequately manned for the purpose.
- To budget expenditure required for above purposes.

Keeping this in view all mine and non-mine accidents occurred in ONGC during the year 1994-1998 have been obtained from various regional SEM's of ONGC and analyzed from various angles.

Although there is reducing trend of accidents during the year 1998 as compared to 1997 which is very encouraging yet it needs further attention to pull it down to zero level. As they said, "With our efforts and will we can make accidents nil".

1. **Safety Measure:** ONGC pays highest priority in safety management system and continuously strive to reduce the rate of accident. To keep it as Low As Reasonably Practicable (ALARP), ONGC has taken up the following steps to improve the safety level in all its work centres:

2. **Code of Practices**

2.1. ONGC's Internal Code of Safe Practices: The International Code of Practices, the prevailing regulations, obligatory conventions and practices as applicable in USA, U.K., Norway have been studied to frame with all the legislative provisions in our national context.

2.2. International and National Code of Practices: In addition to the above, ONGC also follows the relevant standards as under:

- American Petroleum Institute (API)
- American Society of Mechanical Engineers (ASME)
- National Association of Corrosion Engineers (NACE)
- National Fire Protection Association (NFPA)
- American National Standards Institute (ANSI)
- NEC Code
- Bureau of Indian Standards (BIS)
- Oil Industry Safety Directors (OISD)
- Institution of Electrical Engineers (IEE)
- Institute of Electrical and Electronic Engineers (IEEE)

2.3. Code of Driving safety: ONGC has developed its own code on safety practices, which are based on the similar international codes.

Implementation of this being monitored the driving safety committee consisting of senior experienced managers.

2.4. International Safety Management Code: A committee is now functioning to ensure the implementation of the forthcoming international safety management code for OSVs, MSVs and the MODUs. This code is issued by International Maritime Organization (IMO) and Convention and is mandatory for its implementation, India being signatory.

3. Critical Facilities

3.1. Multi Telecommunication Network for Emergency Preparedness: A Multi Telecommunication network exists in ONGC, which is adequate to provide necessary communication requirement. A key during any emergency and its preparedness. Some of these networks are Radio communication (HF sets, ISB, VHF sets) Satellite communications (TELE-NET, IC-NET, EP-NET, V-SAT RABMN) and telephones (normal lines, leased line, hotlines and mobile cellular phones).

3.2. Fire Protection and Suppression: All the facilities at offshore are equipped with adequate fire detection, monitoring and suppression system, strictly adhering to the provisions of SOLAS convention, inspected, maintained and tested to ensure their readiness at the time of any eventuality. ONGC strictly follows the guidelines contained in Fire Protection Systems Inspection, Test and Maintenance manual issued by National Fire Protection Association, NFPA, and USA in both offshore and onshore facilities.

4. Safety Organization and Management Systems

4.1 Safety Organization: To plan, execute, monitor and control the safety and environment functions in ONGC, there is an established 3 Tier set-up at Hqrs, regions and projects of ONGC with adequate manpower, infrastructure and authority. While the administrative control in the region is with Executive Director, the overall functional control is under the Director (Tech.) of ONGC.

4.2. Safety Policy: It is ONGC policy to seek and provide safe and healthy conditions and enlist the active support of all staff in achieving these ends.

4.3. Internal Controls: Regular audits and inspections are carried out on all the facilities with a predetermined frequency to ensure that all the safety systems are in place. The audit also ensures that safe practices are being followed. The observations made during the audits are implemented within the specified time. The implementation status is monitored regularly at project, regional and corporate level.

4.4. Implementation of SMS based on ISRS: To have a systematic safety management online ONGC has introduced the ISRS system in 9 major Production Complexes and Drilling Rigs and achieved level-5 in Uran and Hazira and offshore NQO. ONGC is in the process of providing the similar employees to all its critical installations. This has been extended in onshore drilling rigs, work-over rigs and gradually being implemented in installations.

4.5. External Control

4.5.1. RE-certification of Offshore Facilities

(a) **Drilling Rigs:** Re-certification of drilling rigs is done as per the requirement of Merchant Shipping Act as well as SOLAS conventions of IMO. The survey of offshore rigs is undertaken by the surveyors of the classification societies like ABS, DNV, Lloyds, MMD, in accordance with SOLAS convention, which covers the wide range of measures designed to improve the safety of shipping such as safety of navigation, construction radiography, fire fighting appliances etc. These surveys include annual surveys of Hull, Cargo-gear, load line, machinery etc. besides 2 ½ years Dry Dock Survey, 5 yearly special surveys.

(b) **Production Installations:** Re- certification of the platforms by international certifying agencies has been initiated to confirm the "Fit For Purpose" for the continuance of their operations.

(c) **Ships and Vessels:** Re-certification of all the ships and vessels like surveys vessels, multi support vessels, supply vessels is carried out by surveyors of classifications societies as per the requirement of Merchant Shipping Act.

(d) **Reliability Assessment of Critical Equipment:** The reliability assessment of the critical equipment like Blow Out presenter and control system has been undertaken in the past though the internationally recognized companies/ classification societies like MODU SPEC Holland and ABS. The reliability assessment through the third party assessment provides an adequate assurance to the operator about the system, which is functional and fit for use.

4.5.2. Regulatory / Advisory Control for Onshore

(a) The comprehensive safety regulations for onshore operations are covered under the Oil Mines Regulations (OMR 1984, amended in 1996) which are framed under the Mines Act, 1952. The statutory authority to regulate OMR is the Directorate General of Mines Safety (DGMS) under Ministry of Labour, which undertakes regular audits and inspections.

(b) In addition to this Oil Industry Safety Directorate (OISD) under MOP and NG undertakes ESA (External Safety Audit) regularly.

The observations are closely monitored at the highest level of the organization and MOP and NG. The implementation status is of the highest order to the extent of 96 per cent.

4. Regional Contingency and Disaster Management Plan: As per international practice in vogue, Regional Contingency and Disaster Management Plan have been drawn for offshore/ onshore operations after considering different risk scenarios to combat and mitigate effects of any eventuality. Regional Contingency Plan for offshore is a joint co-order plan wherein besides ONGC, other agencies like Navy, offshore operator, IB Police, Coast Guard, State Authorities etc. are also associated.

5. Risk of Accidents to a Level As Low as Reasonably Practicable (ALARP): The principal of ALARP is followed in ONGC. A concept review group is functioning in ONGCs Institute of Engineering and Ocean Technology (IEOT). The HAZOP and QRA (risk analysis) of the installations are undertaken at the concept stage and also subsequently. As required Risk analysis for LPG complex, Uran was undertaken during 1988, 1996, Hazira during 1992, 1998, BHN 1990, NQO 1991, BHS 1994, ICP, SH Heera complexes in 1995 by KLG-TNO and SCA WIN BPB, S/Laxmi, R-12 installations in 1995 by DNV Technical. The implementation of the recommendations are undertaken in phases.

6. Accident / Incident Analysis: Accidents at installations are reported to concerned agencies and Enquiries are conducted to ascertain the causes, circumstances etc., and to suggest the remedial measures to avoid such recurrence. Recommendations suggested are followed religiously in a time bound manner.

7. Personal Protective Equipment (PPE): In accordance with various statutory requirements, duly approved PPE required for personal safety and safeguard against Occupational Health Hazards are provided to the working personnel and their usage is ensured.

8. Periodical Medical Examination: Each employee has to undergo a Periodical Medical Examination, whose Periodicity depends on age bracket of the employee. The PME reports are critically analyzed and corrective actions are taken, wherever necessary.

9. Statutory and Development Training: At all the operational sites and offices in ONGC, more than adequate qualified and experienced manpower is available. This takes care of manpower, which is required during the whole year and also round the clock operations, which is very vital for safety.

Institute of Petroleum Safety and Environment Management (IPSEM) an institute of repute caters to the need of safety and environment training of the personnel deployed at various units of

ONGC including offshore operations. Out of various such programmes, such as survival at sea, fire fighting and first aid are specially designed for offshore personnel and also cover the onshore applications.

Institute of Management Development (IMD), Dehradun, Institute of Drilling Technology (IDT), Dehradun and Regional Training Institutes are also imparting training on SHE management. IDT, Dehradun is also imparting advanced a well control safety training on computerized simulator to its personnel working on the rigs. These trainings are accredited by international agencies like International Association of Drilling Contractors (IADC). Mines Vocational Training (MVT) as per OMR. The curriculum duly approved by DGMS is being conducted through our Regional Training Centers regularly.

Conclusion

The E and P operations of ONGC at offshore / onshore are being carried out strictly adhering to the rules and regulations, both international as well as national, wherever applicable following the guidelines of the best international practices and the path of continuous improvement through adoption of Safety Management System based on ISRS with reference to benchmarking of its performance with Oil Majors.

Accident Records and Injury Rates

The annual summary reports are used by the companies to evaluate members' experience for the presentation of awards. Award Plan is for Recognising Good Industrial Safety Records.

Safety performance is relative. Only when a company shares its injury experience with that of similar companies, or with that of the entire industry of which it is a part, or with its own previous experience can it obtain a meaningful evaluation of its safety accomplishments.

To make such comparisons, a method of measurement is needed which adjusts to the effects of certain variables, and which contributes to differences in injury totals alone, cannot be used.

First, a company with many employees may be expected to have more injuries than a company with a few employees. Second, if the records of one company include all the injuries treated in the first aid room, whereas the records of a similar company include only injuries serious enough to cause lost time, obviously the first total will be larger than the second.

A standard procedure for keeping records, which provides for these variables, is included in ANSI Z16.1. First, this procedure uses frequency and severity rates which relate disabling injuries, and days charged as a result of them, to the number of man-hours worked; thus these rates automatically adjust for differences in the hours of exposure to injury. Second, this procedure specifies the kinds of injuries, which should be included in the rates.

These standardised rates, which are easy to compute and to undertand, have been accepted generally as uniform procedures in industry and permit necessary and desired comparisons.

A chronological arrangement of these rates for a company will show whether its level of safety performance is improving or getting worse.

Within a company, the same sort of arrangement by departments will not only show the trend of safety performance for each department, but may reveal to management information which will make safety work more efficient.

A comparison of current injury rates with those of similar companies and with those of industry as a whole will provide the safety professional with a more reliable evaluation of the safety performance of his company than he could obtain merely by reviewing numbers of injuries.

Standard Formulas for Rates

The injury frequency rate and the injury severity rate are based on standard formulas have been as set forth in ANSI Z16.1.

Frequency Rate: The disabling injury frequency rate relates the injuries to the hours worked during the period and express them in terms of a million-hour unit by use of the following formula:

(Number of disabling injuries × 1000,000)/ Employee-hours of exposure

Severity Rate: The disabling injury severity rate relates the days charged to the hours worked during the period and expresses them in terms of a million-hour unit by use of the following formula:

(Total days charged × 1000,000) / Employee-hours of exposure

Average Days Charged: The frequency and severity rates show, respectively, the rate at which time is charged. A third measure included in the standard procedure shows the average severity of the disabling injuries. It is called the average days charged per disabling injury and may be calculated by either of the following formulas:

(Total days charged)/(Total disabling injuries) or
(Severity Rate)/ (Frequency Rate)

Disabling Injury Index: As an aid to those companies expressing a desire to combine frequency and severity into a single measure, the following index is shown:

Disabling Injury Index = (F× S)/ 1,000

Where F is the disabling injury frequency rate and S is the disabling injury severity rate. This measure combines both frequency and severity to yield an index of total disabling injury experience.

In the from shown it can be correctly applied only for ranking total experience from "best" to "worst". If the measure is to be used to determine percentage of improvement, or for comparing the degree of difference between two units, the square root of the index must be taken before such comparisons are made.

Calculation of Employee-hours: Employee-hours used in calculating injury rates is the total number of hours worked by all employees, including those of operating, production, maintenance, transportation, clerical, administrative, sales, and other departments.

Employee-hours should be calculated from the payroll or time clock records. If this method cannot be used, they may be estimated by multiplying the total employee-days worked for the period covered by the number of hours worked each days.

Accident Rate in NISOC

The accidents rates during the last five years are as follows:

In 1999 the number of NISOCs' companies was from 11 reduced to 5, in which Kharg was included. In 2000 Kharg was separated from NISOC and AMA divided into two companies, as KOGC and MOGC. So, the following data covers the changes.

At Installations Personnel Accident

Table 3.1: Personnel Accident in NISOC

S.No.	*Year*	*No. of Accidents*	*Days Lost*	*F*	*S*	*DII*
1.	1996	190	24156	3.12	830	2.59
2.	1997	218	24156	2.584	466	1.204
3.	1998	164	31283	1.033		
4.	1999	251	49338	3.77	945	3.562
5.	2000	189	24578	3.09	550	1.70

F= Frequency Rate S= Severity Rate DII= Disabling Injury Index

Table 3.2: Road Accident in NISOC

S. No.	*Year*	*No. of Accidents*	*F*
1.	1996	507	-
2.	1997	570	-
3.	1998	504	4.5
4.	1999	433	3.77
5.	2000	354	4.21

There is not meter worked from 1996 till 1998.

Table 3.3: Fire Accident in NISOC

S. No.	*Year*	*No. of Accident*
1.	1996	284
2.	1997	211
3.	1998	339
4.	1999	330
5.	2000	170

The above figures include departmental and contractual employees.

Table 3.4: Accidents Rates in ONGC (1998-2000)

The accidents rates during last three years is as follows:

At Installations

S. No.	*Year*	*No. of Accident*
1.	1998	167
2.	1999	134
3.	2000	161

Table 3-5: Road Accidents in ONGC 1998-2000

S. No.	*Year*	*No. of Accident*
1.	1998	07
2.	1999	16
3.	2000	32

The above figures include departmental and contractual employees.

Causes of Accidents

Hazards are present everywhere i.e., homes, roads, industries etc. and NISOC and ONGC are not exceptions to it. So long as these hazards are controllable and manageable, no incident/accident occurs. The loss of control over these hazards either due to personal factor or environmental factor results into dis-equilibrium of man, machine and environment. This causes release of energy from the system in uncontrollable manner and hits the person, machine, equipment, property or all. The severity of damage/loss depends upon the intensity of energy.

Accidents are the indicators of unsafe conditions and unsafe practices adopted by the human beings at work place. The correction of either or both conditions may avert the possibility of occurrence of similar accidents in future.

Though the accidents are undesirable but these continue to occur at the work place unless systematic and sustained efforts are made. Hence, fact finding, investigation and objective analysis of accidents assumes greater significance. Examples of exposure sources which may result in an injury in the form of a disease-like condition are:

- chemical exposures (solvents, cleaning agents, degreasing agents, etc.)
- physical exposures (noise, radiation, heat, cold, inadequate lighting, lack of oxygen, etc.)
- physiological exposures (heavy loads, bad work postures or repetitive work)
- biological exposures (viruses, bacteria, flour, animal blood or leather, etc.)
- psychological exposures (work in isolation, threat of violence, changing working hours, unusual job demands, etc.). (Stellman, 1998: p. 56.3-4).

Fire extinction and suppression can be examined in terms of the theory of fire. The gas phase combustion processes (i.e., the flame reactions) are very sensitive to chemical inhibitors. However, if a flame-retarded material becomes involved in an existing fire, it will burn as the high heat fluxes overwhelm the effect of the retardant. Extinction of a fire may be achieved in a number of ways:(a) stopping the supply of fuel vaporous, (b) quenching the flame by chemical extinguishers (inhibiting), (c) removing the supply of air (oxygen) to the fire (smothering), (d) "blow-out". (Stellman, 1998: p. 41.5).

A variety of techniques are available which can be used to minimize the incidence of heat disorders and reduce the severity of cases when they do occur. Interventions fall into five categories: maximizing heat tolerance among exposed individuals, assuring timely replacement of lost fluid and electrolytes, altering work practices to reduce exertional heat load, engineering control of climatic conditions, and use of protective clothing.

Factors outside the worksite which may affect thermal tolerance should not be ignored in the evaluation of the extent of exposure and consequently in elaborating preventive strategies. For example, total physiological burden and the potential susceptibility to heat disorders will be much higher if heat stress continues during off-hours through work at second jobs, strenuous leisure activities, or living in unremittingly hot quarters. In addition, nutritional status and hydration may reflect patterns of eating and drinking, which may also change with season or religious observances. (Stellman, 1998: p. 42.10).

Cold stress may be present in many different forms, affecting the extremities, skin and lungs.

Cooling of the whole body or parts of the body results in discomfort, impaired sensory and neuro-muscular function and, ultimately, cold injury. Cold discomfort tends to be a strong stimulus to behavioural action, reducing or eliminating the effect.

On exposure to cold, behavioral measures do reduce the cooling effect and, eventually, allow the maintenance of normal thermal balance and comfort. Insufficient measures evoke thermoregulatory, physiologically compensatory reactions (vasoconstriction and shivering). The combined action of behavioral and physiological adjustments determines the resulting effect of a given cold stress. (Stellman, 1998: p. 42.29).

Human beings have evolved an essentially diurnal; that is, the body is mainly "programmed" towards daytime work performance and for night-time recreation and rest. Internal mechanisms (sometimes called the body or biological clock) control the physiology and biochemistry of the body to fit in with a 24-hour environment. These cycles are called circadian rhythms. The disruption of circadian variations in physiological function caused by having to be awake and at work at biologically unusual hours, as well as to sleep during the daytime, is one of the major stresses associated with shiftwork. (Stellman, 1998: p. 43.2)

Hazardous noise levels are easily identified and it is technologically feasible control excessive noise in the vast majority of the cases by applying off-the-shelf technology, by the redesigning the equipment or process or by retrofitting noisy machines. But as they say, all too often, nothing is done. There are several reasons for this. First, although many noise control solutions are remarkably inexpensive, others can be costly, especially when the aim is to reduce the noise hazard to levels of 85 or 80 dBA.

Loss of hearing is certainly the most well-known adverse effect of noise, and probably the most serious, but it is not the only one. Other detrimental effects include tinnitus (ringing in the ears), interference with speech communication and with the perception of warning signals, disruption of job performance, annoyance and extra-auditory effects. Under most circumstances, protecting workers' hearing should protect against most other effects. This consideration provides additional support for companies to implement good noise control and hearing conservation programmes.

Noise-induced hearing impairment is usually considered an occupational disease or illness, rather than an injury, because its progression is gradual. On rare occasions, an employee may sustain immediate, permanent hearing loss from a very loud event such as an explosion or a very noisy process, such as rivetiny. (Stellman, 1998: p. 47.2-4.2)

Electrical accidents may be caused by the entire range of voltages present in workplaces. Every industrial sector has its own set of conditions capable of causing direct, indirect, unipolar, bipolar, arcing, or induced contact, and ultimately, accidents. In rare cases, asphyxia may be the cause of death. This may result from prolonged tetanus of the diaphragm, inhibition of the respiratory centres in cases of contact with the head, or very high current densities, for example as a result of lightning strikes (Gourbiere et al. 1994). If care can be provided within three minutes, the victim may be revived with a few puffs of mouth-to-mouth resuscitation.

On the other hand, peripheral circulatory collapse secondary to ventricular fibrillation remains the main cause of death.

The International Electro Technical Commission (1987; 1994) has produced curves describing the effect of current intensity and transit time on the probability (expressed as percentages) of fibrillation and the hand-foot current path in a 70-kg male in good health. These tools are appropriate for industrial currents in the frequency range of 15 to 100 Hz, with higher frequencies currently under study. For transit times of less than 10 ms, the area under the electrical signal curve is a reasonable approximation of the electrical energy. (Stellman, 1998:p. 40.3) Unfortunately, even under the best circumstances, electrical equipment is subject to failures that may result in human injury or material damage.

Safe operation of electrical installations is the result of good initial design, not the mere retrofitting of safety systems. This is a corollary of the fact that while current flows at the speed of light, all electromechanical and electronic systems exhibit reaction latencies, caused primarily by thermal inertia, mechanical inertia and maintenance conditions. These latencies, whatever their origins, are sufficiently lengthy to allow humans to be injured and equipment damaged (Lee, Capelli-Schellpfeffer and Kelly 1994; Lee, Cravalho and Burke 1992; Kane and Sternheim 1978).

It is essential that equipment be installed and maintained by qualified personnel. Technical measures, it should be emphasized, are necessary both to ensure the safe operation of installations and to protect humans and equipment.

Proper operation of electrical installations requires that machinery, equipment, and electrical circuits and lines be protected from hazards caused by both internal (i.e., arising within the installation) and external factors (Andreoni and Castagna 1983). Internal causes include:

- over voltages
- short circuits
- modification of the current's wave-form
- induction
- interference
- over currents
- corrosion, leading to electrical current leakage's to ground
- heating of conducting and insulating materials, which may result in operator burns, emissions of toxic gases, component fires and, inflammable atmospheres, explosions
- leaks of insulating fluids, such as oil
- generation of hydrogen or other gases which may lead to the formation of explosive mixtures. (Stellman, 1998:p. 40.10-11)

Environmental health hazards, like occupational health hazards, may be biological, chemical, physical, biomechanical or psychosocial in nature. Environmental health hazards include traditional hazards of poor sanitation and shelter, as well as agricultural and industrial contamination of air, water, food and land.

These hazards have resulted in a loss of health impacts, ranging from catastrophic direct effects (e.g., the recent cholera epidemic in Latin America and the chemical poisoning outbreak in Bhopal, India (Bhopal, India 1985, has Environmental Hazards in Methylisocyanate, as Acute Lung Disease, which caused 2,000 deaths and 200,000 poisoned), to chronic effects (e.g., in Love Canal, USA). Environmental health hazard thus include the indirect effects of industrial disruption of the adequate food and housing, as well as the degradation of the global systems on which the health of the planet depends. (Stellman, 1998:p. 53.2)

Risk measurement must be made on the basis of information regarding the number and seriousness of injuries which have occurred in the past, yielding to a retrospective measurement. The risk of injury to individuals may be described two types of data:

Management of risk provides a calculated frequency of injuries and a measurement of the seriousness of the injury. This could be described as the number of lost work day cases (or fatalities per number of workers (e.g., in Denmark, the risk of dying in an occupational accident is 3 fatalities per 100,000 employees).

Type of risk or element of danger assessment provides not only an indication of the exposure sources and other harmful factors which may cause an accident, but also indication of the circumstances leading to injury or damage. Work performed at a height, for example, will involve a risk of falling, with serious injury as a possible result. Similarly, work with cutting tools involves a risk of cuts from contact with sharp components, and work with noisy machines for a long time may result in hearing damage.

However, it is one thing to know what has happened in the past. It should be noted that the very knowledge of the exposure sources and other potentially harmful factors which may cause damage or injury in connection with tasks of various sorts, as well as knowledge of the factors that can either heighten or reduce those risk factors that influence risk measurement, can provide a basis for recognition of the risk. The factors which are of greater relevance in determining risk are:

- factors which determine the presence or absence (or potential) of risks of any sort.
- factors which either increase or minimize the probability of these risks resulting in accidents or injuries.
- factors affecting the seriousness of accidents associated with these risk.
- To clarify the first point, it is necessary to identify the causes of the accident, namely, exposure sources and other harmful factors;

the two latter points constitute the factors which influence the measurement of risk.

- The primary factors in the working environment are the direct causes of harm, either by way of occupational diseases or occupational accidents.

Safety Protection

In the manufacturing process, people and objects interact. The term object is used in the broader sense as expressed in the customary designation "people- (machine)-environment system". This includes not only technical instruments of work, machines and materials, but all surrounding items such as floors, stairs, electrical current, gas, dusts, atmosphere and so on).

Because it is apparent that questions of accident prevention can be solved not in isolation, but only in the context of their relationship with production and the working environment, the following principles for accident prevention can be derived:

(1) accident prevention must be built into production planning with the goal of avoiding disruptions.

(2) the ultimate goal is to achieve a production flow that is as unhindered as possible. This results not only in reliability and the elimination of defects, but also in the workers' well-being, labour-saving methods and job safety.

Some of the practices commonly used in the workplace to achieve job safety and which are necessary for disruption-free production include, but are not limited to the following:

- Workers and supervisors must be informed and aware of the dangers and potential hazards (e.g., through education).
- Workers must be motivated to function safely (behaviour modification).
- Workers must be able to function safely. This is accomplished through certification procedures, training and education.
- The personal working environment should be safe and healthy through the use of administrative or engineering control, substitution of less hazardous materials or conditions, or by the use of personal protective equipment.
- Equipment, machinery and objects must function safely for capabilities.
- Provisions should be made for appropriate emergency response in order to limit the consequences of accidents, incidents and injuries. (Stellman, 1998: pp. 56.30-31)

Researchers and practitioners from mutiple disciplines primarily form epidemiology, engineering, ergonomics, biomechanics, behavioural psychology, safety management and industrial hygiene - are engaged in the study of the factors associated with the worker (the host); the environment; the type and source of energy involved (the agent); and the tools, machines and tasks (the vehicles) that combine to cause or contribute to workplace injury.

The most important audiences for risk and prevention information are the population at risk, and the various individuals and organizations that have the power to change or influence workplace risk through their decisions, programmes and policies. These audiences, which include the workers, employers, safety and health practitioners, regulators, insurers, legislators and policymakers, are targeted when researchers develop new information regarding the existence or scope of occupational injury problems, or recommendations aimed at reducing risk. (Stellman, 1998:pp. 60.2-3)

The public health approach is one model which provides a framework for occupational safety research. The public health approach involves:

- The identification, characterization and description of injury cases, hazards and exposures through surveillance.
- the in-depth analysis of specified injury problems in specified workers population in order to identify, quantify and compare risk and causal factors.
- the identification and development of prevention strategies and interventions.
- the evaluation of preventive strategies in laboratory and field experiments.
- the communication of information on risk and the development of strategies and programmes for reducing risk and preventing injuries.

Ideally, workplace safety problem may be identified and solved systematically by means of this process.

Safety analysis is another relevant model for addressing workplace injury.

When effective preventive strategies are identified or developed, they are the keys to implementing the strategies. Occupational safety research produces two types of information that are useful to individuals and organizations outside the research community: risk information and prevention information.

Risk messages may include the notification that risk exists; information about the scope or nature of risk; information about the individuals or populations at risk; information about when, where, has the risk exists; and information about the factors that influence or contribute to risk and their relative importance. Risk information is a principal product of surveillance and analytical research.

Prevention massages include information on methods of reducing risk and may cover a broad range of strategies and interventions. (Stellman, 1998: pp. 60.2-3)

1. Safety Policy

According to Safety Regulations (19) Safety is considered as an integral part of all functions. Management and supervisors of all levels are responsible for the effectiveness of the following accident prevention principles:

1. Safety work environment to be provided through proper design operation and maintenance of plants, equipment and facilities. Hazards which cannot be isolated should be guarded against through the use of appropriate personal protective equipment.
2. Employees must be selected and placed in the jobs consistent with their physical and mental capabilities to perform them safely.
3. Employees will be thoroughly indoctrinated and continuously trained in the accident prevention and fire protection requirements of their work assignment.
4. Suggestions for improving the safety of operations will be encouraged and promptly handled by the supervisor of the originator.
5. Jobs which are known to be hazardous will be deveioped. These instructions will be reviewed and revised as required.
6. Periodic safety inspections must be conducted to identify and correct unsafe acts conditions.
7. Motor vehicle accident prevention shall be promoted by training employees to drive defensively and identifying and rehabilitating problem drivers.
8. Proponents of contracts will ensure that accident and fire prevention requirements are adequately covered and fulfilled.
9. Provisions will be made for responding to emergencies which will provide optimum protection of personnel and property.
10. All work injuries, property damages and fires will be immediately reported and thorough investigation conducted to identify causes and initiate effective corrective action.

11. Off-the-job safety will be promoted to prepare employees to protect themselves and their families from accident.
12. All levels of management must demonstrate interest in accident prevention by actively participating in and promoting the principles of the company's safety programme.
13. All employees, supervisors and management personnel shall be held accountable for their safety performance. It will be an important factor in the appraisal of their overall job performance and reward.
14. Every organization will have a formal programme designed to contribute to the company's goal of accident-free operations.

2. Personal Safety Protective Equipment
Prevention and Control Measures

1. Hazards and risks to workers' safety and health should be identified and assessed on an ongoing basis. Preventive and protective measures should be implemented in the following order of priority:

(a) eliminate the hazard/risk;
(b) control the hazard/risk at source, through the use of engineering control or organizational measures;
(c) minimize the hazard/risk by the design of safe work systems, which include administrative control measures; and
(d) where residual hazards/risks cannot be controlled by collective measures, the employer should provide for appropriate personal protective equipment, including clothing, at no cost, and should implement measures to ensure its use and maintenance.

2. Hazard prevention and control procedures or arrangements should be established and should:

(a) be adapted to the hazards and risks encountered by the organization;
(b) be reviewed and modified if necessary on a regular basis;
(c) comply with national laws and regulations, and reflect good practice; and
(d) consider the current state of knowledge, including information or reports from organizations, such as labour inspectorates, occupational safety and health services, and other services as appropriate.

3. Emergency Prevention, Preparedness and Response: Emergency prevention, preparedness and response arrangements should be established and maintained. These arrangements should identify

the potential for accidents and emergency situations, and address the prevention of risks associated with them. The arrangements should be made according to the size and nature of activity of the organization.

4. Procurement: Procedures should be established and maintained to ensure that:

(a) Compliance with safety and health requirements for the organization is identified, evaluated and incorporated into purchasing and leasing specifications;

(b) National laws and regulations and the organization's own requirements are identified prior to the procurement of goods and services; and

(c) arrangement are made to achieve conformance to the requirements prior to their use. (ILO, 2001: p.11)

Investigation of Work-related Injuries, Ill Health, Diseases and Incidents, and their Impact on Safety and Health Performance:

1. The investigation of the origin and underlying causes of work-related injuries, ill health, diseases and incidents should identify any failures in the management system and should be documented.
2. Such investigations should be carried out by competent persons, with the appropriate participation of workers and their representatives.
3. The results of such investigations should be communicated to the safety and health committee, where it exists, and the committee should make appropriate recommendations.
4. The results of investigations, in addition to any recommendations from the safety and health committee, should be communicated to appropriate persons for corrective action, included in the management review and considered for continual improvement activities.
5. The corrective action resulting from such investigations should be implemented in order to avoid repetition of work-related injuries, ill health, diseases and incidents.
6. Reports produced by external investigative agencies, such as inspectorates and social insurance institutions, should be acted upon in the same manner as internal investigations, taking into account the issues of confidentiality. (ILO, 2001: pp.14-5)

Suitable protection clothing and safety equipment shall be provided and the crew engaged in handling acids or corrosive material, welding and exposed to any hazards must be fully equipped with protection clothing and safety equipment. In many operations some protection is required:

1. The District Head Safety and Fire has to maintain an up-to-date list of safety equipments available from stores, and advise supervisors on choice of equipments.
2. Employees issued safety clothing must wear it on appropriate jobs. Failure to do so should warrant suspension. Continued or repeated failure to use safety clothing merits discharge.
3. Employees issued safety shoes must wear them on the job. An employee who has lost his shoes may buy one pair through the company at the current price.
4. Articles of safety equipment which are not strictly clothing, such as gloves, masks, safety goggles, etc, must also be used on jobs for which they are issued. Failure to do so warrants suspension. Repeated or continued failure merits discharge.
5. When a worker needs to replace an issued article of safety, clothing or equipment, he must return the worn-out article to receive a new issue. Should he be unable to, the article may be issued to him, but its full cost will be deducted from his pay. This is entirely apart from any penalties for failure to wear or use the issued article.
6. Those charged with issuing safety goods must be both fair and reasonable. Articles like gloves can be lost; some kinds of work may quickly wear out particular items. This policy is intended to guard against abuses and not to penalize the worker, for legitimate use or loss. A good guide is repetition. A worker who repeatedly reports for early replacement or continually loses his issue may be disposing of it illegally and deserves disciplinary action.
7. All safety clothing or articles issued to workmen shall be recorded including, the name, number, date and the type of equipment issued.
8. All employees shall be notified of the above rulings through their supervisors and through the Workers' Representatives of Reconciliation Committees.

Clothing

1. Protective clothing ranges from overalls giving protection against dirt and grease to specialized garments for shielding against acids and other chemicals, special suits for protection against fire, blanket cloth garments for insulation against heat and extreme

cloud, leather aprons toward off sparks and hot metal, and rubber aprons for wet work.

2. Men working on or near moving machinery should wear close fitting overalls. Sleeves, if worn, should be clear of the wrists and too loose-fitting to be caught by moving parts. Long coats, or loose-fitting jackets and sleeves should not be worn, and the use of mufflers and head scarves with loose-hanging ends which might be caught between moving parts should not be permitted.

Hand Protection

Many types of gloves and gauntlets are available for handling chemicals, hot objects and electrical conductors. In certain cases where delicacy of touch is required or where gloves might become saturated with liquid, it may be advisable, instead, to use a suitable barrier cream which will give the desired protection if applied and treated with care.

Foot Wear

1. Men handling steel work, pipes etc., or the type of jobs with 60 per cent to hazard should be issued with safety boots with reinforced toe-caps to prevent crushed toes.
2. Rubber boots should be worn by chemical workers and others liable to contact dangerous liquids. Such footwear should also be available for wet situations. Clogs may be found suitable for furnace men and for men handling some types of chemicals.

Head Protection

Several types of head protection will be required, including:

1. Safety helmets for protection against falling objects.
2. Air-fed helmets for use in atmospheres deficient in oxygen, in dusty areas, or where the atmosphere is otherwise unfit to breathe.
3. Updraft helmets to give protection against chemical and liquid sprays.
4. Welding helmets to protect against sparks and injurious light rays.

All employees working in construction and maintenance sites, Production and NGL Units. Drilling Rigs and on Jetties shall wear safety helmet.

Eye Protection

1. Eye protection equipment is provided by the company for the protection of employees performing certain kinds of works. Some

works are such that it is mandatory for the employees to use the eye protection equipment. Employees shall be instructed on the eye hazards of each job and the proper type of equipment to be used. Eye protection equipment is generally thought of in the terms of goggles primarily used for:

- Flying particles
- Corrosive and irritating liquid and gases
- Injurious light radiations
- Splashing and flying molten metals

One type of goggle, shield or face mask will never protect the eyes against all of these conditions. For this reason the selection of the right type of eye protection is important.

2. Care must be taken that goggles can be worn with maximum comfort. Many eye injuries result from reluctance to use uncomfortable, ill-fitting or unsuitable goggles.
3. The employee is to be provided with suitable type of goggles. Goggles issued must be worn where any exposure to eye hazards exists. Violators of this rule must be a subject to disciplinary action.
4. Employees with defective vision wearing ordinary prescription glasses to be issued with clip-on lens and those employees whose type of work necessitates will continuously to wear safety goggles, may be issued with prescription safety goggles if required.
5. Faces shield of clear transparent plastic, attached to a head frame, which has a head band, protect against very light particles, for the entire face, do not protects against very light particles, liquid splashes and sparks. These shields offering protection for the entire face, do not protect against dust, gases, or heavy impact. Goggles and/or spectacles may be worn underneath the shield.
6. The following works require the mandatory use of goggles or other approved types of eye protection by the employees performing the work and by the employees assisting in the work or working the immediate vicinity where they are exposed to similar hazards.
   - 6.1. Chipping, breaking, cutting, picking or drilling concrete, bricks, stone, roads, cast iron, etc.
   - 6.2. Grinding or dressing of, aggressive in grinding wheels, even though they are equipped with protection shields.
   - 6.3. Working inside furnaces and heaters.
   - 6.4. Dusty and dis-cleaning operation.

6.5. Unloading or shoveling dusty materials such as soda ash, sulfurs, cement, clay, catalysts from truck.

6.6. Handing of acid, caustics or other corrosive and irritat ing materials.

Electric and gas welding, burning or cutting. Electric welders shall use welding helmet or hand shield, equipped with lens of approved density of shade. Spectacle type goggles shall also be worn under welding helmet. For cutting or gas burning, cup type gaggles must be used.

Sand Blasting

Exposure to any type of flying particles.

7. It is also necessary that under certain conditions in the following type of operations eye protection be worn:

- Machine tool operation.
- Using power drive or hand wire brushes. Scrapping desiccating and similar operations.
- Riveting.
- Handling scrap.
- Forging.
- Blowing-out-ended pipe.
- Using hammer, strike wrenches and chisels.
- When pulling with pliers, when cutting wire, band, etc., under tension or when handling wire where a hazard exists of loose end flying.
- When working with glass apparatus maintained underpositive pressure or under vaccum.
- When cleaning with air driven tools.
- Spraying paint.
- Insulating work.
- Masonry work.
- Handling hot asphalt.
- Taking samples of crude oils and light hydrocarbons.
- All supervisors or others whose duty requires them to be present near operations where goggles are necessary must also wear them.
- All goggles shall be washed and sterilized before they are reissued to another employee.
- The removal of foreign body from the eye shall only be done by a doctor.

Breathing Apparatus

(A) The function of breathing apparatus is to enable wearer to enter and work in atmospheres which are:

- Short of oxygen.
- Containing any gases in concentrations that would be dangerous to a worker.

(B) All employees working in Const. and Maint. Jobs, employees entering production and NGL units, employees working on drilling rigs and jetty installations must wear safety hats.

1. Puretha Gas Maskes: Puretha canister type which shall only be used as a protection against known gases and vapours in low concentrations (1% or less). The life of canister depends upon concentration of gas for which it has been used. Canister in general use must only remain in service for ten hours, or six months from date of issue, it is therefore required that a record card be fixed on the canister to mark the time used.
2. Self Contained Compressed Air Breathing Apparatus: These type of breathing apparatus consists of a cylinder contained natural air under pressure, a main valve on the cylinder, when opened, passing high pressure air to an automatic pressure reducing valve. The air is controlled to the wearer by an automatic demand valve in the face mask. Duration of air supply depends on the capacity of cylinder and is governed by the type of work being carried out. Depending on type of work the air supply may last between 25 minutes, to an hour.
3. Blowman Breathing Apparatus: Blowman Breathing Apparatus or fresh air mask is a metal case and a rotary blower, lengths of supply tubing, a belt or harness life-line, a breathing tube and a face mask. Air from surrounding atmosphere is pumped through the supply tubing into the face mask, and so to the wearer. It will give full protection in any concentration of gas or shortage of oxygen if the following instructions are followed:

3.1. The air pump must be sited up-wind of the contaminated area so that fresh air is pumped to the wearer.

3.2. A life-line firmly attached to the harness or belt must be used. This will serve to relay signals and to rescue the wearer from area if necessary.

3.3. While a wearer is in a gaseous area, there must be one person turning the pump handle, and one person tending the supply tubing and life line and acting as standby (Three persons to each Blowman). In some cases a full time standby may be required.

3.4. A maximum of 50 metres of supply tubing is imposed.

3.5. An additional Blowman with supply tubing and life line equal in length, to that in use, must be available on the spot for emergency use.

4. Self Rescue: Self contained breathing apparatus similar to Item 2 above is also available but in a light and easy operatable from. Air cylinder of this type can supply the air to the wearer between 7 to 9 minutes. This type of breathing apparatus will be usually carried by employees working in an expected hazardous condition and in case of emergency employees can escape to a safe area.

5. Breathing Apparatus Trailer Unit for Continuous Work in any Circumstances of Gas or Shortage of Oxygen: The unit can supply air to six or more employees working in a hazardous atmosphere. The main air supply is through large cylinders man folded together. Air through main supply tube after pressure reduction, flows to a supplying manifold in which individual supply tubes will be connected by special quick release couplings. An electric or motor driven compressor is also mounted on trailer unit which will continue to supply the air to the system.

Life Lines and Safety Harness

Safety belt and harness and life-lines shall be carefully inspected by the job supervisor each time before using. At least once every three months all safety belts, harness and life-lines must be inspected by a qualified employee.

Where altitude hazard exists, proper precautions must be taken by using life-lines and safety belts or safety harness or providing standard platform or scaffolds. Life-line must be fastened to some substantial anchorage, preferably above the working level.

Ear Protection

1. Ear protection in general use fall into two groups, the plugs or insert type and the cup or muff type. The insert type placed into ear canals varies both in design and materials. Since ear canals vary in size insert type may be designed or moulded to the size and the shape of individuals, ear channels and shall be fitted by a trained personnel.
2. Employees working in high level noise areas who are issued with ear protection shall wear them when they are entering in such work areas.
3. The supervisors shall discourage all employees from improvising any kind of inserts other than approved devices. (Appendix,

Table 3-A: Safety Protective Equipment Table)

3. Education and Training

Education focuses on theory or principles. Training gets into the specifications of how to turn principles into effective action.(Geller, 2001: p.47) Education and training provide individuals with the basic theoretical and practical knowledge required for the successful exercise of their trade or occupation and their integration into the working environment. Because of the importance of occupational health and safety, measures should be taken to include these subjects in all levels of education and training including higher technical, medical and professional education. Occupational health and safety training should meet the needs of all workers, and should be promoted in a manner that is appropriate to national conditions and practice. (ILO, 2001: pp. 35-52)

Employers' and workers' organizations should take positive action to carry out training and information programmes with a view to preventing potential occupational hazards in the working environment, and to controlling and protecting against existing resins such as those due to air pollution, noise and vibration. The public authorities have the responsibility to promote training and to act as a catalyst by providing resources and specialized personnel where necessary. Such a support is essential for developing countries.

Occupational health and safety training is a long-term task, and one that is never completely finished. It is a continuous exercise because initial training, even under the best of conditions, cannot cover all foreseeable and unforeseeable situations. If the goals of occupational health and safety policy are to be achieved, there is a need for the continuing involvement of employers and workers. National tripartite seminars can be an effective means of associating employers and workers in the policy-making process. The consensus developed by such seminars increases the commitment to implement the agreed measures.

Managers, supervisory staff and workers all need to be trained. Workers and their representatives in the undertaking should be given appropriate training in occupational health and safety.

Training in occupational health and safety should not be treated in isolation; it should feature as an integral part of job training and be incorporated into daily work procedures on the shop floor. Management must ensure that all those who play a part in the production processes are trained in the technical skills and their exposure should therefore always include a component of occupational health and safety.

4. Management Responsibilities in Occupational Health and Safety Training

It is the responsibility of the management to:

- Give each worker practical and appropriate instruction taking account his skills and professional experience, in each case defining the objective to be achieved in terms of ability to perform a specific function;
- Provide training involving the acquisition of knowledge and know-how to be applied in a specific job and corresponding to the qualifications required; this may consist of initial training for entry to a particular trade or profession, or adaptive training associated with a modification of the work station, the introduction of new methods or a transfer to another job;
- Give refresher courses to update the knowledge acquired through training; and
- Provide future training, thus enabling workers to acquire new knowledge, supplement existing knowledge, or specialize in a particular area by acquiring more detailed knowledge. (ILO, 2001: pp. 35-52)

Labour education has proceeded according to well-recognized principles of adult learning theory, including the following:

- Adults are self-motivated, especially with information that has immediate application to their lives and work. They expect, for example, practical tools to help them solve problems in the workplace.
- Adults learn best by building on what they already know so that they can incorporate new ideas into their existing vast reservoir of learning. Adults wish to be respected for their experience in life. Therefore, effective methods draw on participants' own knowledge and encourage reflection on their knowledge base.
- Adults learn in different ways. Each person has a particular learning style. An educational session will work best if participants have the opportunity to engage in multiple learning modalities: to listen, look at visuals, ask questions, simulate situations, read, write, practice with equipment and discuss critical issues. Variety not only ensures that each cognitive style is addressed but also provides repetition to reinforce learning and, of course, combats boredom.
- Adult learn best when they are actively engaged, when they "learn by doing". They are more responsive to active, participatory

methods than to passive measures. Lectures and written materials have a place in full repertories of methods. But case studies, role plays hands-on simulations and other small group activities that allow each individual to be involved are more likely to result in the retention and application of new learning. Ideally, each session involves interaction between participants and includes occasions for learning new information, for applying new skills and for discussing causes of problems and barriers to solving them. Participatory method requires more time, smaller groups and perhaps different instructional skills than those that many trainers currently posses. But to increase the impact of education, active participation is essential. (Stellman, 1998: p.18.8)

5. Competence and Training

According to the OSH competence includes education, work experience and training, or combination of these:

1. The necessary OSH competence should be defined by the employer, and arrangements established and maintained to ensure that all persons are competent to carry out the safety and health aspects of their duties and responsibilities.
2. The employer should have, or should have access to, sufficient OSH competence to identify and eliminate or control work-related hazards and risks, and to implement the OSH management system.
3. Under the arrangement referred to in paragraph 1, training programmes should: (a) cover all members of the organization, as appropriate; (b) be conducted by competent persons; (c) provide effective and timely initial and refresher training at appropriate intervals; (d) include participants' evaluation of their comprehension and retention of the training; (e) be reviewed periodically. The review should include the safety and health committee, where it exists, and the training programmes, modified as necessary to ensure their relevance and effectiveness; and (f) be documented, as appropriate and according to the size and nature of activity of the organization.
4. Training should be provided to all participants at no cost and should take place during working hours, if possible.

6. Training Reinforcement

No matter successful the training has been in meeting its objectives, its effect will decline with time if reinforcement is not provided in the workplace on a regular and consistent basis. Such reinforcement should be the routine responsibility of supervisors, managers and joint safety and health committees. It can be provided through regular monitoring of performance on the job, recognition of proper performance and routine reminders through the use of short meetings, notices and posters. (Stellman, 1998: p.18.7)

7. Training Evaluation

The purpose of evaluating training is simply to establish whether the training objectives have been met and, if so, whether this has resulted in solving the problem addressed by those objectives. Preparation for training evaluation should begin at the training design stage. In other words, the problem to be addressed by training must be clear, the training objectives must be specific and the *status quo* prior to training must be known.

Evaluation of training can be done at various levels. At the first level, the aim is simply to asses employees reactions to the training programme. Did they like the programme, the instructor and the course material, were they bored, did they feel that they had learned something? This approach may useful in assessing whether or not the programme was perceived to be of value by the students. Such evaluations are most useful of conducted through an attitude survey and should not generally be administered by the course instructor. Participants are unlikely to provide candid answers at this point even if questionnaires are anonymous. As an aid to this type of evaluation, students can be allowed to test themselves on the training content.

The next level of evaluation is the assessment of whether or not the learning objectives have been met. Learning objectives are related to the content of the training and they define what the student should be able to do or know when training is completed. Learning objectives are usually developed for each part of the course content and are shared with students so that they know what they should expect to learn. Evaluation at this level is designed to assess whether or not students have learned what is defined in the learning objectives. This can be done by testing participants at the end of the course. Knowledge, concepts and abstract skills can be assessed in written tests whereas practical skills can be assessed by direct observation of students demonstrating the skill. Where this level of evaluation is used, it is absolutely necessary to have prior knowledge of the knowledge or skills baseline of the students before training begins.

The third level of evaluation is the assessment of whether or not the knowledge and skills learned in the training are actually being applied on the job. Such assessment can be made through direct observation at specified intervals of time following training. Evaluation of application on the day following training may produce a result quite different from that based on an evaluation some three months later. It is important to note, however, that if the evaluation shows a lack of application after three months, it may not be the training itself which is defective; it may be due to a lack of reinforcement in the workplace itself.

Finally, the highest level of evaluation is the determination of whether or not the problem addressed by the training has been resolved. If the problem identified was a high rate of musculoskeletal injuries in the shipping and receiving area, is there evidence of the desired drop in the injury rate? Here again, timing is important. In this case, it may take time for the training to become effective. The rate may not drop for a number of months because such injuries are often cumulative; and so the rate for some time may reflect conditions prior to training. Furthermore, the training may result in greater awareness of the problem leading to increased reporting soon after training.

Ideally, all four levels of training evaluation should be built into the training design and implementation. However, if only one level is used, its limitations should be clearly understood by all concerned.

Where training is designed and provided by an external agency, the organization can and should nevertheless evaluate its potential usefulness by applying criteria based on the principles. (Stellman, 1998: p.18.7)

8. General Considerations for Preventive and Protective Measures

The incidence of accidents and work-related diseases and injuries in most occupational sectors is still regrettably high; there is therefore an urgent need for preventive and protective measures to be instituted at workplaces in order to guarantee the safety and health of workers. Occupational accidents and diseases not only cause great pain, suffering or death to victims, but also threaten the lives of other workers and their dependants. Occupational accidents and diseases also result in:

1. loss of skilled and unskilled but experienced labour;
2. material loss, i.e., damage to machinery and equipment well as spoiled products; and
3. high operational costs through medical care, payment as of compensation, repairing or replacing damaged machinery and equipment.

Workplace health and safety programmes should aim at eliminating the unsafe or unhealthy working conditions and dangerous acts which account for nearly all occupational accidents and diseases.(Alli, 2001:p. 93)

8.1. Duties of employers when workers are exposed to hazards: In situations where workers are exposed to hazards, employers have the duty to:

- Inform the workers of all the known hazards associated with their work, the health risks involved and the relevant preventive and protective measures;
- Take appropriate measures to eliminate or minimize the risks resulting from exposure to those hazards;
- Provide workers with suitable protective equipment, clothing and other facilities where adequate protection against risk of accident or injury to health, including exposure to adverse conditions, cannot be ensured by other means; and
- Provide first aid for workers who have suffered from an injury or illness at the workplace, as well as appropriate transportation from the workplace and access to appropriate medical facilities. (Alli, 2001: 95)

As we have seen, accidents can be caused by a number of variables: errors in operator-machine design, work condition, or worker behaviour.

8.2. Reporting of Occupational Accidents, Injuries and Diseases: One of the tasks of the competent authority is to ensure the establishment and application of procedures for the notification of occupational accidents and diseases by employers and, when appropriate, insurance institutions and others directly concerned, as well as the production of annual statistics on occupational accidents and diseases. Consequently, national law or regulations in many countries provide for:

(1) the reporting of occupational accidents and diseases to the competent authority within a prescribed time;

(2) standard accidents as well as dangerous occurrences; and

(3) the compilation and publication of statistics on accidents, occupational diseases and dangerous occurrences. (Alli, 2001: p.76)

8.3. First Aid: First aid means the immediate measures taken at the site of an accident by a person who may not be a physician but who is trained in first aid, has access to the necessary equipment and supplies, and know what must be done to ensure that professional medical care will follow his or her intervention.

When a serious accident happens, the first few minutes may be decisive in terms of lives being saved or injuries avoided. Therefore, taking natio0nal law and practices into account, occupational health services in enterprises should:

(1) provide first aid and emergency treatment in cases of accident or indisposition of workers at the workplace; and

(2). collaborate in the organization of first aid. (Alli, 2001: p. 87)

8.4. Research: Within the limits of their resources, occupational health services should contribute to research by participating in studies or inquiries in the enterprise or in the relevant branch of economic activity. Such research should be subject to prior consultation with employers' and workers' representatives and might, for example, aim to collect data for epidemiological purposes or for orienting the activities of the occupational health service. The results of measurements carried out in the working environment and the assessments of workers' health may also be used for research purposes, subject to the agreement of the employer and the workers or their representatives in the enterprise or the safety and health committee. Most importantly, the privacy of the workers must be protected.

There is a need for action-oriented research programmes, in particular to:

(1) provide accurate statistics on the incidence of occupational accidents and diseases and their causes;

(2) identify the hazards associated with all forms of new technology, including chemical substances;

(3) describe and analyze the working conditions of workers in poorly protected occupations and sectors; and

(4) investigate relationships between working conditions, occupational safety and health, and productivity, including the impact of improved conditions on employment and economic growth.

Where guidelines for research programmes are developed on a tripartite basis, the links between research and action are likely to be strengthened. Mechanisms to promote such tripartite collaboration should be put in place. (Alli, 2001: p. 90-1)

4
Review of Literature

According to Arnalee Yassi and Tord Hjellstrom, development, and industrialization in particular, have made immense positive contributions to health, including greater personal and social wealth, as well as vastly improved health and education services, transportation and communication, Unquestionably, on the global scale, people are living longer and are healthier than they were centuries and even decades ago. However, industrialization has also had adverse health consequences not only for workforces, but for the general population as well. These effects have been caused either directly by exposure to safety hazards and harmful agents, or indirectly through environmental degradation locally and globally.

Environmental health hazards, like occupational health hazards, may be biological, chemical, physical, biomechanical or psychosocial in nature. Environmental health hazards include traditional hazards of poor sanitation and shelter, as well as agricultural and industrial contamination of air, water, food and land.

These hazards have resulted in a loss of health impacts, ranging from catastrophic direct effects (e.g. the recent cholera epidemic in Latin America and the chemical poisoning outbreak in Bhopal India (Bhopal, India 1985, has Environmental Hazard in Methylisocyanate, as Acute lung Disease, which affected 2,000 deaths and 200,000 poisoned), to chronic effects (e.g. in Love Canal, USA). Environmental health impacts thus include the indirect effects of industrial disruption of the adequate food and housing, as well as the degradation of the global systems on which the health of the planet depends. (Stellman, 1998:p. 53.2.

Chisholm and Eskenzal (1983) found that, workers at the Three Mile Island nuclear reactor reported higher levels of tension during the 1979 crisis. This was probably a reaction to the crisis, rather than a direct precipitating factor. Unusually high levels of stress were also observed among residents of Three Mile Island during the 1979 crisis (Baum, Fleming, and Singer, 1983; Cleary and Houts, 1984; Davidson, Baum, and Collins, 1982).

It is important to obtain data on health effects for prevention and for prioritization of approaches to solve occupational health problems. However, most of the available morbidity data may not be applicable for developing countries, as they originate from the developed countries.

In developing countries, the nature of the occupational health effects from workplace hazards may be different from those in the developed countries. Overt occupational diseases such as chemical poisoning and the pneumoconiosis which are caused by exposures to high levels of workplace toxins, are still encountered in significant numbers in developing countries, while these problems may have been substantially reduced in the developed countries.

In fact, the morbidity burden from acute pesticide poisoning in some developing countries, such as Sri Lanka, may even surpass that of traditional public health problems such as diphtheria, whooping cough and tetanus.

Thus, some surveillance of occupational health morbidity is required from the developing countries. The information would be used for the assessment of the magnitude of the problem, prioritization of plans to cope with the problems, allocation of resources and for subsequent evaluation of the impact of interventions.

Unfortunately, such surveillance information is often lacking in the developing countries. It should be recognized that surveillance programmes in developed countries may be inappropriate for developing countries, and such systems probably cannot be adopted in their entirety for developing countries because of the various problems which may impede surveillance activities. (Stellman, 1998: p. 32.10)

These will be largely concerned with: (a) the selection of appropriate experimental groups, and the control of such influences as age, experience and environmental factors, (b) the definition of events which are to be regarded as accidents, and the completeness and accuracy of these data, (c) the stability or consistency of accident records in successive periods as a measure or criterion of personal accidents-proneness; (d) the adequacy of existing instruments of statistical analysis, and the precautions which must be taken against the use of techniques which are suspect, to say the least, when applied to frequency distributions associated with accident data.

The investigators conclude that "such methods could be employed, provided there was a good labour supply, for an occupation in which it was particularly desirable to have workers with a low degree of accident-proneness on accident of its dangerous nature". (Arbous,1951: 376-7)

According to John W.F. Cowell, the primary functions of the employee health service are treatment of acute injuries and illnesses occurring in workplace, conducting fitness-to-work examinations (Cowell 1986) and the prevention, detection and treatment of work-related injuries and illnesses. However, it may also play a significant role in preventive and health maintenance programmes.

A variety of communication techniques and presentation styles may be used. A series of attractive, easy-to-read pamphlets can be very useful where there are budget constraints. (Stellman, 1998: p.15.17)

According to Ian M.F. Arnold and Louis Damphousse, Prevention of disease and injury is driven by the occupational health and industrial hygiene and safety team with input from all interested parties. Methods used frequently do not differentiate between work-related and non-work-related prevention. Prevention is considered to reflect an attitude or quality of an employee - an attitude that does not cease or start at the plant fence line. A further attribute of this philosophy is the belief that prevention is amenable to continual improvement, a belief furthered by the company's approach to auditing its various programmes. (Stellman, 1998: pp. 15.20-1)

According to Wiliam B. Burn and Robert J. McCumey, occupational health services are determined through a system of needs assessment. Factors that affect which the type of occupational health service are to be utilized include the potential risks of normal operations, the demographics of the workforce and management's interest in occupational health. Health service are dependent on the type of industry, the physical, chemical or biological hazards present, and the methods used to prevent exposure, as well as government and industry standards, regulations and rulings. (Stellman, 1998: p.16.35)

According to Steven Hecker, a 1981 study of worker safety and health training in the industrial nations begins by quoting the French writer Victor Hugo: "No cause can succeed without first making education its ally" (Heath 1981). This observation surely still applies to occupational safety and health and is relevant to organization personnel at all levels.

Education focuses on theory or principles. Training gets into the specification of how to turn principles into effective action. (Geller, 2001: p.478)

As the workplace becomes increasingly complex, new demands have arisen for greater understanding of the causes and means of prevention of accidents, injuries and illnesses. Government officials, academics, management and labour all have important roles to play in conducting research that furthers this understanding. The next critical step is the effective transmission of this information to workers, supervisors, managers, government inspectors and safety and health professionals. Although education for occupational physicians and hygienists differs in many respects from the training of workers on the shop floor, there are also common principles that apply to all.

National education and training policies and practices will of course vary according to the economic, political, social, cultural and technological background of the country. In general, industrially advanced nations have proportionally more specialized occupational safety and health practitioners at their disposal than do the developing nations, and more sophisticated education and training programmes are available to these trained workers. More rural and less industrialized nations tend to rely more on "primary health care workers", who may be workers representatives in factories or fields or health personnel in district health centres. Clearly, training needs and available resources will vary greatly in these situations. However, they all have in common the need for trained practitioners.

The primary tools needed to achieve the goals of reducing occupational injuries and illnesses and promoting occupational safety and health have been characterized as the "three E's" - engineering, enforcement and education. The three are interdependent and receive varying levels of emphasis within different national systems. The overall rationale for training and education is to improve awareness of safety and health hazards, to expand knowledge of the causes of occupational illness and injury and to promote the implementation of effective measures. The specific purpose and impetus for training will, however vary for different target audiences.

On-the-job training at the worksite is appropriate for workers as supervisiors facing specific hazards found onsite. If the training of significant length, a comfortable classroom facility within the worksite is strongly recommended. in cases where locating at the workplace may intimidate workers or otherwise discourage their full participation in the class, an offsite venue is preferable. Workers may feel more comfortable in a union setting where the union plays a major role in designing and delivering the programe. However, field visits to actual work locations which illustrate the hazards in question are always a positive addition to the course.

Education and training cannot solve all occupational safety and health problems, and care must be taken that the techniques learned in such programmes are in fact applied appropriately to the identified needs. They are, however, critical components of an effective safety and health programme when employed in conjunction with engineering and technical solutions. Cumulative, interactive and continuous learning is essential to prepare our rapidly changing work environments to meet the needs of workers, especially as regards the prevention of debilitating injuries and illnesses. Those who labour in the workplace as well as those who provide support from outside need the most up-to-date information available and the skills to put this information to use in order to protect and promote workers health and safety. (Stellman, 1998: p.18.2-5)

Accident Pronenss

The significant history of the concept of accident-proneness goes back to 1919 when Greenwood and Wood (1919) and Greenwood and Yule (1920) made the first through-going approach to the analysis of accidents statistics. Their findings and conclusions were later critically examined and extended by Newbold (1926) in her classic contributions to the subject in 1926 and 1927.

According to F. Eggetter, (1982) most accidents arise from human error. (Foreman, 1983)

- Vernon in 1936 stated: The accident-proneness of various individuals is not a fixed quality but is liable to be affected by any and every change in their bodily condition. The condition is influenced by external changes of environment as well as by internal changes of physical and mental health". This statement clearly implies that accident-proneness is a variable attribute, whereas in 1939 the same authors state, "accident liability is influenced by many other personal qualities besides inherent accident-proneness. It depends on general health ... age and experience, fatigue etc...". (Arbous, 1951: pp. 345-51)

Wesman (1968), maintained that all ability tests (tests of achievement, general intelligence, and special abilities) measure only what the examinee has learned. Second, he proposed to define intelligence as an attribute that is the summation of learning experiences. Therefore, according to Wesman, intelligence can be fully measured only by sampling ham every domain of experience in which learning has occured.

Undoubtedly 'accident proneness' originally described by Greenwood and Woods (1919), has been the most important concept in the study of individual differences in accident causation. In reviewing the history and status of this controversial concept. MCKena (1983) referred to two problematic issues. First, inappropriate statistical techniques have persistently been used to investigate proneness. The unequal liability to accidents within the population is described reasonably well by a negative binomial distribution and better than by a distribution (Boyle, 1980a); but acceptance of the negative binomial model rests on the assumption, usually untenable, that exposure and biases in accident reporting are equally distributed across the population in question. Second, the concept is used loosely and inconsistently. McKenna (1983) has proposed replacing the term 'proneness' with the more neutral 'differential accident involvement'. The adoption of his proposal could circumvent the long-standing in congruency between the meaning of the concept and the way it should be investigated. Also it would probably weaken the practice of attempting to show that small groups of individuals are allegedly responsible for the majority of accidents. (Sheehy and Chapman, 1987: p. 204)

Tiffin (1952), Lawsche (1952), and Schaeffer (1941) found positive and significant relationship between a general attitude of "safety mindedness" and accident free performance on the job. Several other researchers have found positive correlation's between accidents and many of the factors associated with job satisfaction and morale, e.g., high accident rates are found in departments which have low promotion possibilities, low mobility rates, and autocratic work climates (Case and Stewart, 1957). Ghiselli and Brown, (1948), had reported a slight correlation between mechanical comprehension and accidents. Interests and accidents were shown to be slightly related (Moffie, 1955). Most personality scales have been even less successful in either identifying the accident-prone or discriminating between accident and non-accident groups (Goldstein, 1962). (Crawford, 1965: p. 560)

The existing theory of accident-proneness started from a knowledge of the observed facts which consisted of a frequency distribution of the number of accidents occurring per individual within a given group in a given environmental situation, and in given period of time. This merely recorded the number of individuals who had 0, 1, 2, ..., n accidents in the given time period.

The accident proneness concept enables one to differentiate between persons with the hope of producing beneficial results. The implied advantage of this theory is that after having spotted who the accident-prone cases are in a group, their removal from the group should result in a degrease in the relative frequency of accidents sustained by the remainder.

Opposition to the concept of accident proneness, and particularly to the notion that a single general personal trait is responsible for accidents, has come mainly from psychometricians and statisticians (Mintz and Blum, 1949; Maritz, 1950).

What is observed in the manner suggested, is due to the inextricable mingling of the effects of environment with the effects of "personal attributes". At best, is it only a measure of average accident proneness relative to a specific environment? Many writers stressing these facts would term a measure of average accident liability in sharp distinction to any proposed measure of accident proneness.

In theory, it is possible that a safety first campaign might by explanation and education affect every individual in the same manner. Everybody remains equally accident prone although less prone to have accidents. Again, everybody "learns by experience", and it is possible mathematically if not psychologically for everybody to learn alike. (Arbous,1951: pp. 390-9)

Brown (1984) stated, that in the present report, it couldn't be considered that accident proneness as a general trait of the individual has been substantiated. Simply because an individual had a high rate for accidents of one kind, it does not necessarily follow that he will have a high rate for accidents of another kind. Rather, if there were any tendency to retain liability to have accidents under many different circumstances, the facts would indicate that such a tendency is of very minor importance as a factor in the determination of accidents. (Brown, 1984: p. 20)

Oldhan and Fried (1987), said, "Recent research has shown that physical and psychological conditions of the environment work together to have an important impact on workers behavior and attitudes".

The accident consistency variable is the number of accident incurred by an individual plus the number of years that employee incurred at least one accident. Each of these measures will be used separately in past research, as Hansen (1988), proposed that this composite variable reflects the "consistency" of one's accidents tendency by adding a measure of temporal frequency (number of years with accident) to a measure of quantity (number of accidents). Jorekog and Sorbom (1979, 1984), recommended three indices to judge the fit of path analytic model to the data.

The relationship between status and accident rate and time on the job on both measures of proficiency the married operators are slightly superior to the single ones. The number of divorced operators is small, but they too appear to be more proficient than the single operators are. The common standards used in hiring motor coach operators, namely, that the desired employee should score high on an intelligence test, be young, with considerable education, and married, do not appear to have much validity. Married operators are slightly superior to single operators both in terms of accident rate and time remaining on the job, and the older operators tend to stay on the job for longer periods of time than the younger ones, but none of the other relationship deviates appreciably from zero. (Brown,1948: p. 478)

According to Shahani, (1987), the worker who appears to be accident-prone and one job could have an excellent safety record on a different job. This is essentially the idea behind accident liability theory: an individual's risk of having an accident varies from situation to situation, as well as over time.

While there is no evidence to suggest that accident proneness is a genetic trait (McKenna, 1983), the question remains open as to whether personality characteristics and accident liability are related. Probably characteristics influence stress coping styles which in turn affect accident involvement. For example, Studenkis (1981) reported that, among coalminers in low, medium, and high accident rate the experience of an accident produced a temporary sharp increase in anxiety among the miners. However, in mines with extremely high accident rates the opposite occurred, and possibly this is because through unsound statistical reasoning.

Various studies have reported associations between indices of accidents, illness, and personality. So, for example, Stuart and Brown (1981) found that levels of self reported stress correlated with accident and disease liability; Schenk and Rausche (1979) found that neuroticism discriminates between high and low accident drivers; Allodi and Montgomery (1979) found that a positive history of medical, surgical, and psychosomatic episodes differentiated a group of 255 workers who had accidents from 215 no-accident controls; Jimenez (1977) found that workers with three or more accident during a 6 –month period had higher levels of aggressiveness than a comparison of no-accident group; and Mayer (1981) found a week non-significant relationship between qualitative performance on the Porteus Maze Test and incidence of reported accidents among 80 workers. (Sheey,1987: p. 205)

There are substantial reports to the effect that workload increases the level of perceived stress and the probability of accidental injuries (Cellier, 1980). Usually, however, the occurrence of an accident itself causes additional stress (Hart and Bartolussi, 1984), as does the supervening criticism from supervisors and managers (Franasczuk and Kopaczewska, 1978).

Considerable practical advantage would be gained if one could predict in any subsequent period which individuals are in fact going to sustain most of the accidents. The practical man, despite all theoretical explanations, will in the end need this information as a basis for his future accident-prevention policy.

The fundamental idea that the occurrence of one accident will alter the probability of having the next seems to be an obvious one, which should be associated with the theories of learning.

In general nature is infinitely variable; human beings are never "exactly alike", the environment they work in at any time is never quite the "same" for each individual. Apparently it is meant to indicate a personal trait in an individual as opposed to some characteristic of the environment in which he works. No individuals enter a "hazardous occupation". All work under "similar conditions" and accidents occasionally occur. "More" suggests that we expect to be able to measure or at least to rank this quality of "accident proneness".

The probability that an individual has an accident within a very short interval of time depends on the number of accidents that he has had previously.

General theory suggests that the beginner, after making one mistake becomes very much more careful.

In accident statistics the observed fact is that some people tend to have more accidents than other people do.

Usually what is required is a cooperative effort between experts and those who are most directly affected by their assessments. In this way a rational risk appraisal is more likely to be possible and the tangible safety benefits are more likely to endure. (Sheehy and Chapman, 1987: pp. 207-8)

Perception of Risk

When dealing with accidents in the workplace, one can estimate the magnitude of the problem retrospectively by comparing the number of accidents (incidence rate) with the severity of the accidents (lost work days). However, if one wants to estimate the magnitude of the problem prospectively, it is done by evaluating the presence of risk factors in the workplace, that is, factors that might lead to accidents.

Knowledge of the relevant risk factors can be obtained by analyzing the detailed information provided with each accident record as to where workers and operators were located when the accident occurred, what injuries occurred and other particulars surrounding the accident.

Risk measurement must be made on the basis of information regarding the number and seriousness of injuries that have occurred in past, yielding a retrospective measurement.

Management of risk provides a calculated frequency of injuries and a measurement of the seriousness of the injury. This could be described as the number of lost work day cases or fatalities per number of workers (e.g., in Denmark, the risk of death in an occupational accident is 3 fatalities per 100,000 employees).

Type of risk or element of danger assessment provides not only an indication of the exposure sources and other harmful factors which may cause an accident, but also indication of the circumstances leading to injury or damage. Work performed at a height, for example, will involve a risk of falling, with serious injury as a possible result. Similarly, work with cutting tools involves a risk of cuts from contact with sharp components, and work with noisy machines for a long time may result in hearing damage.

However, it is one thing to know what has happened in the past. It should be noted that the very knowledge of the exposure sources and other potentially harmful factors which may cause damage or injury in connection with tasks of various sorts, as well as knowledge of the factors that can either heighten or reduce those risk factors that influence risk measurement, can provide a basis for recognition of the risk. The factors which are of greater relevance in determining risk are:

- factors which determine the presence or absence (or potential) of risks of any sort.
- factors which either increase or minimize the probability of these risks resulting accidents or injuries.
- factors affecting the seriousness of accidents associated with these risks.
- To clarify the first point, it is necessary to identify the causes of the accident, namely, exposure sources and other harmful factors; the two latter points constitute the factors which influence the measurement of risk.
- The primary factors in the working environment which are the direct causes of harm, either by way of occupational diseases or occupational accidents.

Stanley Tucker Hughes, in 1993, in his research "The Perception of Risk for non-Lethal Events and its Relation to Risk-taking Behavior (Risk Perception, Product Safety Warnings) found that risk factors obtained (1) when risk is defined as death were the same as when risk was defined as injury, (2) for both a broad and narrow class of product were the same, (3) A subject is perception of a product's risk could be modified through manipulation of risk variables. (4) explored the possibility of using risk perception variables to modify risk-taking behavior through the use of product tables that decried a product in terms of risk variables.

The link hypothesized here between risk and accident is perceptual: discrepancies between subjective estimates of risk and their objective counterparts leave people poorly prepared to detect and cope with potential hazards. The larger the underestimation of objective risk the greater the probability that potentially dangerous situations will become accident situations. Conversely, one might predict that when subjective distributions approximate objective distributions the incidence of accidents should be minimized. However, in practice the incidence does not then approach zero (see Ostberg, 1980). This is partly because objective assessments of risk are not inherently more reliable than subjective assessments (Sheehy and Chapman, 1985).

From the standpoint of prevention the distinction between subjective and objective risk remains important. Objective risk is normative, in the sense that it is based on events that are known to have happened, and it cannot be disproved because it is a post-accident assessment. The shape of the objective risk distribution is altered by additional accidents and by usual accidents, but whatever its shape it cannot be declared untenable. Subjective risk is context-sensitive and reflects anticipations which can easily be shown to be wrong. Thus, subjective and objective risk serve different functions and it would be wrong to presume the superiority of objective risk.

Brown (1980) has argued that conventional hypotheses about the relationship between subjective and objective risk (see Naatanen and Summala, 1975) are oversimplified. In particular he maintains that subjective risk is weighted by the perceived likelihood of correcting errors. Subjective risk is a function of decision error probabilities and error correction probabilities. Thus, increasing people's awareness of the discrepancy between assessed objective risk and their perceptions of that risk will not necessarily bring about a reduction in accidents. Often safety requires taking sufficient precautions to permit opportunities to rectify errors.

A methodological problem that has plagued the past accident research is "differential exposure to risk". The older an employee is, the more likely that he or she will hold a job with greater responsibility and skill requirements.

Metts (1982) studied 302 work injuries and found that smokers had a relatively greater risk of accident involvement. One way of interpreting this finding would be to treat the difference as providing an explanation for differential accident liability. A better interpretation, pursued by Metts, is to see the difference as requiring explanation. Metts reported that the relationship between smoking and accident liability was due to specific conflict on certain kinds of tasks, rather than smoking as such. (Sheehy and Chapman,1987: pp. 204-5)

A salient possibility demanding investigation is that accidents may be precipitated by the drug and alcohol use associated with attempts to manage a crisis.

If there is a strong link between critical life events and accident liability then, from a management point of view, the most efficient method of reducing excessive risk of accidents is probably through education about substance abuse. Most people are not aware of their general vulnerability during periods of intense stress (see Levenson, 1980). For example, it may be commonly recognised that stress is associated with sleep loss, but it is not so well recognised that sleep loss is associated with industrial accidents (Lavie, Kremerman, and Wiel, 1982). The link between accidents and sleep loss may be causal on some occasions but on others it may be mediated by different stress-provoking factors. Making individuals more aware of their vulnerability may in itself be sufficient to facilitate extra caution.

Plez (1976) quotes West German statistics which suggest that alcohol is a contributing or major cause of 7-10 per cent of causes of industrial injury, and in the USA Parker and Brody (1981) found that 10 percent of women and 19 per cent of men were occupational alcoholics. (Sheehy and Chapman, 1987: pp. 206-7)

In order to quantify actual risk, data on workplace injuries must be related to a measure of exposure to risk, such as number of hours worked, a labour supply measure which may be available from other surveys. The rate of nonfatal workplace injuries for a group of workers may be calculated by dividing the number of injuries recorded for that group by the number of hours worked during the same time period. The rate obtained this way represents the risk of injury per hour of work:

$$\textit{Injury rate} = \frac{\text{No injuries incurred during specific time period}}{\text{Hrs. worked by all group members during time period}}$$

A convenient way of comparing the risk of injury among various group of workers is to compute the relative risk:

$$\textit{Relative Risk (RR)} = \frac{\text{Injury rate for selected group of workers}}{\text{Injury rate for a reference group of workers}}$$

The reference group may be a special group of workers, such as all managerial and professional specialty workers. Alternatively, it might consist of all workers. In any case, the relative risk (RR) corresponds to the rate ratio commonly used in epidemiological studies (Rothman 1986). It is algebraically equivalent to the percentage of all injuries which occur to the special group divided by the percentage of hours accounted for by the special group. when the RR is greater than 1.0, it indicates that members of the selected group are more likely to sustain injuries than members of the reference group; when the RR is less than 1.0, it indicates that, on an average, members of this group experience fewer injuries per hour. (Stellman, 1998: p. 32.18)

Accident Prevention

According to Renald Skiba, Job safety involves the interrelationship between people and work; materials, equipment and machinery; the environment; and economic considerations such as productivity. Ideally, work should be healthful, not harmful and not unreasonably difficult. For economic reasons, as high a level of productivity as possible must be achieved.

In the manufacturing process, people and objects interact. The term object is used in the broader sense as expressed in the customary designation "people- (machine)-environment system". This includes not only technical instruments of work, machines and materials, but all surrounding items such as floors, stairs, electrical current, gas, dust, atmosphere and so on).

Because it is apparent that questions of accident prevention can be solved not in isolation, but only in the context of their relationship with production and the working environment, the following principles for accident prevention can be derived:

1. Accident prevention must be built into production planning with the goal of avoiding disruptions.
2. The ultimate goal is to achieve a production flow that is as unhindered as possible. This results not only in reliability and the elimination of defects, but also in the workers' well-being, labour-saving methods.

The following principles are important in understanding how accident prevention concepts relate to disruption-free production:

1. Accident prevention is sometimes considered a social burden instead a major part of disruption prevention. Disruption prevention is better a motivator than accident prevention, because improved production is expected to result from disruption prevention.
2. Measures to ensure workplace safety must be integrated into the measures used to ensure disruption-free production. For example, the instructions on hazard must be an integral part of the general directions governing the flow of production at the workplace.

Assuming that workers as well as their objective environments can be carriers of hazards or dangers, accident prevention would basically consist of eliminating the hazards or dangers, or impeding the consequences by keeping the carriers apart or by minimizing the effects of the energy. (Stellman, 1998: pp. 56.30-31)

According to Linnea lillienberg, a workplace hazard can be defined as any condition that may adversely affect the well-being or health of exposed persons. Recognition of hazards in any occupational activity involves characterization of the workplace by identifying hazardous agents and groups of workers potentially exposed to these hazards. The hazards might be of chemical, biological or physical origin. Some hazards in the work environment are easy to recognize-for example, irritants, which have an immediate irritating effect after skin exposure or inhalation. Others are not so easy to recognize, for example, chemicals which are accidentally formed and have no warning properties. Some agents like metals (e.g., lead, mercury, cadmium, manganese), which may cause injury after several years of exposure, might be easy to identify if you are aware of the risk. A toxic agent may not constitute a hazard at low concentrations or if no one is exposed. Basic to the recognition of hazards are identification of possible agents at the workplace, knowledge about health risks of these agents and awareness of possible exposure situations. (Stellman, 1998: p. 30.10)

According to Abdul Raouf, accident is defined as unplanned occurrences which result in injuries, fatalities, loss of production or damage to property and assets. Preventing accidents is extremely difficult in the absence of an understanding of the causes of accidents.

According to W.H. Heinrich (1931), who developed the so called domino theory, 88 per cent of all accidents are caused by unsafe acts of people, 10 per cent by unsafe actions and 2 per cent by "act of God". He proposed a "five-factor accident sequence" in which each factor would actuate the next step in the manner of toppling dominoes lined up in a raw. The sequence of accident factors is as follows; (1) ancestry and social environment, (2) worker fault, (3) unsafe act together with mechanical and physical hazard, (4) accident, (5) damage or injury.

The removal of a single domino in the row would interrupt the sequence of toppling.

Heinrich suggested that removal of one of the factors would prevent the accident and resultant injury; with the key domino to be removed from the sequence being number 3. Although Heinrich provided no data for his theory, it nonetheless represents a useful point to start discussion and a foundation for future research. Multiple causation theory is an outgrowth of the domino theory, but it postulates for a single accident there may be many contributory factors, causes and sub-causes, and that certain combinations of these give risk to accidents. According to this theory, the contributory factors can be grouped into the following two categories: (1) Behavioural; this category include, lack of knowledge, lack of skills and inadequate physical and mental condition. (2) Environmental; this category includes improper guarding of other hazardous work elements and degradation of equipment through use and unsafe procedures.

The major contribution of this theory is to bring out the fact that rarely, if ever, is an accident the result of a single cause or act.

According to the pure chance theory, every one of any given set of workers has an equal chance of being involved in an accident. It further implies that there is no single discernible pattern of events that leads to an accident. In this theory, all accidents are treated as corresponding to Heinrich's acts of God, and it is held that there exist no interventions to prevent them.

Accident proneness theory maintains that within a given set of workers, there exists a subset of workers who are more liable to be involved in accidents. Researchers have been able to prove this theory conclusively because most of the research work has been poorly conducted and most of the findings are contradictory and inconclusive. This theory is not generally accepted. It is felt that if indeed this theory is supported by any empirical evidence at all, it probably accounts for only a very low proportion of accidents without any statistical significance.

Those who accept the energy transfer theory put forward the claim that a worker incurs injury or equipment suffered damage through a change of energy, and that for every change of energy there is a source, a path and a receiver. This theory is useful for determining injury causation and evaluating energy hazards and either preventive, limiting or ameliorating with respect to the energy transfer.

The "symptoms versus causes" theory is not as much a theory as an admonition to be heeded if accident causation is to be understood. Usually, when investigating accidents, we tend to fasten upon the obvious causes of the accident to the neglect of the root causes. Unsafe acts and unsafe conditions are the symptoms - the proximate causes - and not the root causes of the accident.

The belief that accidents are caused and can be prevented makes it imperative for us to study those factors which are likely to favour the occurrence of accidents. By studying such factors, the root causes of accidents can be isolated and necessary steps can be taken to prevent the recurrence of the accidents. These root causes of accidents can be grouped as "immediate" and "contributing". The immediate causes are unsafe acts of the worker and unsafe working conditions. The contributing causes could be management-related factors, the environment and the physical and mental condition of the worker. A combination of causes must converge in order to result in an accident. However, an understanding of the "cause and effect" relation of the accident-causing factors is required before continuous improvement of safety processes can be undertaken.

Accident causation is very complex and must be understood adequately in order to improve accident prevention. Since safety lacks a theoretical base, it cannot be regarded as being a science yet. These theories are nonetheless necessary, but not sufficient, for developing a frame of reference for understanding accident occurrences. (Stellman, 1998: pp. 56.6-7)

According to Robert F. Herrick, the entire topic of personal protection must be considered in the context of control methods for preventing occupational injuries and diseases. Personal protection should be considered the method of last resort in reducing the risks found in the workplace. In the hierarchy of methods which may be used to control workplace hazards personal protection is not the method of first choice. In fact, it is to be used only when the possible engineering controls which reduce the hazard (by methods such as isolation, enclosure, ventilation, substitution, or other process changes), and administrative controls (such as reducing work time at risk for exposure) have been implemented to the extent feasible. There are cases, however personal protection is necessary, whether as a short-term or long-term control, to reduce occupational disease and injury risks. When such use is necessary, personal protective equipment and devices must be used as part of a comprehensive programme which includes full evaluation of the hazards, correct selection and fitting of the equipment, training and education for the people who use the equipment, maintenance and repair to keep the equipment in good working order and overall management and worker commitment to the success of the protection programme.

Protective equipment and devices are essential parts of a hazard control strategy. They can be used effectively, provided their appropriate place in the hierarchy of controls is recognized. The use of protective equipment and devices must be supported by a personal protection programme, which assures that the protection actually performs as intended in conditions of use, and that the people who have to wear it, it can use it effectively in their work activities. (Stellman, 1998: pp. 31.2-3)

According to Cary L. Cooper and Sue Cartwright, any organization which seeks to establish and maintain the best state of mental, physical and social well being of its employees needs to have policies and procedures which comprehensively address health and safety. These policies will include a mental health policy with procedures to manage stress based on the needs of the organization and its employees. These will be regularly reviewed and evaluated.

There are a number of options to consider in looking at the prevention of stress, which can be termed as primary, secondary and tertiary level of prevention and address different stages in the stress process (Cooper and Cartwight, 1994). Primary prevention is concerned with taking action to reduce or eliminate stressors (i.e., source of stress), and positively promoting a supportive and healthy work environment. Secondary prevention is concerned with the prompt detection and management of depression and anxiety by increasing self-awareness and improving stress management skills. Tertiary prevention is concerned with the rehabilitation and recovery process of those individuals who have suffered or are suffering from serious ill health as a result of stress.

To develop an effective and comprehensive organizational policy on stress, employers need to integrate these three approaches (Cooper, Liukonen and Cartwright 1996). (Stellman, 1998: p. 34.65)

Heinrich states that the occurrence of an injury accident invariably results from completed sequence of factors culminating in the accident itself. He postulates five factors or stages in the accident sequence, with the injury invariably caused by the accident and the accident in turn the result of the factor that immediately precedes it. The five factors or stages in the sequence of events are: (a) ancestry and social environment, leading to (b) fault of person, constituting the proximate reason for (c) an unsafe act and/or mechanical hazard, which results in (d) The accident, which leads to (e) the injury.

Heinrich links these five stages to five dominoes standing on edge in a line next to each other, so that when the first domino falls it automatically knocks down its neighbour which in turn knocks down its next neighbour and so on. Removal of any one of the first four will break the sequence and so prevent the injury. He suggested that accident prevention should aim to remove or eliminate the meddle or third domino, representing the unsafe act, mechanical or physical hazard, thus preventing the accident. (Ridley, 1994, L. Banlor: p. 168)

Rasmussen (1982) reflect attempts to achieve a dasher integration of human error theories and accident and safety theories. In a recent review of the concept of 'deviation' in accident control Kjellen (1984) has outlined some preliminary considerations for the design of comprehensive information systems for accident prevention. (Sheey, 1987: pp. 210-18)

Psychological intervention can be associated with any of the three categories of prevention. Traditionally, training has been viewed as a primary preventive measure, although aspects of first aid training and crisis management constitute secondary preventions; rehabilitation programmes are an example of tertiary prevention. However, although psychological interventions can have a partial role to play in each of the three preventive categories, strategic countermeasures cannot materialise in any of the categories unless there is a co-ordinate, multidisciplinary effort. In order this to occur it will be necessary to specify how the three classes of prevention are related. These relationships are not likely to prove simple: for instance, Saari and Lahtela (1981) found that workers' job experience was an important predictor of accident occurrence, but experiential factors have been found to be unrelated to injury severity (Bennett and Passmore, 1985).

The idea that society tolerates certain 'acceptable' risks (see Sheehy and Chapman, 1984) has important implications for accident prevention. Only rarely have those implications been explicitly recognised in the theory of accident prevention. Cliff (1984) has proposed a tripartite classification of preventive measure - primary, secondary, and tertiary to acknowledge the significance of acceptable accident rates. Primary prevention involves human factors, including engineering and legal innovations, designed to avoid accidents. Secondary prevention presumes that the primary measures will often fail to eliminate accidents and so includes measures designed to pattern the kind and severity of injuries likely to be sustained in an accident: the provision of protective clothing and safety goggles and design and placement of bumpers on cars are examples of secondary prevention. Tertiary prevention presumes that both primary and secondary measures will often fail; it has been defined as the prevention of serious pathological consequences (Waters and Cliff, 1983), and it demands exceptionally sophisticated and expensive resources to ensure that victims recover and lead a normal life. At any one time, groups of accidents can be described in terms of the proportion of accidents prevented by primary, secondary, and tertiary measures, and this distribution is one measure of society's acceptance of the costs of accident prevention. Sheehy and Chapman (1985) have argued that some kinds of prevention are judged unacceptable because of the enormous social costs involved.

It seems that errors are a constant feature of all behaviour. Studies show also that they occur in the causes of approximately two-thirds of work-related fatal accidents.

Risk messages may include the notification that risk exists; information about the scope or nature of risk; information about the individuals or populations at risk; information about when, where, how the risk exists; and information about the factors that influence or contribute to risk and their relative importance. Risk information is a principal product of surveillance and analytical research.

Prevention massages include information on methods of reducing risk and may cover a broad range of strategies and interventions.

The most important audiences for risk and prevention information are the population at risk, and the various individuals and organizations that have the power to change or influence workplace risk through their decisions, programmes and policies. These audiences, which include the workers, employers, safety and health practitioners, regulators, insurers, legislators and policymakers, are targeted when researchers develop new information regarding the existence or scope of occupational injury problems, or recommendations aimed at reducing risk. (Stellman, 1998: pp. 60.2-3)

Ruch, K.E., (1994) says, results of statistical analysis showed a low to moderate but statistically significant relationship between organizational work place factors and proactive work behaviour. Situational work place factors being studied also had a low but statistically significant relationship to proactive work behaviour. (Involvement in situation activities provided the strongest relationship to proactive work behaviour. And equipment problems, as greatest reactive managerial work behaviour and has posed the greatest opportunity for intervention. Also managers work behaviours can be correctly classified as either reactive or proactive based upon organizational and situation factors.

Safety Norms

According to Saxena, (1978):

1. Safety Rules: in every industrial establishment, safety rules should be drawn up for each occupation represented in the establishment.
2. Discipline: In every industrial establishment, any person who renders distinguished service in promotion of industrial safety and hygiene should be suitably recognized, and any person who violates any safety rules should be reprimanded and, if defiance is serious or repeated, suitably punished.
3. Suggestions: In every industrial establishment, the management should encourage workers to give suggestions for the improvement of safety and hygiene.
4. Workers' Safety Delegates: In every industrial establishment, workers should be entitled to appoint their members to be a safety delegate.
5. Safety Committees: In every industrial establishment, there should be a safety committee.
6. Safety Officials: In every industrial establishment, where a sizeable number of employees work or where the accident hazard is high,

a safety officer should be appointed.

7. Accident Records: Every industrial establishment should keep records of all lost time accidents, minor accidents and dangerous occurrences.
8. Industrial Establishment Medical Service.
9. Personnel Services in industry.

The root of the term "ergonomics" stems from the Greek "nomos" meaning rule, and "ergo" meaning work. One could propose that ergonomics should develop "rules" for a more forward-looking, prospective concept of design. In contrast to "corrective ergonomics", the idea of Prospective Ergonomics is based on applying ergonomic recommendations which simultaneously take into consideration profitability margins (Laurig 1992).

The basic rules for the development of this approach can be deduced from practical experience and reinforced by the results of occupational hygiene and ergonomics research. In other words, Prospective Ergonomics means searching for alternatives in work design which prevent fatigue and exhaustion on the part of the working subject in order to promote human productivity (" ...for the benefit of ourselves and others"). This comprehensive approach of Prospective Ergonomics includes workplace and equipment design as well as the design of working conditions determined by an increasing amount of information processing and a changing work organization. Prospective Ergonomics is, therefore, an interdisciplinary approach of researches and practitioners from a wide range of field united by the same goal, and one part of a general basis for a modern understanding of occupational safety and health (UNESCO 1992).

"Designing for everyone" puts special emphasis on an ergonomic approach that is based on the characteristics and capabilities of the worker, a concept often overlooked in practice. The ILO Encyclopedia are directly related to ergonomics, such as Heat and Cold, Noise, Vibration, Visual Display Units, and virtually all chapters in the sections, Accidents and Safety Management and Management and Policy.

Ergonomics is the systematic study of people at work with the objective of improving the work situation, the working conditions and the tasks performed. The emphasis is on acquiring relevant and reliable evidence on which to base recommendation for changes in specific situations and on developing more general theories, concepts, guidelines and procedures which will contribute to the continuously developing expertise available from ergonomics. (Stellman, 1998: pp. 29.2-5)

According to Gordon Atherley and Dilys Robertson, training can and will produce positive results if it is based on clearly defined needs specific to the workplace and if it is delivered with a view to those needs and the ways in which adults learn. This is, of course, true for safety and health training as well. The principles of safety and health training are no different from those which apply to any form of industrial training. Indeed, a good case can be made for the integration of skill training along with safety training wherever possible. Safety and health training which fails to produce positive results because it is not based on sound analysis is, at best, a waste of time and money. At worst, such training may result in false confidence, thus increasing the risk of accidents.

The sorts of problems that lend themselves to solution by means of training include the following:

1. Those that are identified after accidents have already happened. In this case, problems may be identified through review of accident statistics, accident investigation reports or, more broadly, through the failure to meet organizational goals for safety and health.
2. Problems that can be anticipated. Dangers can be identified before actual harm is done, for example, hazards can be foreseen when new machinery, substances or processes are introduced into the workplace, where there exist processes that have never been thoroughly analyzed or where existing practice conflicts with known safe procedures.
3. The existence of external requirements. New legal requirements which either impose specific safety and health training duties or other requirements suggesting the need for training are examples of external requirements. The development of new industry code of practice or national or international standards affecting safety and health are other examples. (Stellman, 1998: p.18.5)

Labour education has proceeded according to well-recognized principles of adult learning theory. Adult learn best when they are actively engaged, when they "learn by doing". They are more responsive to active, participatory methods than to passive measures. Lectures and written materials have placed in full repertoires of methods. But case studies, role plays, hands-on simulations and other small group activities that allow each individual to be involved are more likely to result in the retention and application of new learning. Ideally, each session involves interaction between participants and includes occasions for learning new information, for applying new skills and for discussing causes of problems and barriers to solving them. Participatory method requires more time, smaller groups and perhaps different instructional skills than those that many trainers currently posses. But to increase the impact of education, active participation is essential. (Stellman, 1998: p.18.8)

There are basically two approaches to deal with human errors that will inevitably occur in the work place. The first is the personnel approach, which involves selecting only those workers whose skills and abilities are suited to the operation of machines and equipment needed to perform the job, or developing training programmes to teach workers to perform the job safety with a minimum number of errors. The second strategy, which is more likely to be used by human factor psychologists, is the design approach. This involves designing equipment, procedures, and environments that reduce the likelihood of errors or the consequences of errors that do occur. This approach should help develop safe and efficient operator-machine systems. (Brown, 1948: p. 478)

Klancko, Robert John, (1977), Discusses the profession of safety, as practiced today, which evolves from two schools - both very old, and both important - but requiring totally different levels of skill. The subject encompasses the effect of the work environment upon the work-heat stress, cold stress, toxicity, air contaminant radiation, noise, etc. Safety of the past - classical safety - although a necessity is becoming less emphasized; environmental health safety is maturing. As a result, the prerequisites for a safety professional are changing. Another field previously given little attention, but gaining increasing importance, is financial planning and forecasting.

In collective agreements, increasing emphasis is put on the improvements of the occupational environment, reduction of psychological tension and removal of accidents possibility by reduction of working hours (International Labour Conference, 1980, p. 4).

Although it does not have any foundation is psychobiology, biorhythm theory has attracted the interest of some safety practitioners (Pittner and Owens, 1975; Schwarz, 1976). The theory suggests that the percentage of accidents occurring on 'critical days' (days on which 'cycles' of intellectual, emotional, and physical capacity change) will be much higher than the percentage occurring on other days. A large number of non-significant findings has been reported (e.g., Carvey and Nibler, 1977; Khalil and Kurucz, 1977; Persinger, Cooke, and Jones, 1978; Soutar and Weaver, 1983), and critics have suggested that positive findings may be due to unreliable coding methods (Chaffin and Skadburg, 1979).

Educational counter-measures may be needed to counter that attitude and to promote a balanced picture of the effects of environmental factors; a positive attitude towards accident avoidance should be encouraged. For example, biorhythm can easily be confused with circadian rhythm.

Disturbances to circadian rhythm associated with shift work have been linked to increased accident rates but even these effects may be eliminated by well-established safety programmes (Levin, Oler, and Whiteside, 1985). (Sheehy and Chapman,1987: p. 209)

Syroit (1985) has shown that, although the effectiveness of an educational intervention (viz. video safety programme) can produce observable changes in attitudes to safety at the shop floor, serious accident rates tend to remain unaltered until senior management is positive in its responsibility for managing safety. For example, amongst naval personnel increased levels of responsibility are associated with lower accident rates (Hoiberg, 1980).

Beaumont (1983) has suggested that, compared with management, unions tend to have a more viable approach to safety because they tend to see problem-solving and negotiation strategies as complementary activities, whereas management tended to see them as substitutes. Thus, a managerial approach to safety is usually a problem-solving one and this usually leads to a top-down imposition of a safety solution.

A frequently used safety device is the safety sign. John G. Casual, in1994, in his thesis, said, "Danger signals for work places - auditory danger signals, requires that any auditory alarm or warning be audible to all individuals in the workplace, including those suffering from a hearing loss and/or wearing hearing protection devices (HPDs). (Riggio, 1990: p. 372)

Gianota, C., (1988) discusses a method for improving safety, that is, a hazard and operability (HAZOP) study. This helps to identify potential hazards in the plans, which the design team may have missed. He looks at the use of an expert system to carry out the mundane tasks of hazard analysis.

Rajaram, N.S.; Tsehaie, H., (1985), discusses, Industrial equipment-machinery and vessels as well as controls - is configured as series of man-machine systems. Given sufficient time, access to information- and a relined atmosphere, most humans are capable of making sound decisions.

However, none of these prerequisites is likely to be present during the emergency situations in which they are most needed. Expert systems, a technology derived from applied artificial intelligence, may provide a means of minimizing human error and mitigating its possible consequences.

Their problems were discussed with them in a sympathetic manner which enabled them to understand them better, these problems were discussed, created a new attitude of mind on the part of the workers to the problem of accidents, and encouraged them to think of safety in new terms, and to regard their work habits in a new light. (Arbous, 1951: p. 390)

In accounting for the effectiveness of a number of safety innovations in the industrial gases industry, Griffiths (1985) has summarised the significance of the management contribution as follows: 'safety in industry is above all a responsibility of management, and understood other measures will not be successful in abolishing accidents and injuries' (p.61). In a detailed study, of safety management, Stevenson (1980) suggested that one of the strongest barriers to effective managerial involvement in safety is a reluctance to accept safety as an important performance criterion.

Fire extinction and suppression can be examined in terms of the theory of fire. The gas phase combustion processes (i.e., the flame reactions) are very sensitive to chemical inhibitors. However, if a flame-retarded material becomes involved in an existing fire, it will burn as the high heat fluxes overwhelm the effect of the retardant. Extinction of a fire may be achieved in a number of ways: (a) stopping the supply of fuel vaporous, (b) quenching the flame by chemical extinguishers (inhibiting), (c) removing the supply of air (oxygen) to the fire (smothering), (d) "blow-out". (Stellman, 1998: p.41.5)

The enforcement activity has been hindered by two factors. First, even the best safety programme will be ineffective if workers are not motivated to accept it, and there are many reasons that workers might find it easier to behave unsafe other than safety. The second factor hindering enforcement is that OSHA's budget has never allowed it to have a truly adequate inspection and enforcement staff.

Sanders and McCarmick (1993) argue that it is often easier to design a safe workplace than it is to make workers behave safety, but workers must learn to use their work equipment, and in so, doing are likely to make errors and have accidents.

Greenlund, K.J., (1993), in his research mentioned that how WHS issues are tied to control and power in the work place. Management initiated WHS programmes also helped employers maintain control and power even where workers were involved in such programmes.

He suggested the need for improving intervention into WHS problems through greater worker power within and between nations and greater planning of economic activity, which takes health and safety into account. These can be accomplished by establishing true participatory democracy in the work place.

Cohen (1977) suggested that successful safety programmes be not just characterized by their high internal validity and external face validity but by their integration into other work programmes and practices.

McKemma (1978), McKenna and Hale (1982) and Perusse (1980) have all reported that the main effect of first aid training is to facilitate a more rational attitude towards responsibility allocation. In turn this probably affects individuals' motivations to eliminate perceived hazard. Kjellen and Baneryd (1983) reported that worker discussion groups also facilitated greater individual acceptance of responsibility for safety, and this suggests that safety programmes might be directed more towards encouraging individuals to see safety as a matter of personal responsibility. What is implied here is more than simply changing people's attitudes towards safety.

Ananyev, N.I.; Sergeev, V.N.; Navrotskoya, N.I., (1989), the authors demonstrate the efficacy of physical exercise during the workday in restoring work capacity. It was found that the application of specially developed physical exercises during breaks in the work day resulted in a more rapid restoration of work capacity and a decreasing fatigue in workers participating in the exercise programme as compared with the control group.

Sunstrom (1986) says, unfortunately, poor design in an operator-machine system is often not discovered until there is a serious accident or breakdown in the system.

Sutton and Rafaeli (1987), says in open office designs, the evidence indicates that workers may sense a lack of privacy and control over their space in such settings. This may lead to dissatisfaction with the work environment and may negatively affect work behaviour.

Sanders and McCormick (1993), says, human factor researchers have, therefore, studied such variables as workers energy expenditure, strength, endurance, speed, accuracy of movements, and workload. Knowledge gained through this research has promoted the design of work places that maximize human performance, and minimize such outcomes as fatigue, and stress, and the errors to which they contribute. (Mackeven,1995, pp. 458-64)

Approximately half of electrical accidents are occupational in region, with the other half occurring at home and during leisure activities.

Electrical accidents may be caused by the entire range of voltages present in workplaces. Every industrial sector has its own set of conditions capable of causing direct, indirect, unipolar, bipolar, arcing, or induced contact, and ultimately, accidents. In rare cases, asphyxia may be the cause of death. This may result from prolonged tetanus of the diaphragm, inhibition of the respiratory centres in cases of contact with the head, or very high current densities, for example, as a result of lightning strikes (Gourbiere et al. 1994). If care can be provided within three minutes, the victim may be received with a few puffs of mouth-to-mouth resuscitation.

According to Renzo Comini, (Prevention and Standards): The many components making up electrical installations exhibit varying degrees of robustness. Regardless of their inherent fragility, however, they must all operate reliably under rigorous conditions. Unfortunately, even under the best circumstances, electrical equipment is subject to failures that may result in human injury or material damage.

Safe operation of electrical installations is the result of good initial design, not the mere retrofitting of safety systems. This is a corollary of the fact that while current flows at the speed of light, all electromechanical and electronic systems exhibit reaction latencies, caused primarily by thermal inertia, mechanical inertia and maintenance conditions. These latencies, whatever their origins, are sufficiently lengthy to allow humans to be injured and equipment damaged (Lee, Capelli-Schellpfeffer and Kelly 1994; Lee, Cravalho and Burke 1992; Kane and Sternheim 1978).

It is essential that equipment be installed and maintained by qualified personnel. Technical measures, it should be emphasized, are necessary both to ensure the safe operation of installations and to protect humans and equipment.

Proper operation of electrical installations requires that machinery, equipment, and electrical circuits and lines be protected from hazards caused by both internal (i.e., arising within the installation) and external factors (Andreoni and Castagna 1983). Internal causes include: (1) over voltages, (2) short circuits, (3) modification of the current's wave-form, (4) induction, (5) interference, (6) over currents, (7) corrosion, leading to electrical current leakage's to ground, (8) heating of conducting and insulating materials, which may result in operator burns, emissions of toxic gases, component fires and, inflammable atmospheres, explosions, (9) leaks of insulating fluids, such as oil, (10) generation of hydrogen or other gases which may lead to the formation of explosive mixtures. (Stellman, 1998: pp. 40.10-11)

According to Leon J. Warshaw and Jacqueline Messite, (Health Protection and Promotion in the Workplace: An Overview); it has often been said that the workforce is the most critical element in the productive apparatus of the organisation. Even in highly automated plants with their smaller number of workers decrements in their health and well-being will sooner or later be reflected in impaired productivity or, sometimes, even in disasters.

According to Sarah A. Nurneley, Although human being possess considerable ability to compensate for naturally occurring heat stress, many occupational environments and/or physical activities expose workers to heat loads which are so excessive as to threaten their health and productivity.

A variety of techniques are available which can be used to minimize the incidence of heat disorders and reduce the severity of case when they do occur. Interventions fall into five categories: maximizing heat tolerance among exposed individuals, assuring timely replacement of lost fluid and electrolytes, altering work practices to reduce exertional heat load, engineering control of climatic conditions, and use of protective clothing.

Factors outside the worksite which may affect thermal tolerance should not be ignored in the evaluation of the extent of exposure and consequently in elaborating preventive strategies. For example, total physiological burden and the potential susceptibility to heat disorders will be much higher if heat stress continues during off-hours through work at second jobs, strenuous leisure activities, or living in unremittingly hot quarters. In addition, nutritional status and hydration may reflect patterns of eating and drinking, which may also change with season or religious observances. (Stellman, 1998: p. 42.10)

According to Inguar Holmer, Pre-Ola Granberg and Goran Dahlstram, a cold environment is defined by conditions that cause greater than normal body heat losses. In this context "normal" refers to what people experience in everyday life under comfortable, often indoor conditions, but this may vary due to social, economic or natural climatic conditions. For the purpose of this, environments with an air temperature below 18 to 20°C would be considered cold.

Cooling of the whole body or parts of the body results in discomfort, impaired sensory and neuro-muscular function and, ultimately, cold injury. Cold discomfort tends to be a strong stimulus to behavioural action, reducing or eliminating the effect.

On exposure to cold, behavioural measures reduce the cooling effect and, eventually, allow the maintenance of normal thermal balance and comfort. Insufficient measures evoke thermoregulatory, physiologically compensatory reactions (vasoconstriction and shivering). The combined action of behavioural and physiological adjustments determines the resulting effect of a given cold stress. (Stellman, 1998: p. 42.29)

According to Peter Knauth, Shiftwork is work scheduled, either permanently or frequently, outside normal daytime working hours. Shiftwork can be e.g., permanent work at night, permanent work during the evening, or work hours can have changing assignment patterns. Each type of shift system has its advantages and disadvantages, and each is associated with differing effects on well-being, health, social life and work performance.

Human beings have evolved as essentially diurnal; that is, the body is mainly "programmed" towards daytime work performance and for night-time recreation and rest. Internal mechanisms (sometimes called the body or biological clock) control the physiology and biochemistry of the body to fit in with a 24-hour environment. These cycles are called circadian rhythms. The disruption of circadian variations in physiological function caused by having to be awake and at work at biologically unusual hours, as well as to sleep during the daytime, is one of the major stresses associated with shiftwork.

Some shiftwork are also exposed to other workplace hazards, such as toxic agents, or to jobs with high mental loads or physical demands. Only a few studies, however, have addressed the problems caused by the combination of shiftwork and unfavourable working, organizational and environmental conditions where the negative effects of shiftwork could be caused not by the phase difference between circadian rhythms and living conditions, but also the adverse negative conditions that may be combined with shiftwork.

A variety of workplace hazards, such as noise, unfavourable climatic conditions, unfavourable lighting conditions, vibration and combinations of these, can sometimes occur more of three-shift systems, irregular systems and night-shift systems in two-shift systems or daywork. (Stellman, 1998: p. 43.2)

According to Alice H. Suter, Noise is one of the most common of all the occupational hazards. In the United States, for example, more than 9 million workers are exposed to daily average A-weighted noise levels of 85 decibels (abbreviated here as 85 dBA). These noise levels are potentially hazardous to their hearing and can produce other adverse effects as well. There are approximately 5-2 million workers exposed to noise above these levels in manufacturing and utilities, which represents about 35 per cent of the total number of workers in US manufacturing industries.

Hazardous noise levels are easily identified and it is technologically feasible to control excessive noise in the vast majority of cases by applying off-the-shelf technology, by redesigning the equipment or process or by retrofitting noisy machines. But all too often, nothing is done. There are several reasons for this. First, although many noise control solutions are remarkably inexpensive, others can be costly, especially when the aim is to reduce the noise hazard to levels of 85 or 80 dBA.

Loss of hearing is certainly the most well-known adverse effect of noise, and probably the most serious, but it is not the only one. Other detrimental effects include trinities (ringing in the ears), interference with speech communication and with the perception of warning signals, disruption of job performance, annoyance and extra-auditory effects. Under most circumstances, protecting workers' hearing should protect against most other effects. This consideration provides additional support for companies to implement good noise control and hearing conservation programmes.

Noise-induced hearing impairment is usually considered an occupational disease or illness, rather than an injury, because its progression is gradual. On rare occasions, an employee may sustain immediate, permanent hearing loss from a very loud event such as an explosion or a very noisy process, such as riveting. (Stellman, 1998: pp. 47.2-4.2)

According to Michael Griffin, vibration is oscillatory motion. Human responses to whole-body vibration, hand-transmitted vibration and the causes of motion sickness.

While-body vibration occurs when the body is supported on a surface which is vibrating (e.g., when sitting on a seat which vibrates, standing on a vibrating floor or recumbent on a vibrating surface). Whole-body vibration occurs in all forms of transport and when working near some industrial machinery.

Hand-transmitted vibration is the vibration that enters the body through the hands. It is caused by various processes in industry, agriculture, mining and construction where vibrating tools or work pieces are grasped or pushed by the hands or fingers. Exposure to hand-transmitted vibration can lead to the development of several disorders.

Many occupational exposures are intermittent, vary in magnitude from moment to moment or contain occasional shocks. The severity of such complex motions can be accumulated in a manner which gives appropriate weight to, for example, short periods of high magnitude vibration and long periods of low magnitude vibration. Different methods of calculating doses are used.

Occupational exposures to whole-body vibration mainly occur in transport but also in association with some industrial processes. (Stellman, 1998: p. 50.2)

Thim, J; Menges, G., (1983) discusses that the effective accident prevention is only possible through a systematic and specific research of accidents, details are presented on a research project on the above. The first section described the injection molding working system from technical, organizational and psychological aspects. The next section is divided into an accident dependent and accident independent hazard analysis and ergonomic stress analysis. From these three analysis groups, key accident areas were located, which led to the formulation of safety and protection requirements for avoiding industrial accidents.

According to Kikuzi Kimuro, eye and face protection includes safety spectacles, goggles, face shields and similar items used to protect against flying particles and foreign bodies, corrosive chemicals, fumes, lasers and radiation. Often, the whole face may need protection against radiation or mechanical, thermal or chemical hazards. Sometimes a specific eye protection is necessary, either separately or as a complement to the face protection. There are six types of eye and face protection: (1) spectacle type, either with or without side shield, (2) eye cup (goggle) type, (3) face shield type, covering eye sockets and the central portion of the face, (4) helmet type with shielding of the whole front of the face, (5) hand-held shield type, (6) hood type including the diver's helmet type covering the head completely. (Stellman, 1998: p. 31.2)

According to Toyahiko Miura, (Foot and Leg Protection), injuries to foot and leg are common to many industries. The dropping of a heavy object may injure the foot, particularly the toes, in any workplace, especially among workers in the heavier industries such as mining, metal manufacture, engineering and building and construction work. Burns of the lower limbs from the molten metals, sparks or concessive chemicals occur frequently in foundries, iron - and steelworks, chemical plants and so on. Dermatitis or eczema may be caused by a variety of acidic, alkaline and many other agents.

Improvements in the work environment have made the simple puncturing and laceration of the worker's foot by protruding floor nails and other less common sharp hazards, but accidents from working on damp or wet floors still occurs particularly when wearing unsuitable foot wear. (Stellman, 1998: pp. 31.6-7)

According to Isabell Balty and Alain Mayer, Head injuries are fairly common in industry and account for 3 to 6 per cent of all industrial injuries in industrialized countries. They are often severe and result in an average lost time of about three weeks. The injuries sustained are generally the result of blows caused by the impact of angular objects such as tools or bolts falling from a height of several metres; in other cases, workers may strike their heads in a fall to a floor or suffer a collision between some fixed object and their heads.

The chief purpose of a safety helmet is to protect the head of the wearer against hazards, mechanical shocks. It may in addition provide protection against other, for example, mechanical, thermal and electrical. (Stellman, 1998: pp. 31.8-9)

According to John R. Franks and Elliott H. Berger, An earplug is a device worn in the external ear canal. Premolded earplugs are available in one or more standard sizes intended to fit into the ear canals of most people. A formable, user-molded earplug is made of a pliable material that is shaped by the wear to fit into the ear canal to form an acoustic seal. A custom-molded earplug is individually made to fit the particular ear of the wearer. Earplugs can be made from vinyl, silicone, elastomer formulations, cotton and wax, spun glass wool, and slow-recovery closed-cell foam. (Stellman, 1998: p. 31.11)

According to S. Zack Manasdorf, there are general categories of bodily hazards for which specialized clothing can provide protection. These general categories include chemical, physical and biological hazards.

Protective clothing is a commonly used control to reduce worker exposures to potentially toxic or hazardous chemicals when other controls are not feasible. Many chemicals pose more than one hazard (for example, a substance such as benzene is both toxic and flammable). For chemical hazards, there are at least three key considerations, that need attention. These are (1) the potential toxic effects of exposure, (2) likely routes of entry, and (3) the exposure potentials associated with the work assignment.

Use First foremost, the selection and proper use of protective clothing should be based on an assessment of the hazards involved in the task for which the protection is required. In the light of assessment, an accurate definition of the performance requirements and the ergonomic constraints of the job can be determined. Finally, a selection that balances worker protection, ease of use and cost can be made. (Stellman, 1998: p. 31.16)

According to Thomas J. Nelson, in some industries, air contaminated with potentially harmful dusts, fumes, mists, vapours or gases may cause harm to the workers. The control of exposure to these materials is important to decrease the risk of occupational diseases caused by breathing the contaminated air. The best method to control exposure is to minimize workplace contamination. (Stellman, 1998: p. 31.21)

Griffiths (1985) said, safety in industry is above all a responsibility of management, and unless this is understood other measures will not be successful in abolishing accidents and injuries.

According to Herbert I. Linn and Alfred A. Amendola, Researchers and practitioners from multiple disciplines - primarily epidemiology, engineering, ergonomics, biomechanics, behavioural psychology, safety management and industrial hygiene - are engaged in the study of the factors associated with the worker (the host); the environment; the type and source of energy involved (the agent); and the tools, machines and tasks (the vehicles) that combine to cause or contribute to work place injury.

Human Factors

According to Ane-Marie Feyer and Ann M. Williamson, human factors are the major components of the causes of accidents in the workplace. Estimates of the actual extent of the involvement vary markedly, but a study in the early 1980s of the causes of all work-related fatalities occurring in Australia over three years revealed that behavioural factors were involved in more than 90 per cent of fatal accidents. In view of data like these, it is important to have an understanding of the role of human factors in accidents. Traditional models of accident causation placed superficial emphasis on human factors. Where human factors were included, they were depicted as linked to error occurring in the immediate sequence of events leading to the accident. A better understanding of how, why and when human factors become involved in accidents enhances our ability to make predictions about the role of human factors and helps to prevent accidents.

A number of models have been put forward that attempt to describe the part that human factors play in accidents.

The two main components (contributing factors and event sequences) of this human factors model should be envisaged as occurring on a notional time line on which the order- contributing factors followed by a sequence of errors - is fixed, but the time base on which they occur is not. Both of these components are essential parts of accident causation.

In this context, the term Human Factors covers a wide range of elements involved in the interaction between individuals and their working environment. Some of these are direct and observable aspects of the ways in which work systems function that do not have immediate adverse consequences. Design, use and maintenance of equipment, the provision, use and maintenance of personal protective and other safety equipment and standard operating procedures originating from management or workers, or both, are all examples of such ongoing practices. (Stellman, 1998: pp. 56.8-9)

Allport, (1937), Realizing that every individual is different and that human behaviour is very complex. Certain psychologists, impressed by the individuality and complexity of personality, have despaired of finding general principles or laws to explain personality. They dismiss the homothetic approach - the search for general laws of behaviour and personality - as unrealistic and inadequate to the task of understanding the individual. Instead they have advocated the ideographs approach, by which every person is considered to be a lawful, integrated system to be studied in its right. Individual patterns of likes and dislikes usually begin to develop long before adult experiences with particular occupations..

Sigmund Freud and other psychoanalysts have viewed human personality as a kind of battleground where there combatants- the id, ego, and superego vie for supremacy. In comparison to Freud, modern psychoanalysts place more emphasis on social learning and culture than biological instincts as determinants of personality. Individual patterns of likes and dislikes usually begin to develop long before adult experiences with particular occupations.

Zimring (1981), says, Poor human factors design has been responsible for many industrial accidents and injuries.

Spettell and Liebert (1986), stress approaches to achieving a better adjustment between the worker and the workplace. The first is based on individual differences and involves selecting people who have the characteristics thought necessary or desirable for specified work demands (this is the personnel-selection approach). The second approach is that of training people in the necessary skill, knowledge, or attitudes. This is the personnel training approach. The third approach is modifying the workplace to provide a better match with abilities and characteristics. This is the engineering psychology or work-design approach. These criteria of interest are that of creating a safe work environment. Given that, 50 per cent to 80 per cent of all attributable to human error, an examination of accidents from a human perspective is most reasonable.

Peay James M., (1981), discusses, the role of human factors in reducing human error injuries and implicit assumptions about human behaviour impacting upon workplace design. A brief overview of current human factors (ergonomics) research demonstrates that ergonomics and training enhance safety.

Asange, P.M. (1988), in his research, says, Human reliability parameters are most varied, unpredictable and somewhat puzzling in nature, such that research in human behaviour under various stresses and environmental conditions presents a wide field of investigation and tend to involve the realms of human psychology and physiology.

The relationship between industrial accidents, personality traits and cognitive characteristics has been intensely studied since the early 1900s (Hansen, 1988, Shaw and Sichel, 1971). The research has mainly sought to identify the differences between the employees with and without accidents (Landy and Trumbo, 1980).

The results obtained by researches on accidents which involve personality and cognitive variables have often been controversial and inconclusive, especially when causal conclusions were made in advance (McKenna, 1983).

None of the personal or sociological data yielded significant differences between the two groups of patients. The only measure in any way predictive of accident behaviour involved patient's beliefs about locus of control. The most compelling explanation for this observation is that people who may be categorized as internalizes tend to give accounts of their accidents that themselves to be culpable, while externalizes produce stories that depict themselves as blameless victims of outside factors. Such attribution process may reflect stable personality characteristics (Brewin, 1982) and as such could introduce artifacts or errors to investigations of accident causation that rely on victims own statements of events.

It might seem obvious to say that industrial accidents are usually a consequence of human error, but the implications of such a statement need to be emphasised. Human behaviour is multicausal: there are many facts to it; and errors can be complex. Hence, any attempts to identify 'the' cause of an accident, or even to identify clusters of primary causes, are destined to fail. In accident investigations 'cause' is often a difficult notion.

Principles of human factors are based on a thorough understanding of human capabilities and limitations (such as perceptual processes and cognitive and physical abilities), the technical capabilities of machines, and the relationship between the two.

Edwards (1981), in examining the detailed structure of two accident surveillance systems, found that the model of accident causation implicit in each was one which emphasised victim culpability: however, that model was supported by the bias towards collecting information on victim characteristics in isolation from other pertinent features of accidents. With such incestuous derivations accident statistics are unlikely to provide appropriate tests of accident causation hypotheses. (Sheehy and Chapman,1987: pp. 201-2)

Brown (1948), stated, the range of individual differences in general intellectual ability and amount of education was nearly twice as great among war time applicants as among those seeking employment in the pre-war years. This increased range of individual differences permits an evaluation of selective devices under optimal conditions. Under these circumstances we propose here to evaluate four factors (intelligence test score, age, amount of education, and marital status.

A variety of test and non-test data on an individual's background, current situation and future prospects may be obtained in an effort to understand his or her capabilities and personality. Such information is useful in diagnosis, prediction, and in planning and evaluating the results of training, clinical treatment, and other intervention procedures.

Kohlberg (1969, 1974), argues that the development of individual morality follows a sequence of three levels, consisting of two stages each, similar to Piaget's levels or stages in cognitive development. In the first stage of the last level (morality of self-accepted moral principles), morality is viewed in terms of acceptance of a contract or democratically determined agreement. In the second stage of the last level, the individual has developed an internal set of principles and a conscience that directs judgment and behaviour.

Bennett himself preferred to emphasize judgment in his definition, whereas others have referred to intelligence as the ability to think abstractly, the ability to learn, or the ability to adapt to one's environment. Spearman (1927) formulated a two-factor theory of intelligence, which he felt could explain the pattern of correlation among the group of cognitive tests that he analyzed. In its simplest form, the theory states that performance on cognitive task depends on a general factor (g) plus one or more specific unique to the particular task.

As we have seen, there is considerable research support for a polygenic model of the inheritance of general mental ability. Most psychologists would probably accept the notion that heredity establishes a potential for mental development, but whether or not this potential is realized depends on motivation and experience. Ferguson's (1956), transfer hypothesis is an attempt to explain how general mental ability gradually differentiates into a number of specific factors. This hypothesis states that the different abilities isolated by factor analysis are the results of over learning and differential positive transfer in certain areas of experience.

Piaget holds that cognitive growth, which takes place by the actions of assimilation and accommodation on the external world, occurs in four periods composed of a series of stages. These four periods constitute a hierarchy of development in that successful equilibrations in proceeding periods are necessary in order for an individual to progress to succeeding ones. (Aiken,1979: pp. 156-8)

As indicated by Entin (1994), increased differentiation of self, whether in a family or corporation, has important ramifications in reducing stress, anxiety and burnout.

Individuals need to be more in control of their own lives and take responsibility for their actions; and both individuals and corporations need re-examine their value systems. Dramatic shifts need to take place. If we do not heed the statistics, then most assuredly burnout and stress will continue to remain the significant problem it has become for all society. (Stellman, 1998: pp. 5.15-16)

According to Catherine A. Heaney, A cognitive disorder is defined as a significant decline in one's ability to process and recall information. The DSM IV (American Psychiatric Association 1994) describes three major types of cognitive disorder: delirium, dementia and amnesic disorder. A delirium develops over a short period of time and is characterized by an impairment of short-term memory, disorientation and perceptual and language problems. Amnesic disorders are characterized by impairment of memory such that sufferers are unable to learn and recall new information. However, no other declines in cognitive functioning are associated with this type of disorder. Both delirium and amnesic disorders are usually due to the physiological effects of a general medical condition (e.g., head injuries, high fevers) or of substance use. There is little reason to suspect that occupational factors play a direct role in the development these disorders.

Cognitive Ability

Guiford (1967), proposed that performance on any cognitive task can best be understood by analyzing it into the kind of mental operation or process performed, the type of content or test material on which the mental operation is performed, and the resulting product of performing particular operation on a certain type of test content. Since in Guilford's model there are five possible kinds of operation (cognition, memory, divergent thinking, convergent thinking and evaluation), four types of content (figural, symbolic, semantic, and behavioural), and six products (units, classes, relations, systems, transformations, and implications), it implies the existence of 5*4*6=120 possible factors comprising the structure of intellect.

Vernon (1960), a general cognitive factor (G) is at the highest level, with two major group factors- verbal- educational (V:ED) and practical mechanical- spatial (K:M) - at the next level. The V:ED and K:M factors are further broken down into a number of minor group factors. For example, V:ED comprises ability such as verbal fluency, numerical ability, and perhaps creativity. Some of the minor group factors under K:M are mechanical knowledge, psychomotor ability, and spatial ability. Finally, at the lowest level of the hierarchy are specific factors peculiar to certain tests.

Noting the significant positive correlation's among measures of different special abilities, Vernon (1960) concluded that general intelligence is more important than special abilities in determining occupational success.

The fact remains that people often perform much well on certain kinds of tasks than on others. Whether they perform differently because of differences in motivation or differences in the special abilities required by certain occupations or both, is debatable.

Because there is so much confusion over the distinction between aptitude and achievement, the term ability may be preferable to either of the first two terms.

Individual differences in abilities are obviously not the only factors influencing performance. For example, the correlation between a mechanical ability test and a measure of job performance may be lower in a small plant than in a large one, or higher for men than for women. Other differences among groups of persons that affect the correlation between a test and a criterion are interests, emotional stability, level of achievement motivation, and values. Such situational and organizing variables, which are known as moderator variables, influence the magnitude of the correlation between test and criterion.

They have been more helpful in predicting performance on repetitive jobs such as routine assembly and machine operation than on complex jobs involving higher-order cognitive and perceptual abilities.

The Thurstone and Likert attitude-scaling procedures are popular methods; a third technique - Guttman's scalogram analysis - is that all the items comprising the scale are on a single dimension, so that the respondent who endorses one item will be met with cognitive test items than with attitude statements and other affective test items. Individual patterns of likes and dislikes usually begin to develop long before adult experiences with particular occupations. (Aiken, 1979: p. 214)

Most of the research has sought to identify worker characteristics that differentiated between the employees with and without accidents (Landy and Trumbo, 1980).

The results of accident research involving personality and cognitive variables have often been controversial and inconclusive, especially when causal conclusions were advanced (Mc-Kenna, 1983). Many personal characteristics have been associated with accidents.

Throndike (1975), formulated a theory and devised a test CAVD (the letters CAVD stand for completions, arithmetic, vocabulary, and understanding directions and discourse) as an expression of his viewpoint that intelligence is a composite of many different abilities interconnecting in the brain.

Thurstone, in his centered method of factoring and oblique rotation to the correlation's among many different cognitive measures, extracted seven important group factors. This primary mental ability, as he perhaps unfortunately labeled them, are V (verbal meaning), N (number facility), R (inductive reasoning), P(perceptual speed), S (spatial relations), M (memory), and W (verbal fluency). (Aiken, 1979, pp.153-4)

Bennett Mechanical Comprehension Test (by G.K. Bennett et al; The psychological corporation). A form of this well-contracted test, one of most popular measures of mechanical ability, also appears on the Differential Aptitude Tests battery. Bennett measures understanding of mechanical relationships and physical laws in practical situations. The problems consist of drawings and questions concerned with the operation of such relationships or laws. There are several forms of the test (AA, BB, CC, WI, S, and T). The usual time limit is 30 minutes, and the reliabilities are in the 80s. The manuals for the various forms of the test give perceptual norms for selected groups of industrial applicants, industrial employees, and students. Since the average score and reliability of the test are lower for females than for males, separate norms are given by sex. Evidence for the validity of the Bennett is found in its modest correlation's (.30-.60) with performance in a variety of occupations requiring mechanical ability. (Aiken,1979: pp. 172-3)

According to G.K. Bennett in The Manual of Forms S and T, of the Bennett Mechanical Comprehension Test (BMCT), like the earlier form of the test; measure the ability to perceive and understand the relationship of physical forces and mechanical eliminates in practical situations. This type of aptitude is important for a wide variety of jobs and for engineering training, as well as for many trade school courses.

The notion that a certain minimum level of ability is required for success in specific occupation is one that the designers of the General Aptitude Test Battery have stressed. Beyond such a minimum ability level-whatever it is-work habits, interests, and other variables become more important in determining competence.

Wesman (1968), maintained that all ability tests (tests of achievement, general intelligence, and special abilities) measure only what the examinee has learned. Second by, he proposed to define intelligence as an attribute that is the summation of learning experiences. Therefore, according to Wesman, intelligence can be fully measured only by sampling, has every domain of experience in which learning has occurred. (Aiken,1979: pp. 183-6)

The results of the Thorndike and Hagen investigation and similar follow up studies demonstrate that the pattern of scores on a multiple-aptitude test serves as a rough indicator of the examinee's suitability for a particular job. But occupational success cannot be accurately predicted from test scores alone. The range of tasks comprising most jobs is great enough so that people within a fairly wide span of abilities can adopt. Thus, scores on aptitude tests alone, without taking into account motivation, interests, personal history, or individual occurrences, are insufficient for vocational counselling.

Accident Behaviour and Experience

However, many studies involving personality and cognitive variables failed to control for the potentially confounding effects of age (Mc Kenna,1983).

Age should be causally related to involvement in counselled because younger people tend to have more emotional and maturity problems than older people (Wolman, 1976). Also, it was proposed that counselling status, above and beyond its association with, GSM and Distractibility, would be predictive of accident involvement. In other words, additional traits of the counselled employee would be linked to accidents (Manuso, 1983).

Age and Experience: The effects of these two factors on accident frequency have usually been studied together because it is difficult to disentangle their influences, except under experimentally controlled conditions, which cannot always be applied because of the constitution of groups in the real industrial situations.

As Vernon (1936) has pointed out, "the apparent lock of reduction with increasing experience may have been due to the groups of workers studies contained very few new workers' force have seen that it is they who are particularly responsible for high accident rates". It would appear from the above that experience (per se) is important particularly in the early initial stages of employment, but that after a given period its influence becomes negligible.

"The results were not screwy, but the experimenters-a" screwy "person being by definition one who is not acting in accordance with the customary human values of the situation in which he finds himself".

In most work-group studies a minority was responsible for the majority of accidents.

Bennett and Passmore, (1985), Saari and Lahtela (1981) found that workers' job experience was an important predictor of accident occurrence, but experiential factors have been found unrelated to injury severity. (Sheey,1987: p. 212)

The conclusion that youth is associated with greater accident potential can be questioned. Younger workers tend to have less job experience than older workers. Therefore, it becomes a question of whether their higher accident rate is caused by a characteristic of youth, whether it is simply the result of lack of experience and knowledge about the job (Power, Hale, Martin, and Simon, 1971), or whether it is caused by an interaction of the two factors, as suggested by Denning (1983). Brown and Ghiselli (1984) considered experience to be more important than age in accident.

For each operator accident rate was calculated as the number of accidents in which he was involved divided by the number of months he was employed and on duty. The relationship between this accident rate and months of experience on the job appeared to be linear. Although this relationship is low, the accident rate for each man was corrected by the experience factor. (Brown,1948: p. 478)

In recent years, instruments constructed exclusively for vocational counselling in the skilled, semiskilled, and unskilled occupations have become available, perhaps the simplest of these nonprofessional interest inventories is the Gordon Occupational Check List (by L.V. Gordon), a checklist of activities representing 240 jobs not requiring college training. Inventories such as the Gordon can be helpful in counselling. Individual patterns of likes and dislikes usually begin to develop long before adult experiences with particular occupations.

Aldrich, Donald C., (1990), stated that, experience gained from a long history of working safety in chemical appertains in being applied to manage safety, health and environmental hazards associated with advanced composites. Although composites bring new hazards, applying proven techniques, can reduce risks to acceptable levels. The policies and practices, which DuPont uses to protect its employees and the application of this expertise to assist subcontractors, customers, and others in the industry, will be discussed.

Accident Behaviour and Age

Accident analysis and investigation go to prove that at every kind of work and every place of employment, new men are injured. The new men are more likely get hurt than the trained ones. In addition, fatigue, and stress, as well as other personal variables are all related to the incidence of work accidents.

Almost all of the research on age and accidents agree that accident rates are highest for the youngest workers in an industry. Younger workers tend to have less job experience than older workers do. Therefore, it becomes a question weather higher accident rate is caused by a characteristic of youth, weather it is simply the result of a lack of experience and knowledge about the job (Pawell, Hale, Martin and Simon, 1971) or whether it is caused by an interaction of the two factors. So the younger worker will have higher accident rates than older. The current study predicted that younger workers would have the greatest accident liability. The current study tested the hypothesis that more experienced workers would have a lower accident rate than less experienced employees. Increasing experience causes workers to be placed in positions of greater accident potential, and that the greater experience of those in high-risk jobs gives the initial impression that more experience is associated with more accidents.

There is also a tendency for younger workers to have higher accident rates than older workers, due perhaps to lack of maturity and a more carefree or reckless attitude (Riggio, 1990: pp. 420-1).

Some surveys show that younger workers have greater number of accidents than older workers (Gorden, Akman, and Brooks, 1971). Others show that accident rates increase from middle age to old age (Cooke and Blumenstock, 1979). (Mackeven, 1995: p. 458)

In addition, age should be causally related to involvement in counselling because younger people tend to have more emotional and maturity problems than older people (Wolman, 1976).

The means and standard deviations for accidents, age and personality variables were also calculated for the male patients when separated into three occupational groups comparing the sedentary with the heavy manual workers, the latter group showed a significantly higher mean number of accidents. Although there was also a tendency, which did not reach significance, for the heavy manual workers to be more extraverted.

The accidents reported did not produce significant differences between the mean scores, for age and personality variables, of the men who reported one or more serious accidents and the men who reported only minor accidents.

The means and standard deviations for accident, age and personality variables for men and women were used. The mean Neuroticism and Extraversion scores obtained for the male group are similar to those previously reported as samples of normal population (Extraversion=12.1+−4.4; Neuroticism=9.1+−4.8; Eysenck and Eysenck, 1964).

The importance of motivational factors in particular was underscored in a recent study by Harbert Greenberg ("Job Study findings", 1976). It was concluded from the results of what makes a person suited or unsuited to a particular job is not primarily youth, education, previous experience, or ethnic-group membership, but rather the dynamics within the person. Thus, the findings indicate that if one has "right" the job training can make him or her as effective as someone who has more education and experience. (Aiken, 1979: p. 188)

For this purpose it becomes imperative to study the cases of accidents reports in oil industries, the nature of the organizational role and stress, the required safety rules and regulation of organizations jobs, besides how does it influence the satisfaction of person on his job to have peace of mind to do his work.

5
Research Methodology

The present chapter states precisely the main issue involved in the study of safety of values, sampling features, explanation of the means and methods used to test the hypotheses and relevance of a sort methodology. This chapter also deals with the methodology selected for the present investigation. An attempt has been made to present a summary review of the statement of problem, its rationale and objectives, the samples, tools and the techniques used, data collection, sample testing and statistical treatment of data.

Empirical studies demand the use of some statistical tools and techniques depending upon the objectives set forth for the study. Here we have developed hypotheses for the study which primarily attempts at ascertaining the relationship between value congruency, bio-data variables and employee commitment. This relationship is ascertained by resorting to the bivariate analysis of the data collected from the sample respondents. Besides the study also focused on the lack of humanitarian aspects of organisational and managerial set up in the companies as well as the differences in using the factor analysis, stepwise regression, and other statistical techniques.

This proposes to examine broadly the factors, which are responsible for accident involvement in NISOC. The primary data for analysis was generated through structured questionnaires' from different levels of workers and managements. It was further substantiated by personal interviews of selected organisations in Iran. Secondary data (case studies, research and books studies, articles, reports etc.) was used to reinforce the analysis.

Suitable statistical techniques such as frequency distribution (Mean, standard deviation, etc,) and stepwise, inferential statistics (Factor analysis, reliability, correlation, stepwise regression) and statistical influences have been used to analyze the primary data and to test the hypotheses and make generalized inferences. The study concludes with a package of recommendations for organizations to prevent accidents and improve the safety programme in future.

The present study is done in two successive stages. First stage was to standardize the questionnaire and make it comprehensible. Sample size is 60 and 120 and the random sampling procedure is applied. The second stage was to execute the questionnaire along with three standard test of BMCT and FIT, as empirical work based on 600 employees as a selected stratified random sample. The samples of organization has been chosen as random from NISOC's employees.

In this research, factors responsible for the occurrence of accidents have been divided into two categories:

1. *Technological Factors (Direct Factors)* such as safety norms,
2. *Human Factors (Indirect Factors)* such as Employee Age, Job Experience and Understanding of Mechanical Dynamics, (UMD).

The researcher's aim was to study some of the related compilations of these characteristics including (Safety Norms, Employee Age, Job Experience and Understanding of Mechanical Dynamics), with accident involvement on NIOC's employees. Because it is believed that these factors have relationship with accident involvement in NIOC's employees.

5.1. Organizational Site

Since the present study reviews the study of "**The Realtionship of Human Factors and Safety Norms with Involvment in Industrial Accidets**" therefore, it is always thought appropriate to conduct the study in an organization in which safety played crucial role in determining efficiency and effectiveness. For this purpose National Iranian South Oil Company (NISOC) of Iran was selected. The NISOC is the largest company of NIOC (The NISOC, which was the biggest Oil Industry of Iran, with several Oil Refinery companies, Petrochemical companies, Drilling companies, Pipe Mill companies, Gas companies, Crude Oil companies, etc.) after 1999 was divided into a central Headquarter and five other subsidiary Oil companies AMA-KOGC- MOGC- AOGC- GOGC and Mis.OGC (for details, see page 4-5). These sub-companies are responsible for about 57 per cent of the total output of the NISOC industry and, for our concern, carry a long history of various kinds of major and minor accidents. Out of NISOC oil industry of Iran, which has the total six independent sub-companies, three Adreh Marhazi Ahawaz (AMA), Karoon Oil and Gas Company (KOGC) and Murun Oil and Gas Company (MOGC), have been chosen for the present study. It is assured that the conclusion was good for the NISOC industry as field of study.

NISOC is one of the leading industrial concerns in the government sector which is engaged in oil production and oil storage strategically to cater the demands of other countries, besides fulfilling Iran's domestic requirements. It also manufactures varied kinds of oil and gas and derivatives related to oil and gas. It is one of the biggest pioneer organizations in Iran. The main factories of NISOC's company are situated at Khzastan in south-west of Iran 900 km from Tehran. Considering the objective, data were collected from NISOC. After systematically going through fifteen years' accident reports of NISOC, I have selected five years reports, (i.e., from 1996 to 2000) for a detailed analysis.

5.2. Statement of the Problem

There are many reasons which are more fundamental when an individual joins the organization and becomes involved in its functioning. There are certain aspects of many personal and organizational factors due to his own self or which he might either feel satisfied or dissatisfied. The dissatisfaction and related lack of concentration can cause workers or professionals to meet accidents.

The study here is proposed to understand the nature of the accidents and the relation of accidents' factors due to which accident occurs in Oil Industries. The study can work as sample for other industries. Here the relationship of industrial accidents with demographic technological variables (in general Safety Norms), Human variables such as Cognitive Ability (UMD), and, Individual Characteristics (Employee Age and Job Experience) has been studies.

A. *Cognitive Ability;* including "UMD", has relationship with Accident Involvement on NISOC's employees. The "UMD", has been chosen under cognitive abilities factors. This characteristic is the ability of understanding the relation between physical force and mechanical factors in practical situation, in NISOCs' employees.

The FIT (Mechanics) and BMCT (S and T) are tests that measure understanding of UMD. Higher FIT and BMCT's scores are associated with better accident records. This situation is reasonable in that the BMCT assesses UMD, which are of obvious applicability in production and maintenance work. In addition to this, it is reasonable to assume that those with the best mechanical reasoning skills would be placed in jobs with high accident potential. If the proposed relationship between cognitive ability and accident were true, these employees would be unlikely to incur accident.

B. *Individual Characteristics;* including Employee Age and Job Experience, have relationship with Accident Involvement in NIOC's employees. Almost all of the research on age and accidents agree that accident rates are highest for the youngest workers in an industry. Younger workers tend to have less job experience than older workers have. Therefore, it becomes a question of weather higher accident rate is caused by a characteristic of being youth, whether it is simply the result of a lack of experience and knowledge about the job (Pawell, Hale, Martin and Simon, 1971) or whether it is caused by an interaction of the two factors. So the younger worker will have higher accident rates than older. The current study predicted that in NISOC the younger workers will have the grėatest accident liability. The current study tested the hypothesis that more experienced employees would have a lower accident rate than less experienced employees. Increasing experience causes workers to be placed in positions of greater accident potential, and that the greater experience of those in high-risk jobs gives the initial impression, that more experience is associated with more accidents. Age, job experience and their relationships of in this case is compensated by the level of accident risk.

C. *Safety Norms,* such as Safety Standards, Rules and Discipline, Worker's Safety Delegate, Safety Equipment, Safety Personnel Equipment, Safety Committees, Safety Officials, Safety Methods, Training, Tools, etc., have relationship with Accident Involvement in NISOC's employees. So these factors have been tested too in the present study.

5.3. Rationale of the Problem

Developing countries like Iran and India can achieve the pinnacles of advancement only if they can increase their safety measures appreciably. Economists, scientists, sociologists and engineers have addressed themselves to this very significant but monumental task over the years. In the past few decades, the psychologists and behavioral scientists have also joined the fray to make their respective contributions for discovering an efficient and viable solution to the problem. In the safety process, apart from personnel, machinery, building, raw materials and technology, the human resource in the form of manpower and labour plays a very important role.

In Iran, manpower is the most replenishable and easily available resource. It is one of the factors of production and if it is adequately developed, it has immense potential for increasing productivity.

Industrial safety has taken firm root in the precepts and practices of oil industries behaviour over the years. It includes training section, placement, technological factors, prevention of human causes, and other practices. The conflict that a person could experience in the job due to various kinds of rules, regulations and expectations from him and also from the nature and quality of his work life. For this purpose, it became imperative to study the cases of accidents reports in oil industries, the nature of the organizational role and stress, the needed safety rules and regulations of organizations. Beside, how does these influence the satisfaction of persons to have peace of mind to do work with less chances of meeting accidents.

The kind of programmes in the NISOC may depend on safety standards, rules and regulations and how they were planned to make it as personnel nature. So, it is necessary to find out the effects of the demographic variables of some Human Factors and Safety Norms with involvement in industrial accidents, on NISOC's employees.

5.4. Objectives of the Present Study

The purpose of this research is to recognize the accidents' factors of Oil Companies and to construct and test a causal model of accident process. The variables included in the model are those associated with accident. The major purpose in this research is to find the relationship among industrial accidents, with safety norms and human factors including Individual Characteristics, and Cognitive Ability in NIOC's employees in Iran. The applied purposes are:

1. To determine the dimensions of the industrial accident and safety measures in the Oil Industry of Iran.
2. To identify the major variables related to the occurrence of accidents and to examine the relationship among industrial accidents, safety norms and human factors including (Individual Characteristics, and Cognitive Ability) in NIOC's employees of Iran, and the causes for industrial accidents in the units through empirical studies.
3. To develop models that postulate the interrelationships among these variables in a causal framework.
4. To construct and test a causal model of the accident process.
5. To suggest practicable measures for the prevention of industrial accidents in NISOC of Iran.

6. To analyze the existing legal and regulatory framework dealing with injuries and deaths of industrial workers.
7. To suggest changes in the rules and regulations, if any.
8. To make necessary suggestions and recommendations for the prevention of accidents.

Although this scenario is preferable to the typical research design, it is also of limited value.

This study developed a new direction for future accident research by its use of causal modeling and by the creation of new scales for the assessment of NISOC's employee's accident potential. In future studies, the global measures social maladjustment and neurotic distractibility etc., may be decomposed into several measures, of individual traits that can then be woven into the refined causal model and tested. This study of pivotal importance since it establishes a new direction for accident research by developing and validating a causal model of accident process and using methodology and analytical technique not previously used. The 5-year span of the study allowed greater variability in accidents, which helped clarify the relationship between accidents and the other variables. The present study is valuable because its subjects are industrial workers in their actual work settings.

5.5. Samples

The present study was designed to obtain an analysis of oil industries in Iran. For this purpose two groups of NISOC of Iran have been chosen (Group I as Victim employees and the Group II as Non-Victim employees).

The matched-group experimental design was used in the present investigation. The matching between the two groups of oil industries was achieved as the basis of certain characteristics such as :

(a) Function: Both groups of employees were maintainers and manufacturing oil product as appeased to service sectors industries.

(b) Products/Produced: Both groups (Non-victim and Victim) were manufacturing oil/petrochemical and gas.

Primary Study

1. Interviews (Open ended) with the victims affected by injuries (by random sample, 60 such cases were interviewed).
2. Self-devised inventory for studying accident (by random sample, 120 people were interviewed).
3. Self-developed questionnaire for studying factors involved in

accident (by stratified random sample, 600 employees were interviewed) (Appendix 5-B).

Secondary Study

Data Collection: The study has been carried out at two stages:

The first stage was for standardizing the questionnaire and making it comprehensible. Two samples were taken; (1) interviewing 60 employees at random without any stratification among the 1989 victim employees who experienced one or more accidents. (2) Perceptions of the victim about the causes of the accidents by random sample 120 non-victim were interviewed. Selecting 120 from among 1989 victim employees who experienced one or more accidents by administered self-devised inventory to get information about their perceptions for the accident they encountered. At this stage, they were asked to write about their accident experiences and to give the suggestions for the prevention of the similar accidents.

The second stage was for the execution of the questionnaire, as empirical work. The questionnaire which were prepared in consultation with employees, the employers and the experts of the field with government organizations and of the Universities. These three standardized tests which were translated in a language comprehensible by the workers to understand " UMD" factor i.e., of BMCT and FIT. In this Stage, 717 employees were involved with the process as stratified random sample. Among the 717 respondents, 497 were the non-victims of the accidents while 220 were the victims having experienced one or more accidents. However, only 600 (365 non-victims + 235 victims) returned the questionnaire and the tests. The range of sample age were from 25 to 60 years, Experience from 3 to 41 years, and Education from 3 to 18 classes levels. (Appendix 6- C1).

Sources of Data: The data have been collected from the available reports of the companies under study and the data have also been obtained from the offices; internal record of the corporation. The empirical study is based on the data generated through a questionnaire for employees. Knowledgeable persons have also been contacted to discuss the research issue and the meetings with them were also quite useful. Thus, the study combines both secondary and primary data and my own observations.

At the beginning of the study, the accidents' reports of last fifteen years, from 1986 till 2000 have been studied. A period of five years (from 1996 till 2000), has been chosen for the detail research, after reviewing the accidents' reports of this period. Then the name of all accidents' involved people in NISOC, have been listed for the chosen samples. Since the

NISOC is a very big oil industry with different sub-companies, and considering the time limitation of study, three main companies have been chosen for to study (AMA, KOGC and MOGC). Each one has several main managerial area, along with different departments. Through the study of accidents' reports, it has been found that the highest rate of accidents during this period (1996-2000) were in (AMA, KOGC and MOGC) Ahawaz and at the surrounding area. So these companies were selected for the study. The data collection was done in two stages and three types of samples were collected from the NISOC, in Iran.

The first sample of the first stage was of 60 victim employees. They were interviewed first. The second sample of first stage was 120 victim employees randomly chosen, out of 1989 victims who gave information in a self-devised inventory having questions related to technological and human factors, in NISOC. They were involved in an accident (from 1996 to 2000).

After sample survey, questionnaire was designed with 177 questions to find real major factors, specially Safety Norms (in general sense), and Individual Characteristics (Employee Age and Job Experience) etc. UMD has been tested with FIT and BMCT (S and T) tests (in Persian) to measure these factors in NISOC's employees and to see their relationship of these factors with accident involvement. Questions were formulated to find out the technological and human factors, on one hand, and to find about the responders' job related accidents for better analysis. As a Pilot Study, the questionnaire was prepared in consultation with 50 employees, the employers, the experts of the field with government organizations specially NISOCs' experts, and other experts from the Universities, for their suggestion.

For collecting finally the needed data, the third sample as 7.5 per cent, with total 724 employees as stratified random sample was chosen from NISOCs' staff. For better scattered sample, the statistical rate of NISOC was under consideration, including the population of each company's and manager's area and their departments. So the population percentage of each managerial area, along with their subordinate departments, was under consideration for the sample. No female was included in this study because there were only a few woman in the sample (7 from AMA) and none of them was involved in any accident.

The prepared edited questionnaire and Tests of UMD, were used for third sample, and were distributed to 717 employees. The first part consisted

497 (which was 69 per cent Non-victim) employees. And the second part, was of 220 (which was 31 per cent victim) employees.

Frequency of Chosen Sample in NISOC

Application type Region	*Non-Victim*	*Victim*	*Total*	*Percentage of Each Co. (%)*
AMA: Managerial Department Manager of Technical Manager of Operational Manager of Services Manager of Engg. & Build Manager of Office Work	243 (27 10 92 79 30 5)	91 (9 4 57 8 11 2)	334 (36 14 149 87 41 7)	100% (11 4 44 27 12 2)
KOGC: Guard Manager of 3) Technical Manager of Operational Manager of Office Work Manager of Accounting	154 (11 2 137 4)	56 (3-51 2)	210 (14 2 188 6)	100% (7 1 89
MOGC: Guard Manager of Techinical Manager of Operational Manager of Office Work Manager of Accounting	100 (7 2 88 1 2)	73 (5 2 65-1)	173 (12 4 153 1 3)	100% (7 2 88 1 2)

Table 5.1: The Frequency of Stratified Random Sample in three Companies

The investigator was lucky to get 600 informants, out of which 365 were Non-victims (68 per cent of entrants, which is 27 per cent less than the chosen sample), and 235 victims (32 per cent of total entrants, which is 16 per cent more than chosen sample), which represents a fairly good sample.

Note: Perhaps during the study, some of the responded were involved in accidents.

Percentage and Frequency of Chosen Sample in NISOC

Region of Sample	*Total of victim*	*% of Total*	*% of Total*
AMA	334 (47%)	91 (41%)	243 (49%)
KOGC	210 (30%)	56 (26%)	154 (31%)
MOGC	173 (24%)	73 (33%)	73 (20%)
TOTAL	717 (100%)	220 (100%)	497 (100%)

Table 5-2: The Percentage of Sample

Percentage and Frequency of Responded Applicants in NISOC

Region	*Non -victim*	*Victim Joined*	*Absent*	*Total*	*% of Co Joined*	*% of Co. Absented*
AMA	204(50%)	90(49%)	40(32%)	294	88%	12%
KOGC	119(26%)	36(19%)	55(44%)	162	74%	26%
MOGC	85(24%)	59(32%)	30(24%)	144	83%	17%
Total	407(100%)	185(100%)	125(100%)	600	84%	16%

Table 5-3: The Represented Applicant Number

Total 603 employees jointed were Interviewed, out of which 600 completed the questionnaire and three tests, and three of them didn't complete the questionnaire.

5.5.1. Demographic Description of Sample

Here the relationship of industrial accident with demographic Technological variables (in general Safety Norms) and Human variables such as Cognitive Ability (UMD), Individual Characteristics (Employee Age and Job Experience) has been studied.

The FIT and the BMCT (S and T) are tests that measure understanding of mechanical dynamics.

The higher FIT and BMCT's Scores are associated with better records of not being victim. This situation is reasonable in that the FIT and BMCT assesses "UMD", which are of obvious applicability in production and maintenance work. If the proposed relationship between cognitive ability (UMD) and accident were true, these employees would be unlikely to indulge into accident.

Background of Sample in NISOC

S.No.	*Background Sample*	*Group I (victim)*	*Group II (Non-victim)*
1.	No. represented = 600	235	365
2.	Sex	Males	Males
3.	Range of the Age	23-59 yrs	29-60 yrs
4.	Range of the Experience	3-41	4-41
5.	Range of Education	3-18	4-18
6.	UMD grade range	0-188	0-153

Table 5-4: Background Variable of Applicants

5.6. Variables

Along with the following variables which were investigated in the present study, different Technical and Human Factors' variables were designed in the questionnaire.

(A) Employee Age
(B) Job Experience
(C) Understanding of Mechanical Dynamics (UMD)
(D) Safety Norms
(E) Accident Risk
(F) Accident Involvement

5.6.1. Independent Variables

The demographic variables like Employee Age, Job Experience, Safety Norms, Organizational Problems and Managerial Problems on the one hand and on the other hand Accident Risk as coming in the middle were measured by means of the information schedule given in the prepared questionnaire and UMD was measured by the FIT and BMCT (S and T) Tests, as independent factors, to see if they have any relationship with Accident Involvement, as depending factor on NISOCs' employees. The greater exposure to risk will lead to higher accident risk and involvement. The measurement of these factors done by the FIT (1960) and BMCT(1970), and the questionnaire prepared by researcher (2002). These were also administered to 717 of NISOCs' employees.

5.6.2. Dependent Variable

The demographic variables like Accident Involved as dependent variable was assessed with the help of the Questionnaire prepared by researcher.

5.7. Tools and Techniques Used

The data collected were analyzed by applying various techniques of analysis. Basically SPSS-11 was used for Data Analysis which includes Reliability, Correlation, Regression, Factor Analysis, (Principle Component, KMO, Barllet, Varimax), etc.

The UMD, is the ability of understanding relation between physical force and knowledge of mechanical symbols, devices and principles and understand mechanical relations, and mechanical factors in practical situation. The BMCT(S and T) and FIT Test are knowledge of tools that measures the UMD factor. The employees, who have higher scores in this characteristic, will be able to understand the logical and arithmetic reasoning and they will be able to have reasonable knowledge of industrial tools and equipment. So they easily will learn how to work and repair the industrial machines and tools.

The questionnaire which was prepared by researcher, with the statistical tools such as SPSS-11 has been applied to measure the Technological and Human factors such as Safety Norms, Organizational Problems, Managerial Problems besides Individual characteristics (Employees Age, Job Experience), Accident Risk, which remain involved in Industrial Accidents.

5.7.1. BMCT (S and T) Descriptive Index

The S and T of the Bennett Mechanical Comprehension Tests (BMCT) was designed by George K. Bennett, 1970, and translated by researcher to measure the ability of understanding relation between physical force and mechanical factors in practical situation, the NISOCs' employees. BMCT also has a wider range of difficulty, equal or better reliability, uptodate illustrations, and simplified scoring. Forms S and T are timed tests, with 30-minute limit, and the score is number of right answers (with no penalty for incorrect responses). The person who scores high in this trait tends to learn readily the principles of operation and repair of complex devices. The surviving 136 items classified into 18 categories are designed in forms S and T were distributed as following:

Table 5-5 : The Categorized List of BMCT

Category	*Number of Items*	*Category*	*Number of Items*
Acoustics	3	Inertia	5
Belt Drive	2	Levers	8
Center of Gravity	7	Optics	6
Centrifugal Force	5	Planes and Slopes	2
Electricity	6	Pulleys Systems	10
Gears	10	Resolution of Force	6
Gravity and velocity	9	Shape and Volume	7
Heat	8	Structures	12
Hydraulics	16	Miscellaneous	14
TOTAL			**136**

Within each category, the items were divided evenly as possible between Forms S and T. A cumulative sum of difficulty value was maintained throughout the process so that for each category the sum of difficulty was as nearly equal as possible. The final values for item statistics, were obtained from the experimental group. An analysis of the reading difficulty level of the BMCT, Forms S and T, showed that both the directions and the test questions fell within the "fairly easy" range. However, the possibility exists that persons with limited reading ability will be unable to demonstrate their true capability in understanding mechanical problems.

Forms S and T are suitable for male applicants for industrial jobs and male applicants for mechanical jobs, already employed in mechanical jobs, candidates for engineering schools, and other adult male group of comparable ability and education, and for women competing on these levels and for the same kinds of jobs. It should be noted that women tend to score lower than men. Mechanical comprehension may be regarded as one aspect of intelligence, if intelligence is broadly defined. Quite probably this relationship results in part because one does not often learn the names and usages of tools or read blueprints without acquiring some understanding of machines. This test is influenced by environmental factors, but not to an extent that introduces important difficulties in interpretation. The practical value of BMCT is enhanced for many situations by its relatively low correlation with other tests (BMCT by George K. Bennett, 1970).

The tests score was by the use of the appropriate key for the each form of test that was given. Only one answer was allowed for each item. It draws a red line through multiple answers and did not count those answers that show red through the key. The counted marks (other than red) that show through the key and record the number in the box marked. Since there were 68 questions for each tests, so the maximum raw score for each form of test was 68.

Scoring

The inventory has 136 answering items classified into 18 categories which are designed in forms S and T. Each category was divided as evenly as possible between Forms S and T, which means 68 items in form S, and 68 items in form T. A cumulative inventory of items has three types of answers, any one of which is "true". Every respondent has to give either one of the three responses for each question (Item), of the inventory. A score of "1" is given for each "true" item. The number in each role of the completed answer sheet can be added. The total can be written at the end in space provided. The number represents the total scores of the (68) role of each form of UMD. Thus the maximum score on the each form that can be obtainable is "68", and the minimum score obtainable is "0". The higher the score, the better is the UMD, and the lower the score, the better is the UMD, and the lower the score, the poorer is the UMD of employee.

Reliability of the BMCT

The internal consistency of the UMD inventory derived by correlating scores of random Split-half, Spearman Brown and Alpha Cronbach of item for 600 number from three separate companies. This implies that scales are not completely orthogonal but somewhat separate facts of UMD (BMCT and FIT). The lowest and the highest mean value were S=0 to 64, T= 0 to 62.

5.7.2. Fit of Mechanics Descriptive Index

This test was designed by John C. Flanagan, 1960, and translated by researcher to measure UMD as knowledge of mechanical symbols, devices, and principles and the ability to understand mechanical relations. This test has 30 questions. Form FIT is timed test, with 15-minute limit, and the score is number of right answers (with no penalty for incorrect responses). Items 1 to 20 consist of questions or incomplete statements followed by several possible answers. Respondents should choose the best answer. The items 21 to 30 are based on diagrams. Each diagram in the test is a number of questions about diagram. Each question has a choice of several possible answers. Respondent should choose the best answer for each question and mark them in the answer sheet within a time limit which was used in the research. This test was used in the result as validity for S and T test of BMCT. This test (FIT), has also been used in a research by Dr. H. R. Orezei in Iran under the supervision of Professor H. Shokrkon, from Sheid Chamran University (Jondi Shehpour University).

Scoring

The inventory surviving 30 items. The inventory five type of answers, and which only one of them is true. Every respondent has to give either one of the five responses for each one.

A score of "1" is given for each "true" item. The number in each role of the completed answer sheet can be added. The total can be written at the end in space provided. This represents the total scores of the (30) role of each form of FIT. Thus, the maximum score on the form that can be obtainable is "30", and the minimum score obtainable is "0". The higher the score, the better is the UMD, and the lower the score, the poorer is the UMD of employee in the NISOC, the lowest and the highest grade were "0" to "25".

Reliability of the Flanagan Industrial Test (FIT)

Test and Retest reliability coefficients (Split-half, Spearman Brown and Alpha Cronbach) were for a group of about 600 employees from three companies of NISOC.

5.7.3. The Questionnaire of Oil Industrial Accidents Factors

As Geller 2001 said, "If you want to get a good idea, get a lot of ideas". So, based on that the oil industrial accidents factors questionnaire has been designed. The questionnaire is based on two main dimensions namely "Technological Factors" and "Human Factors". The researcher designed a questionnaire with 137 questions to find out the related factors of these dimensions. The answers of accident factor are based on a configuration or circumplical model of interpersonal and task-related systems. These dimensions were as follows; 1. Technological Factors, 2. Human Factors. So major factors of these research, specially Safety Norms, (in general sense), and Individual Characteristics (Employee Age and Job Experience), lack of humanitarian aspect of organisational and managerial on one hand and on the other hand, the relationship of these factors with accident involvement in NISOCs' employees was in the mind while designing the questionnaire. Also in designing of these questionnaires, tried to ask different questions, to find out the technological and human factors of NISOC, the involvement of respondent in accidents, and the relation of their job to the questions. After a Pilot Study, and editing, the questionnaires has been shortened finally to 137 questions and distributed to 717 employees, 497 (Non-victim) employees. And 220 (victim) employees of NISOC (Appendix 5-B).

Description of Dimensions

This scale has been developed by Researcher in 2002. The scale consists of (3) dimensions.

Table 5-6: The Dimensions of Major Factors in NISOC

S.No.	*Dimensions*	*Items*
1. Factor 1	Organizational Problems (Human Factor)	71
2. Factor 2	Safety Norms Problems (Technological Factor)	40
3. Factor 3	Managerial Problem (Human Factor)	16

(A) Scoring

The inventory has two categories of responses with each having six types of answers: "very much", "much", "fair", "poor", "very poor" and "none". Every respondent has to give either one of the six response for each categories and questions (Items) of the inventory, a score of "6" is given for "very much", "5" for "much", "4" for "fair", "3" for "poor", "2" for "very poor" and "1" for " none".

Response to each questions are one of the (six) points scale with each item carrying a score from (6) to (1). Total individual item score is obtained through a composite score for each dimension. But totaling scores for the following items should be done only after the scales are reversed, i.e., scores go from (1) to (6) for item none (1). Thus, the maximum score on the questionnaire that can be obtainable is (822) and the minimum score obtainable is (137). The higher the score, the better relationship of questions is to the accidents' involvement. And the lower the score, the poorer relationship of questions is to the accidents' involvement of the NISOC.

(B) Reliability of the Questionnaire

Test and Retest (Stepwise) reliability coefficients were calculated for a group of about 600 employees from NISOC. The scale has accepted reliability.

(C) Construct Validity

The questionnaire collected from the respondents were factor analyzed 600 (365 Non-victim and 235 victim). Test-Retest (Stepwise) reliabilities of the subclass were good when compared over a 5 years period (1996-2000).

The respondents were invited for the tests. They were facilities with nice room having good chairs and tables with refreshments. All the materials of writing (sharpened pencil, eraser, pencils sharpener, and spares etc.), were available for them to they good comparable while answering the questionnaire and tests.

The correlation was between 41 and 66. These low intercorrelations frequently permit the use of teams or batteries of tests with a combined predictive value appreciably higher than could be obtained by the use of any single test.

For three forms studies, comparable scores were obtained by using the equi-percentile method as described by Flanagan.

The standard error of measurement, on the other hand, is relatively independent of the range of ability. For this reason it is a more useful statistic with which to evaluate a test's reliability.

Table 5-6 presents the reliability coefficients obtained in the testing of several groups from the normative sample. In addition to the reliability coefficient, the table in chapter 6 presents the mean, standard deviation, and standard error of measurement for each group.

5.6.4. Validity-Item Analysis

Some evidence about validity is provided by a measure of UMD, BMCT and FIT instrument tests. Each item was correlated with the total score on the instrument for a list of 600 respondents.

The number in each role of the completed answer sheet can be added. The total can be written at the end in space provided.

5.8. Procedure of Data Collections

A separate place was allotted to the investigator in the NISOC Industry premises for data collection. The data was collected in the highest of the relevance and the importance of study. It was emphasized that the results of the study was utilized for research purposes only. All the respondents were assured of an enormity. After the clarification of doubts raised by the respondents, they were given the questionnaires and tests. First several months were spent in establishing report and explaining the importance of the study to NIOC's managers. Then again several months were spent to study, the last fifteen years (from 1986 till 2000) of accident reports in NISOC one of the largest companies of NIOC. Then a period of five years (from 1996 till 2000), has been chosen for the research. After reviewing the reports of the cases of accidents, during this period, the name of all accidents' involved employees during this period in NISOC, has been listed for the chosen samples, and the names were entered in the computer system, for recognition of their last Place and Position in NISOC. Three main companies (AMA, KOGC and MOGC), has been chased for study which there were several main managerial area in each one, alone with different department.

Three sample were used for data collection, in two stages which first two was used for questionnaire preparation and third one for data collection.

The questionnaire was not time limited, but the tests were limited time tests. Some factors such as Age and Experience, have been tested through the data which was collected from responses of the personals' information section of questionnaire.

The standard procedure stated in the manual was followed, instructions which formed the part of the research instrument, were read out. The respondents were requested to answer all the questions honestly and truthfully and asked not to leave and question/statement unattempted.

The results of the SPSS-11 analyses was demonstrated the causal model provides for a good fit to the data in future the initial and cross-validation samples. A SPSS-11 calculates a matrix of modification fiction indices that identify variable paths not proposed in the original model. Actually, the results shows that it was the greater exposure to risk that causes more accidents, as the path coefficients reveal.

5.9. Precautions for Data Collections

The following precautions were taken in mind while collecting the data.

- Following the ethics of data collection in research. It was made sure that subjects were willing to take test.
- A good rapport was established and maintained throughout the procedure of data collections.
- Subjects were made confident that their identities in no case will be revealed.
- The maximum possible care was taken so that no item was omitted by chance or otherwise. Only a very few cases the respondents were asked to complete omitted items and suggestions.

After collecting back all the questionnaires and tests, each applicants was scoring (experimental subjects was graded). The higher scores should be associated with better accident record. The number below certain grade have been cancelled, and the rest of them have been analyzed. Along with the questionnaire, the UMD Tests, such as FIT and BMCT was used for testing a UMDs' factor, and the other factors such as Age and Experience, have been tested through the data which was collected from the questionnaire. The subject ranged was from low educated to high educated. However, the task were concentrated more about the victim employees. For analyzing, the Stepwise, and the SPSS-11 has been used.

5.10. Limitation

Owing to the formalities involved in big organization, people from all department of a particular NISOC could not be taken. The sample may not be truly random. The sample was taken on the basis of non-probability incidental sampling technique which is characterised by collecting data from the available individuals of the populations, the main consideration being that must should be of victims.

In a study like this which deals with personnel and confidential matters it is perhaps impossible to avoid altogether all sampling errors. Hesitation to put down factors on papers in such organization (in fact it is everywhere) is a part of Human Nature , People hesitated in giving their identity to the questionnaires. So the researcher didn't asked respondent to give their name, in designed questionnaire.

Moreover the length of the questionnaire was too big to welcome anyone to do it peacefully and show by interest. So they really were encouraged the investigator by praising as well as criticising the questionnaire and tests. Understanding and doing it carefully was not infrequent but this fact made the sample limited. However, an effort was made to get a large and representative sample of respondents.

During the period of study the NISOC has been shifted some of their personel to other subsidiary companies, which this makes a difficulties for researcher to find those one in the samples. Also the retirements, deeds, and resigned employees which were in the victim samples was another problem for researcher.

Every scientific research has been done in particular time, place, and environment position will have problems and limitation in execution. So situations and problems, which will affect the research finding, and exact correctness or acceptance, will be as research limitation.

1. The research finding were based on answers of organisation employees'. Even if employees as respondents were in different various jobs and this covers broadly different organisation and personels' characteristics, but still acceptance of this finding cannot be trustfully assurance for other organization with different situation and charteristics. So the obtained finding will be limited and acceptable only for similar organisation.
2. Second limitation is related to kind of data collection in this research. The mentioned variables for caused of accidents were base on victims 'employees' view, experiences, and suggestion. And amount of effective of factors with accident involvement were based on judgments of chased sample as victims and non-

victims' employees. So exactness and correctness of identifying factors is adherence matrix of mentioned factors by NISOC employees' in this organization. Since suggestion and view of people in different subjects is different, concerning their experiences, the obtained finding can not be completely observable as trustfully desirability.

3. Previous theories and research related to industrial accident have been described different personnel, cognitive, behavior and environment factors which respondents suggestions in this research did not mentioned them. So in the recognized factors, this type of factors has not been seemed. To study the relationship between these factors Industrial accidents, and to find the amount of their effects on industrial accidents, needed another researches. So, even if, finding of this research is valuable in relation with caused of industrial accident, but will not be completely cover all industrial accidents factors.

In a study like this, which deals with personal and confidential matters about the employees, it is perhaps impossible to avoid altogether all sampling errors. Hesitation to put down factors on paper in such organizations (in fact it is everywhere) is a part of Human Nature (specially in my country Iran) culturally people hesitate to give their identity in the questionnaires. So the data regarding Employees' Age, Job Experience, Kind of Education, and Level of Education is missing.

Moreover, the length of third questionnaire was too long to welcome anyone to complete it peacefully and fully. Understanding and doing it carefully was not infrequent but this fact made the sample limited. However, an effort was made to get a large and representative sample of respondents. The investigator was lucky to get responses from 600 applicants, out of which 365 were Non-Accident Involved (61% of entrants), and 235 Accident Involved (39% of total entrants), which represents a fairly good sample.

In the industries in developing countries like Iran, most of minor accidents usually remain unreported, either from employees or employers side. Moreover, employees do not like to give information about accident very trustfully.

5.11. Statistical Treatment of the Data

After collecting back all questionnaires and tests which were 600 entrants (applicants), there were coded and entered in computer program. With correcting all data and deleted fails'(false) information, data preparation for analyzing were done. Then after scoring the questionnaires and tests for the each of the persons in third sample which were 600, the raw data were tabulated for each of the variable being studies. The raw data were analyzed on the basis of:

1. Descriptive statistics
2. Inferential statistics
   2.1. Factor analysis
   2.2. T-Test
3. Correctional statistics
4. Multiple regression analysis

5.11.1. Descriptive Statistics

This consisted of the computations of the mean and standard deviation etc. To determine the central tendencies and dispersion of the distribution of the scores obtained on the variables, study and skewness and kurtosis were tested for both the group I and group II in NISOC for all variables (Appendix 6-C2 to 6-C7 and Table 6-1).

5.11.2. Inferential Statistics

This consisted Factor Analysis for shortened the questionnaire in main factors. To followed Factor Analysis, the KMO, Bartlett's Test of Spercity-Klpan Meir has been used which KMO were 0.97. And the different factor from Factor Loading of 0.35 to 0.45 was measured. Concerning the Scree Plot, the Loading Factor of 0.45 with Egan value of 1 has been chased, which came through three Major Factors. Then the Correlation Matrix between different questions has been used to find up the main factors. After factor analysis and clearance of three major factors' variables, the (t) tests were computed to determine whether significant difference existed in factors and two groups (Non-victim and victim) in the NISOC on background variables, which shows good reliability. (Appendix 6-D, 6-E, 6-F1 to 6-F5, 6-G1 to 6-G5 and Table 6-2)

5.11.3. Correlational Analysis

In order to understand the relationship between different variables selected in the present study. The Pearson Product Moment Correlation were computed. The purpose was to see the relationship between different variables under study. (Appendix 6-H)

5.11.4. Multiple Regression Analysis

Regression is the determination of statistical relationship between two or more variables. In simple regression, two variables are taken, one as independent and one as dependent. While in multiple regression number of independent variables are employed to predict the single dependent variable. To study the Extend of EAI NISOC, as depended and the rest of the variables independent variables, stepwise Multiple Regression (Back 1975). Stepwise has been used in different ways for different factors, such as one to one, one to two, one to three and so on. The equations were obtained for each variables. This analysis was done with the help of SPSS-11 where instructions were given to the computer to select and. enter into the questions only those variables which have got significant predictive values. The remaining variables were kept out of the equation they failed to pass mean tolerance level test (Back 1975). Before shortened the questionnaire for Reliability, Spearman Brown, Guttman (Split-half, Apha- Gronbach has been used for Reliability (Table 5.7).

Table 5-7: The Reliability tables in NISOC of Iran

Statiscal Index		*Correlation Between*	*Reabiltiy*		
Kind	*Factors*		*Spearman Brown*	*Guttman Split-Half*	*Alpha Cronbach*
Total Sample	F1 (71)	0.9218	0.9593	0.9579	0.9862
	F2 (40)	0.828	0.9059	0.9045	0.97
	F3 (16)	0.7678	0.8686	0.8681	0.9445
Accident Involved Sample	F1 (67)	0.9247	0.9609	0.9595	0.9858
	F2 (42)	0.8157	0.8985	0.897	0.9703
	F3 (23)	0.8047	0.892	0.8914	0.9566
Non-Accident Involved Sample	F1 (73)	0.9223	0.9594	0.9594	0.9865
	F2 (34)	0.842	0.9142	0.9131	0.967
	F3 (9)	0.7796	0.8773	0.8709	0.904
Technical Education Sample	F1 (67)	0.9206	0.9587	0.9585	0.9831
	F2 (42)	0.8217	0.9021	0.9007	0.9697
	F3 (23)	0.8386	0.9122	0.9122	0.9622
Non Technical Educated Sample	F1 (75)	0.9226	0.9598	0.9597	0.9867
	F2 (39)	0.8146	0.8679	0.8978	0.9707
	F3 (15)	0.7931	0.8851	0.8791	0.937
T Test (Benett)		0.4418	0.6128	0.612	0.8996
S Test (Benett)		0.556	0.7146	0.705	0.9203
F Test (Flanagan)		0.4245	0.596	0.5946	0.7875

6
Results and Interpretations

The results of the study as contained in this chapter have been thoroughly discussed in the light of the research findings of the many previous studies carried out by other the researcher himself on the similar fields.

Chapter 5 discusses the methodology of the causes of the industrial accidents. This chapter deals with the analysis and results of the investigator. The Chapter ends up by highlighting the practical implications of the study for the Industrial Safety in general and the sample taken from the NISOC organizations in particular.

After scoring the questionnaires for the accident involvement in both groups of non-victim and victim employees of the NISOC, the raw data was analysed on the basis of the statistical technique, mentioned in the Chapter V.

6.1. Descriptive Statistics

In this section, the basic data and descriptive statistics for victim employees in group I and for non-victim employees in group II are being presented. Group I, consists of 235 victims and Group II has 365 non-victim employees for the present study. 137 variables ended in three major factors besides the decisive factors such as UMD, Safety Norms, Employee Age, and Job Experience as hypotheses were taken in this study. Before the analysis, an attempt was made to test the nature of the distribution through the measure of skewness and kurtosis, mean and standard deviation etc. To determine the central tendencies and dispersion of the distribution of the scores obtained on the variables, skewness and kurtosis were tested for the both groups, that is group I and the group II in the NISOC for all the variables. The results for sample which have been categorized in five categories (total, accident involvement, non-accident involvement, technical education and non-technical education), in three companies (AMA, KOGC and MOGC), as presented in Table 6-1 and (Appendix 6-C2 to 6-C7). *The figures show that the value of mean and the*

Table 6-1 : Discriptive Statistics of Total Sample in NISOC

	N	*Range*	*Minimum*	*Maximum*	*Mean*		*Std. Dev.*	*Skewness*		*Kurtosis*	
	Stat.	*Stat.*	*Stat.*	*Stat.*	*Stat.*	*Std. Er.*	*Stat.*	*Stat.*	*Std. Er.*	*Stat.*	*Std. Er.*
Age	600	35	5	60	39.23	0.67	16.39	-1.33	0.100	0.90	0.199
Experience	600	38	3	41	19.98	0.44	10.67	-0.27	0.100	-0.72	0.199
FAC2 (S.N.)	600	185.0	37.00	222.00	165.3	1.52	37.23	-0.89	0.100	0.43	0.199
TT (UMD)	600	161.0	0.00	62	89.85	1.13	27.56	-0.72	0.100	0.89	0.199
SS (UMD)	600	188.0	0.00	64	95.06	1.18	28.82	-1.23	0.100	2.31	0.199
FF (UMD)	600	101.0	0.00	22	52.28	0.94	23.03	-0.40	0.100	-0.03	0.199
ACCT	600	36.00	9.00	45.00	41.79	0.25	5.90	-2.74	0.100	9.18	0.199

skewness of the curve to the left signifies and leads us to conclude that more number of accidents are taking place when the workers are quite young and less experienced. Further, from this analysis we conclude that less observance of safety norms leads to more number of accidents. It is also significant to note that the Understanding of Mechanical Dynamics (UMD) plays an important role in the causation of accidents. This analysis reveals that lower UMD increases the possibility of having more accidents.

For normal distributions, Skewness and Kurtosis should be equal to Zero (Yule and Kendall, 1965).

From Table 6.1, it is evident that most of the variables are not significant different from Zero, thus they satisfy the criterion of normality. However, it is reasonable to assure that the present population, normally distributed for the parametric statistics (t-test correlation, multilinear regression and factor analysis) is employed in the analysis of data.

6.2. Inferential Statistics

Inferential statistics namely "t-test" is applied to compare the mean responses of different variables on both the groups. A summary of the results obtained in the "t-test" for the Accident Involvement variable, UMD, Safety Norms and Employees Age and Job Experience is presented below in the table 6.2. The (t) tests were computed to determine whether significant difference existed in factors and the two groups (Non-victim and victim) in the NISOC on background variables, which shows good reliability.

The Table 6.2 Factor Analysis were for shortening the questionnaire in to main factors. To follow Factor Analysis, the KMO, Bartlett's Test of Spercity-Klpan Meir has been used of which KMO were 0.97. The different factor from Factor Loading of 0.35 to 0.45 was measured. Concerning the Scree Plot, the Loading Factor of 0.45 with Egin value of 1 has been chased, which came through three Major Factors (Appendix 6-D, 6-E, and F1 to F5). After factor analysis, three major factors' variables have been determined.

The factor analysis depicts that 10 of obtained variables were not related to accident involvement in NISOCs' employees. The results for sample have been categorized in five categories (total, accident involvement, non-accident involvement, technical education, non-technical education.

Table 6-2: T-Test between Group of Victim and Non-Victim in NISOC

	Type of Group	*N*	*Mean*	*Std. Deviation*	*Std. Error Mean*
Age	Victim	235	38.67	15.54	1.01
	Non-Victim	365	39.60	16.92	.89
Experience	Victim	235	19.40	9.42	.61
	Non-Victim	365	20.36	11.41	.60
Factor 2(S.N)	Victim	235	164.1596	34.6531	2.2605
	Non-Victim	365	166.0904	38.8256	2.0322
T-Test (UMD)	Victim	235	89.9745	27.3647	1.7851
	Non-Victim	365	89.7562	27.7173	1.4508
S-Test (UMD)	Victim	235	95.0043	28.5985	1.8656
	Non-Victim	365	95.0986	29.0037	1.5181
F-Test (UMD)	Victim	235	51.9872	22.1428	1.4444
	Non-Victim	365	52.4712	23.6141	1.2360

6.2.1. Safety Norms

Test and Results of the "t-test" are presented in Table 6-2 between the Group I and the Group II on safety norms' variables. The Table shows that there is a significant difference between victim and non-victim employees on their Safety Norms (Factor 2) and "Accident Involvement" in NISOC. There are significant differences found in terms of "Accident Involvement". The Table also shows that mean values of the variables are consistent for the subjects in the Group II.

6.2.2. UMD

The results of the "t-test" values between the Group I and the Group II on the variables of UMD have also been depicted in Table 6-2.The table shows that the value of "t" is not significant by difference between victim and non-victim employees on their UMD (T Test, S Test and F Test) and "Accident Involvement" in NISOC. There are not significant differences found in terms of "Accident Involvement". The Table 6.2 also shows that mean values of the variables are consistent for lower the subjects iņ Group I, except for T-Test of BMCT where it is higher for the subjects of Group I.

In this research UMD ad subsidiary objective have been studied to reach this gold, three tests (S, T) of bennett, and (FIT) of Flanagan have been completed by respondents. For scoring of UMD tests, mean of two groups (Accident Involvement) and (Non-Accident Involvement) on three tests by used of "t test" has been compared. Result of previous research in relationship with accident involvement on UMD shows that employees who have higher scores in this characteristics (As Bennett and Flanagan tests), should be associated with better accident records, and these employees will not have many accidents.

In this research UMD as subsidiary objective have been studied, to reach the gold. Three tests of S & T of Bennett and FIT of Flanagan has been completed by responded. For examine of UMD, mean of two group of Victims and Non-Victims, in three tests of (S, T, & FIT), by "t test" as independent have been studied. The (t) tests were computed to determine whether significant difference existed in factors and two groups (Non-victim and victim) in the Oil Company on background variables, which shows good reliability. The result is in table 6.2.1.

Table 6-2-1: "t" Test between Victims and Non-Victims on UMD Tests

Kind of Tests	*Mean of Victims*	*Mean of Non-Victims*	*Difference between Mean*	*t*	*df*	*Sig.(1-tailed)*
T-Test	29.4979	31.1423	-1.6445	-1.703	514	0.0445
S-Test	31.5617	33.0391	-1.4774	-1.401	514	0.081
F-Test	8.7830	8.7224	0.0606	0.155	514	0.4387

As the results shows there was significant different between Victims and Non-Victims employees on (T and S tests at level of a= 0.05 &0.01. This means that mean of tests (S and T) are higher than mean of Accident Involved. But in FIT test, there was not significant different between two groups (Victims and Non-Victims).

6.2.3. Employees' Age

The results of the "t-test" values between the Group I and the Group II on the Employees' Age have also been depicted in Table 6-2. The table reveals that there is a significant difference in terms of Employees' Age for both the groups. It also shows that there is significant defference between the two groups in terms of "Accident Involvement", with respect to the employees' age. Also the mean scores are consistently higher for the Group II.

6.2.4. Job Experience

The results of the "t-test" values between Group I and II, on the job experience has been depicted in Table 6-2. The table reveals that there is significant difference in terms of job experience and "Accident Invlvement" for both the groups. It also shows that there is significant defference between the two groups in term of "Accident Invlvement", with respect to the employees' experience. Also the mean scores are consistently higher for the Group II.

(Table 6.3 (a) : Questions of factor Analysis of Questionnaire (Total) Appendix 6- G2 to 6- G5)

	Row	*Varb*	*Ld. Fac.*	*Subject of Factor 1*
	1	65	0.469	Ignorance of employees of accidents related to their jobs
N	2	67	0.503	Lack of physical characteristics of employees for doing their jobs
U	3	69	0.474	Absence of sense of importance of the work
M	4	70	0.47	Non-independence of choice of work methods
B	5	71	0.494	Non awareness of employees of results of work
E	6	72	0.475	Absence of granting full responsibility of one work to one person
R	7	73	0.501	Giving responsibilities which are more than a personnel's ability
	8	74	0.457	Giving responsibilities which are below personnel's ability
OF	9	75	0.472	Non suitable environment condition of work such as light, heat, adores, cold, sounds, chemical gases, etc
Q	10	76	0.52	Lack of personnel's suggestions about safety problems
U	11	77	0.535	Lack of sufficient of employee's liability
E	12	78	0.602	Lack of suitable pattern for personnel to obey work safety regulation
S	13	79	0.59	Disability of managers in carrying out occupational responsibilities
T	14	80	0.582	Lack of control by supervisors regarding to employee job
I	15	81	0.518	Forcing employees to do non secure work
O	16	82	0.541	Work fatigue
N	17	83	0.564	Sickness of personnel
S	18	84	0.569	Delays in changing shifts
	19	85	0.602	Non-consulting supervisors
F	20	86	0.553	a long time for Being far from family

	Row	*Varb*	*Ld. Fac.*	*Subject of Factor 1*
A	**21**	87	0.576	Carelessness of physicians to medical care & treatment
T	**22**	88	0.527	Lack of channels suggestions' to receive employees' suggestions
O	**23**	89	0.607	Jokes, fun and mocking while working
R	**24**	90	0.51	Improper work exacution by people in carring out their responsibilities
	25	91	0.616	In justice in paying salaries and advantages
1	**26**	92	0.64	Noninterest of executives to obey rules and regulations
	27	93	0.646	Unfriendly relationship of supervisors with their personnel
	28	94	0.636	lack of a friendly atmosphere situation in work area
	29	95	0.638	Existence of fear atmosphere in work area
	30	96	0.696	Forcefultion of supervisors instead of reformatory remindings
	31	97	0.637	to weakness of employees instead of strengthening their Powerful points
	32	98	0.665	Unsuitable punishment for mistakes
	33	99	0.59	Stress of work conditions and factors
	34	100	0.681	Lack of responsibile feeling of supervisors' projects and factories Regarding the health of employees
	35	101	0.678	Non-use of experts' experiences, to exchange with others
	36	102	0.646	Improper attention of supervisors to reports' of problems of tools, equipment and machines
	37	103	0.677	Lack of actual work training during employment
	38	104	0.703	Threatening of personnel by supervisors while working
	39	105	0.695	Not giving information about accidents occurrednce and their cases to employees
	40	106	0.672	Lack of job security
	41	107	0.604	Non efficiency of consulting and environment improvements center to save the employees' problems
	42	108	0.656	Existence of stress' problems in work area
	43	109	0.566	Short managerial periods and in constancy of managements
	44	110	0.659	Non-observance of expertise in professional work
	45	111	0.651	Stress dueto the importance of the given work
	46	112	0.639	Imposition of Pressure of work on personnel's shoulders instead of the system
	47	113	0.676	Lack of vocational or operational systems tocarry out tasks
	48	114	0.664	Lack of constant training of managers and supervisors
	49	115	0.608	Lack of skilled managers to excute organizations' programms
	50	116	0.599	Constant change of organizational policy
	51	117	0.686	Mismatch of employees' characteristics with the job
	52	118	0.639	Dissatisfation with work environment condition

Row	*Varb*	*Ld. Fac.*	*Subject of Factor 1*
53	119	0.492	Unfamiliarity of people with danger signals related to gas and gasoline out of city
54	120	0.471	Anxiety regarding their children's future
55	121	0.599	Dissatisfaction of employees from their supervisors
56	122	0.638	Dissatisfaction of employees from their colleagues
57	123	0.56	Dissatisfaction of employees from getting promoted
58	124	0.543	Dissatisfaction of employees from their salaries and benefits
59	125	0.639	Dissatisfaction of employees from their work
60	126	0.617	Stress because of family sicknesses
61	127	0.608	Anxiety because of family problems`
62	128	0.67	Confusion because unclear of responsibilities
63	129	0.643	Unsuitablityt of duties with moral values
64	130	0.685	expectations from each other, in relation to occupational duties
65	131	0.529	Lack of proportional assesment method
66	132	0.516	Non existence of waive signals such as traffic signs and dangerous signals in area
67	133	0.576	Lack of up to date security standars
68	134	0.587	Absence of motives to obey safety regulations
69	135	0.532	Long overtimes
70	136	0.516	Absence of audio-visual
71	137	0.543	Absence of safety culture in area

Table 6-3 (b) : The Questions of Factor Analysis of Questionnaite (Total)

	Row	*Varb*	*Ld. Fac.*	*Subject of Factor 2*
	1	1	0.556	Carelessness on the job
N	**2**	2	0.64	Lack of regular service and maintenance of tools, machines, and equipment.
U	**3**	3	0.532	Shortage of parts, tools and suitable equipment for the job
M	**4**	4	0.631	Defects and wears of machines, parts, tools and equipment's
B	**5**	5	0.661	Lack of regular control and inspecting on machines, tools, equipment by responsible people
R	**6**	6	0.662	Non-standard machines/equipment and tools
	7	7	0.542	Non-standard roads use of for related work of oil industries
OF	**8**	8	0.649	Execution of work by people unfamiliar with the task.
	9	9	0.637	Non-standard tools, clothes and safety equipment
Q	**10**	10	0.548	Lack of developed technology in oil industries
U	**11**	11	0.651	Shortage of safety and protective tools and equipment
E	**12**	12	0.619	Moving equipment by unfamiliar workers

	Row	*Varb*	*Ld. Fac.*	*Subject of Factor 2*
S	**13**	13	0.635	Shortage of communication facilities in operation of regions
T	**14**	14	0.698	Dirtiness of the work place (trash, grease and ...
I	**15**	15	0.604	Shortage of medical facilities while doing work/ operation with accident risks
O	**16**	16	0.693	Shortage of safety training corresponding to the work conditions
N	**17**	17	0.757	Non attendant of safety and fire extinguishers' officials in accidents' place on time
S	**18**	18	0.718	Non -suitable/secure place for equipment, tools, and machines
	19	19	0.61	Absence of proper assesment of the employees' learning, after training to **F** make sure, they had good training
A	**20**	20	0.687	Non enforcement of employees to use safety / protective facilities
T	**21**	21	0.686	Absence of using individual safety and protective tools/ facilities by employees
O	**22**	22	0.709	Carelessness of inspectors while inspecting machines and equipment
R	**23**	23	0.682	Lack of enough visibily while driving on the roads
	24	24	0.626	Un proportional load with capacity of machines
2	**25**	25	0.627	Incomplete-evacuation of gas before working
&	**26**	26	0.615	Weariness of transfering pipes of gas and gasoline
3	**27**	27	0.519	Technical deficiency of automobile
	28	28	0.562	Use of worn and retted off automobiles
	29	29	0.613	Shortage of safety and protective equipments in machines and installations
	30	30	0.644	Slipperiness of place
	31	31	0.68	Shortage of suitable facilities like water, sand, extinguishers to extinguish fire etc.
	32	32	0.524	Lack of suitable distance and space between machines
	33	33	0.486	Shortage of suitable time table for doing work
	34	36	0.516	Not using suitable facilities to move equipment
	35	37	0.507	Problem of addiction.
	36	38	508	Use of non suitable place for working/operation
	37	41	0.457	Unsuitable safety training
	38	42	0.532	Lack of safety information.
	39	55	0.539	Irrational haste while working
	40	66	0.461	Executive request of doing rapidly work without attention to their risks'

Row	*Varb*	*Ld. Fac.*	*Subject of Factor 3*
1	34	0.604	Problem of personnel's dwellings.
2	39	0.714	Injustice in dividing/giving welfare facilities
3	40	0.631	Supervisors' lack of attention to personnel's suggestions
4	43	0.696	Discrimination in the work area ( ) and giving unjustified advantages
5	44	0.684	Financial problems of personnel.
6	45	0.589	Improper treatment of personnel by supervisors
7	47	0.555	Lack of employees' partnership in related works' decision making
8	48	0.72	Lack of unbiased assessment by supervisors regarding personnel's job
9	50	0.589	Carelessness of supervisors to their personnel's problems and try to solve them
10	51	0.612	Lack of fair rules and regulation for employees' promotions
11	52	0.455	Unsuitability of employees to their work given responsibility
12	53	0.6	Lack of job stimulation in employees for doing their jobs
13	58	0.536.	Lack of executive authority for doing responsible jobs
14	59	0.552	Random decision making of supervisor in important works
15	60	0.596	Ignorance of talents of employees for doing work
16	61	0.58	Lack of a system of encouragement and punishment to do the jobs

6.3. Correlation Analysis

To understand the relationship between different variables selected in the present study. The Pearson Product Moment Correlation were computed. The purpose was to see the relationship between different variables under study. The purpose was to see the relationship of the "Extent of Accident Involvement (EAI)" with UMD, Safety Norms, Employees' Age and Job Experience, for total sample. The results' sample were measured also for the other four categories (accident involvement, non-accident involvement, technical education, non-technical education, in three companies (AMA, KOGC and MOGC), are being presented in Table 6-4 and Appendix 6-H. The results show that there is no significant correlation between "EAI" and (Safety Norms, Age, Experience and "UMD"). But there is strong significant correlation at 0.01 level between Age and "EAI", and Age and Experience. Also there is strong relationship between "UMD" tests (FIT, and BMCT).

Table 6-4: Correlation Table between Relative Factors or Indusrial Accident in NISOC (Total)

St.Index	*Extent of Accident Involve-ment*	*Safety Norms*	*Age*	*Experience*	*Test F (UMD)*	*Test S (UMD)*	*Test T (UMD)*
Variable	p	p	p	p	p	p	p
Extent of Accident Involvement	1						
Safety Norms	.078	1					
Age	**.016	-.011	1				
Experience	.075	-.055	**.647	1			
TEST F (UMD)	.014	.116	-.049	-.059	1		
TEST S (UMD)	-.013	.035	-.048	-.040	**.425	1	**.580
TEST T (UMD)	-.039	-.025	.005	.016	**.398	**.580	1

** Correlation is significant at the 0.01 level (2-tailed).

6.3.1. UMD and Accident Involvement (EAI)

The correlation co-efficient obtained on UMD (T Test, S Test and F Test) with EAI in sample is given in Table 6.4. The Table shows that EAI is negatively related with UMD at 0.01 level of significance with NISOCs' employees.

6.3.2. Safety Norms and Accident Involvement (EAI)

The Table 6.4 shows that the correlation coefficient of the different variables of Safety Norms and EAI is in satisfaction in both the groups. The Table depicts that NISOCs' employees, in all variables of Safety Norms, is negatively related with EAI, and none of other variables are related to each other. And the variables are positively correlated with EAI at 0.01 level of significance.

6.3.3. Employees' Age and Accident Involvement (EAI)

The Table 6-4 shows the correlation coefficient between the variables of EAI with the variable of Employees Age, is in satisfaction in both the groups. The Table depicts that NISOCs' employees, variable of Employees' Age is negatively related with EAI. And the variables are positively correlated with EAI at 0.01 level of significance.

6.3.4 Job Experience and Accident Involvement (EAI)

The table 3.4 shows the correlation coefficient between the variables of EAI with the variable of Job Experience, in is satisfaction with both the groups. The Table depicts that NISOCs' employees, variables of Job Experience is negatively related with EAI. And the variables are positively correlated with EAI at 0.01 level of significance.

6.4. Stepwise Multiple Regression Analysis

Regression is the determination of statistical relationship between two or more variables. In simple regression, two variables are taken, one as independent and the other as dependent. While in multiple regression number of independent variables are employed to predict the single dependent variable. To study the EAI in NISOC, as depend and the rest of the variables independent variables, and in order to arrive at the best possible equation, a stepwise Multiple Regression has been used (Back, 1975).

Stepwise method of regression has been used in different ways for different factors, such as one to one, one to two, one to three and so on. The equations were obtained for each variables. This analysis was done with the help of SPSS-11 where instructions were given to the computer to select and enter in the questions only those variables which have got significant predictive values. The remaining variables were kept out of the equation they failed to pass mean tolerance level test.

Since the EAI variables show significant correlation with EAI and Safety Norms factors among group I and II, an attempt to predict (EAI) and Safety Norms has been made with the help of these variables. The stepwise regression analysis to issue and pick up the best set of predictors variables in determining the statistical significance of their prediction of the criteria using (EAI) as Ontarian stepwise method of regression analysis was applied to the independent variables under study. The moment when "t" value become intolerant, the equation turned out to be the best and predicted (EAI) to the nearest correct value. Once the UMD has been calculated it can be checked for the population under study. Stepwise multiple regression analysis was done taking the entire group of 235 victims

(Group I) and 365 non-victims (Group II) to find out best set of predictors for Accident Involvement separately based on dependent variable. From Group I, EAI was taken as dependent variable and then predicted each one separately while using independent variables like UMD, Safety Norms, Age and Experience similar procedure was adopted for Group II. The results are presented in table 6.5.

Independent variables entered into the regression equation to predict Accident Involvement satisfaction.

The table 6-5 shows that when an independent variable was entered in the regression model Group I, the rest of the variables were included in regression model because of their is level of tolerance of beta coefficient. The normalised beta co-efficient suggested that relative contribution was significant above 1% level.

Table 6.5: Table Regression Sample in NISOC

Variable	*Coefficients*		*Coefficients*	*t*	*Sig.*
	Std. Error	*B*	*Beta*		
Factor 2 (S.N.)	1.02	.009	.064	1.106	.268
AGE	-2.08	.019	-.058	-1.079	.281
Experience	6.58	.119	.119	2.207	.028
Test T (UMD)	-9.46	.011	-.044	-.855	.393
Test S (UMD)	4.09	.011	.002	.038	.970
Test F (UMD)	6.71	.012	.026	.562	.574

Research Finding

The major findings are summarized in the following Table

(a) Factor 1. It has been labeled as "**Lack of attention to the humanitarian aspects in the organization (NISOC), in relation to safety aspects**" with 71 different variables (questions) and loading factor from 0.457 up to 0.703, as Human Factor categories.

(b) Factor 2."**Shortage of Technology;** such as shortage of Safety methods, training, tools, equipments, etc." with 40 different variables and loading factor from 0.457 up to 0.757, as Technological Factor categories.

(c) Factor 3 "**Carelessness from management side towards general personnel's problems**", with 16 different variables and loading factor from 0.455 up to 0.72, as Human Factor categories.

After statistical analysis using of Factor Analysis (SPSS-11), I found the following results:

1. "Safety Norms", which is my first chosen factor, becomes as major factor number 2. Regarding this factor it has been found that with 40 different variables such as safety methods, training, toois, equipment etc., it has relationship to "Accident Involvement". So shortage of this factor will cause accident in NIOCs' employees of Iran, as a Technological Factor.
2. "UMD", which is my second chosen factor. It has been tested with three translated tests of S &T and form A of FIT. It has been found that this factor has relationship with "Accident Involvement". Shortage of this factor will cause accident in NISOCs' employees in Iran, as a Human Factor.
3. "Job Experience" which is my third chosen factor. It has been found that this factor did not have relationship with "Accident Involvement", in NISOCs' employee of Iran as Human Factor.
4. "Employees Age" which is my fourth chosen factor. It has been found that, this factor did not have relationship with "Accident Involvement" in NISOCs' employees of Iran, as a Human Factor.

Also it has been found that besides my above chosen factors, there were many other Human Factors related to "Accident Involvement" in NISOCs' employees, such as;

(A) the 71 variables of major factor 1 that is, "**Lack of attention to the humanitarian aspects in the organization (NISOC), in relation to safety aspects** (NISOC), in relation to safety aspects", and

(B) the 16 variables of major factor 3 that is "**Carelessness from management side towards general personnel's problems**".

Moreover, regarding risk factor it has been found that on the one hand it has relationship with the above factors and on other hand it has relationship with "Accident Involvement". So a risky job will causes an accident in NISOC's employees.

Result and Discussion

The gold of this research was to identify Human and Technological factors causes Industrial Accidents in NISOC of Iran. To reach this gold, different stages have been used and with use of Factor Analysis, the factors and variables which were related to Industrial Accident Occurrence, have been recognized. As table 6-3 shows, three original factors have been obtained, "**Lack of attention to the humanitarian aspects in the organization (NISOC), in relation to safety aspects**", "**Shortage of Technology**", and "**Carelessness from management side towards general personnel's problems**". Factor one with 71, factor 2 with 40, and factor three with 16 variables. In comparing factors and variables of this research with theories and literature of other researches shows that finding of this research has eurhymcy and harmony with previous theories and literatures on causes caused of Industrial accident. Both theories and finding of this research and previous literatures shows two type of variables such as (Human and Technological) caused Industrial accident. This two categories were related to different Technological and Human problems' and difficulties' of manpower in organization. In relationship with Technological factors. Finding of this research have eurhymcy and harmony results with other researches such as Thin and Menges (1982), Sanders and Mc Cormick (1993), Bulty & Mayer, Franks and Beegrs, Manasodrof(as Stellman mentioned in 1998), and these shows that "**Shortage of Technology** are very important in caused of Industrial accidents.

Finding of the other two Human factors on caused of Industrial accident such as "**Lack of attention to the humanitarian aspects in the organization (NISOC), in relation to safety aspects**", "**Carelessness from management side towards general personnel's problems**" in this research also are eurhymcy and harmony with finding of other researches as Hansen (1989), Freguson, Mc Nelly and Booth (1984), Foreman, Allis, and Beavan, Lavie, Kremerman and Wie (1982), Smith and Kirkham (1981), and Stellman (1998). Obtained variable shows that major part of Industrial accident caused are related to problems' and difficulties' of industrial manpower in Organization.

Explanation of the the Research Finding

As finding of research shows, three factor are responsible for caused of accidents, "**Lack of attention to the humanitarian aspects in the organization (NISOC), in relation to safety aspects**", "**Shortage of Technology** ", "**Carelessness from management side towards general personnel's problems**", one as technological factor and two as human factors. Victims' employees mentioned, composed variables of these three factors have been caused industrial accidents, in their organization. Two factors of three recognized factors are shows subjects and problems enclosed the organizational humanities' and one is technological problems'. In theories & researches of caused of industrial accidents, also shows that human and technological factors were responsible for caused of industrial accidents.

Understanding why technological factor causes accidents is not very difficult; non-standard tools, machine, equipment, shortage of safety and protective tools and equipment, or not using them while working, probably will increase accident occurrence as the problems of technological factors. But to understand how human factors causes accidents occurrence, can be approved with several general reasons.

One explanation for effect of human factors caused industrial accidents is different problems which engaged manpower be involved in organization will take main part of their mind power and mentality to be busy on it and make stressful on (boggling/absent mind) employees'.

This mind-boggling will caused them absent mind (mind distraction) and dis-concentration on job process as performance of work.. And the result will probably increase their accident Involvements'. The problems and difficulties of manpower in organizations which make mind-boggling on employees, it will come from two major sources.

(A) First source is related to personal and individual characteristics and Psycho-Physical movement. This means that employees of organization may not have potential, ability, personal characteristics and enough ability of psycho-physical movement such as rhythm and harmony between eyes and hand/foot, and enough lithe of involved limb with job doing, etc. If this be true, engagement of manpower in accident involvement will anticipated. Also manpower need necessary knowledge, experience and skill for doing jobs. Shortage of this charteristics probably will increase caused of accidents' involvement for manpower, and will increase accidents' occurrence.

(B) Second source will be positioned and improper of manpower in work area, or out of work area, specially in the family. Problem such as different jobs' dissatisfactions, feeling an injustice and discrimination, arguments with supervisors, colleagues and employees will caused mind-boggling and it will make them to be prone for accident involvement.

Negative attitude to safety and absent of motives to obey safety regulations will caused manpower in accident involvement. If there be risky attitude in organization manpower and risky behavior seem to be positive, and if, there not be enough motivation for save behavior with safety rules and regulation, occurrence of accidents in organization will be certain.

As you see many different factors will caused engaged of manpower in occupational accidents. So organization executives and specially safety managers of organization should considered on this factors to prevent accident involvement in organization and make safe environment place in organization with any danger or risky.

7
Conclusions and Recommendations

Accidents causation is very phenomenon complex and must be understood adequately in order to improve accident prevention.

Occupational safety and health services are important aspects in developing countries. This is specially so in view of the rapid industrialization of the economy, the vulnerable work population and the poorly controlled health hazards faced at work. Surveillance systems in developing countries should take into account the type of industry and hazards which are important in the country. Simple surveillance mechanisms, employing available and appropriate technology, are often the best options for developing countries.

Protective equipment and devices are essential parts of a hazard control strategy. They can be used effectively, provided their appropriate place in the hierarchy of controls is recognized. The use of protective equipment and devices must be supported by a personal protection programme, which assures that the protection actually performs as intended in conditions of use, and that the people who have to wear it can use it effectively in their work activities.

The importance of training lies in the fact that regulations and warning signs will not prevent risky behaviour unless workers understand dangers and believe that safety measures are worthwhile. Workers, and new recruits in particular, need to be instructed in the safety aspects of their work and kept under close supervision to ensure that they have fully understood the dangers and how to avoid them. This instruction must be supported by effective materials and practical training methods. Specific training materials should be developed to assist action in poorly protected sectors, and emphasis should be placed on the training of trainer.

Developing countries like Iran and India have special needs to which training materials and methods will need to be adapted. In some cases, entirely new materials and methods will be required. This work should utilize research on sectors with particularly high safety risks and experiments identifying the cost-effectiveness and appropriateness of measures. Whenever possible work on developing training methods and materials should be done in consultation with workers' and employers' representatives.

The suggestion and recommendations in this research work is based on more than twenty years of study, teaching and research.

I believe the best suggestion is, as Geller in 2001 said, "Safety" should be as a "Culture": "Total Safety Culture", specially in industries which may have major accidents such as petrochemical, chemical, nuclear power plant, steel, power plant, etc. And I believe the recommendation that Alli and ILO made for major hazard installation in 2001 are the best for the major accident industries too.

So, based on above ideas, the suggestion of researcher is the 50 important principles for understanding the human dynamics of safety. These principles are essential to design, execute, evaluate, and continuously improve interventions to improve safety-related behavior and attitudes for achieving and lay the groundwork for building a "Total Safety Culture". Some of the principles focus on design and implementation. Others explain why we often fail in safety. Most can be used as guidelines for checking potential long-term benefits of specific safety-improvement procedure. All will help appreciate the complex human dynamics of safety and health promotion. And the recommendations can be placed under seven important categories (Geller, 2001). Hopefully, the list will be useful as a review and as a staring band for developing the safety-enhancement process.

7.1. Suggestions

Principle 1: Safety should internally- not externally- be driven.

It makes sense to talk about corporate safety as a mission owned and achieved by the very people it benefits.

Principle 2: Cultural change requires people to understand the principles and how to use them.

Education focuses on theory or principles. Training gets into the specifics of how to turn principles into effective action. Long-term cultural change requires both. Role playing or one-to-one interaction is very important for training because participants get direct feed-back on how they are executing procedures or processes.

Principle 3: Champions of a Total Safety Culture will emanate from those who teach the principles and procedures.

First teach relevant theory and method, then show how others can become instructors, and finally allow opportunities for colleagues and co-workers to teach each other.

Principle 4: Leadership can be developed by teaching and demonstrating the characteristics of effective leaders.

Principle 5: Focus recognition, education, and training on people reluctant but willing, rather than on those resisting.

People resist change for many reasons. It is usually a waste of time trying to force change on these folks. In fact, resistance hardens as more pressure is applied.

Principle 6: Giving people opportunities for choice can increase commitment, ownership, and involvement.

A basic reason for preferring the use of positive over negative consequences to motivate behaviour is that people feel more free. They perceive more choice when working to achieve rewards than when working to avoid penalties (Skinner, 1971).

Principle 7: A Total Safety Culture requires continuous attention to factors in three domains: Environment, behaviour and son.

Principle 8: Do not count on common sense for safety improvement.

Principle 9: Safety incentive programmes should focus on the process rather than outcomes.

Principle 10: Safety should not be considered a priority but a value with no compromise.

Safety becomes a value linked to every priority in the workplace or wherever we find ourselves.

Principle 11: Safety is a continuous fight with human nature.

Because human nature typically encourages at-risk behaviour.

Principle 12: Behaviour is learned from three basic processes: classical conditioning, and observational learning.

Learning new behaviours and attitudes often requires another fight with human nature.

Principle 13: People view behaviour as correct and appropriate to the degree they see others doing it.

Our influence as a social model gives us special responsibility to go out of our way for safety.

Principle 14: People will blindly follow authority, even when the mandate runs counter to good judgement and social responsibility.

People are apt to follow even implicit demands from their supervisor to whom they readily delegate responsibility for injury that could result from at-risk behaviour.

Principle 15: Social loafing can be prevented by increasing personal responsibility, individual accountability, group cohesion, and interdependence.

Given up personal responsibility for safety to another person (Principle 14) could be due to the social mechanisms presumed to influence social loafing.

Principle 16: On-the-job observation and interpersonal feedback are key to achieving a Total Safety Culture.

Principle 17: Behavior-based safety is a continuous "DO IT" process with D = Define target behaviour, O = Observe target behaviour, I = Intervene to improve behaviour, and T = Test impact of intervention.

Good intentions cannot work without appropriate method. As Deming (1991) put it, "Goals without method-what could be worse?" The four-step DO IT process enables continuous improvement through an objective behaviour-focused approach.

Principle 18: Behaviour is directed by activators and motivated by consequences.

Principle 19: Intervention impact is influenced by the amount of response information, participation, and social support, as well as external consequences.

The role of external consequences in intervention design is a bit tricky. Pioneering research by Freedman (1965) demonstrated the need to limit external consequences if we want people to develop internal motivation. This phenomenon has been referred to as the "less-leads-to-more effect" (Baron,1995) and is most likely to occur when people feel personally responsible for their choice of action and the resulting consequences.

Principle 20: Extra and external consequences should not over justify the target behaviour .

Principle 21: People are motivated to maximize positive consequences (rewards) and minimize negative consequences (costs).

Principle 22: Behaviour is motivated by eight types of consequences: positive vs. negative, natural vs. extra, and internal vs. external.

Principle 23: Negative consequences have four undesirable side effects: escape, aggression, apathy, and counter-control.

Principle 24: Natural variation in behaviour can lead to a belief that negative consequences have more impact than positive consequences.

Principle 25: Long-term behaviour change requires people to change "inside" as well as "outside".

Principle 26: All perception is biased and reflects personal history, prejudices, motives and expectations.

If we perceive risk, we will act to reduce it; by acting to reduce risk, we will become more aware of other risks.

Principle 27: Perceived risk is lowered when a hazard is perceived as familiar, understood, controllable, and preventable.

When people perceive a new risk, they adjust their behavior to avoidit. Call it "fear of the unknown". The reverse is also true.

Principle 28: The slogan “all injuries are preventable” is false and reduces perceived risk.

Principle 29: People compensate for increases in perceived safety by taking more risks.

Some people increase their tolerance for risk when feeling protected with a safety device (Wilde, 1994).

Principle 30: When people evaluate others, they focus on internal factors; when evaluating personal performance, they focus on external factors.

Principle 31: When succeeding, people over attribute internal factors, but when failing, people over attribute external factors.

Principle 32: People feel more personal control when working to achieve success than when working to avoid failure.

The value of increasing people’s sense of personal control over safety is obvious.

Principle 33: Stressors lead to positive stress or negative distress depending on appraisal of personal control.

Helping people focus on the stressors they can reduce build, their sense of self-efficacy, personal control, and optimism.

Principle 34: In a Total Safety Culture everyone goes beyond the call of duty for the safety of themselves and others - they actively care.

Everyone actively cares for the safety and health of others.

Principle 35: Actively caring should be planned and purposeful and focus on the environment, person, or behavior.

Principle 36: Direct, behavior-focused actively caring is proactive and most challenging and requires effective communication skills. Proper training and practice as a safety coach increases our ability to actively care for safety in this most beneficial way.

Principle 37: Safety coaching that starts with caring and involves observing, analyzing, and communicating, and leads to helping.

Help another individual reduce the possibility of personal injury.

Principle 38: Actively caring can be increased indirectly with procedures that enhance self-esteem, belonging and empowerment.

Principle 39: Empowerment is facilitated with increases in self-efficacy, personal control, and optimism.

In order to truly feel more empowered, people need to perceive they have the skills, resources, and opportunity to take on the added responsibility (self-efficacy), believe they have personal impact over their new duties (personal control), and expect the best from their efforts to be more responsible (optimism).

Principle 40: When people feel empowered, their safe behavior spreads to other situations and behaviours.

We need to intervene in special ways to promote safety as a value, that is facilitating empowerment is one special way to increase generalization and cultivate safety as a value.

Principle 41: Actively caring can be increased directly by educating people about factors contributing to bystander apathy.

Principle 42: As the number of observers of a crisis increases, the probability of helping decreases.

This principle reflect the need to promote a norm that it is everyone's responsibility to actively care for safety. We can never assume someone else will correct and at-risk behavior or condition.

Principle 43: Actively caring behavior is facilitated when appreciated and inhibited when unappreciated.

Principle 44: A positive reaction to actively caring can increase self-esteems, empowerment, and sense of belonging.

Principle 45: The universal norms of consistency and reciprocity motivate everyday behaviours, including actively caring.

Social influences can be used to directly increase actively caring behaviour. The next three principles offer more direction.

Principle 46: Once people make a commitment, they encounperson-ter internal and external pressures to think and act consistently with their position.

Principle 47: The consistency norms is responsible for the impact of "foot-in-the-door" and "throwing a curve."

When an individual agrees with a relatively small request, for example, to serve on safety committee, you have your foot in the door. To be consistent, the person is more likely to agree later with a large request, perhaps to give a safety presentation at a plant-wide meeting. Similarly, when people sign a petition or promise card that commits them to act in certain way, say to actively care for the safety of others, they experience pressure from the consistency norm to follow through.

Principle 48: The reciprocity norm is responsible for the impact of the door-in-the face technique.

One good act will likely lead to another.

Principle 49: Numbers from programme valuations should be meaningful to all participants and direct and motivate intervention improvement.

The last two principles relate to the critical issue of programme evaluation.

In safety, the Total Recordable Injuries Rate (TRIR) is the most popular evaluation number used to rank companies for safety rewards. It is calculated by multiplying the number of workplace injuries by 200,000 and dividing the answer by the total person-hours worked in that time period (U.S. Department of Labor, 1994). What an obvious example of an abstract number with little meaning! The most direct measure of ongoing safety performance comes from behaviour observations, and I recommended ways to obtain meaningful feedback numbers from such process evaluation. Such evaluation tool are not as objective and directly applicable to process improvement as feedback charts from behavioural observations. Results of the surveys to measure perceptions, attitudes, or personal straits can be meaningful to programme participants if explained properly. If given before and during an intervention process, questionnaires can reflect changes in the "inside" factors that impact programme acceptance, participation, and future success.

Principle 50: Statistical analysis often adds confusion and misunderstanding to evaluation results, thereby reducing social validity.

Complex statistics are appropriate and often necessary for research journals. If the purpose of a programme evaluation is to improve a safety process, we need provide number that give the most meaningful feedback to programme participants - the people in the best position to improve the process.

Recall also the lesson from Sandman (1991) and Slovic (1991) that group statistics have minimal impact on risk perception. If our objective is to increase risk awareness and motivate safe behaviour, the most influential evaluation tool one can use is actually anecdotal. The most moving feedback usually comes from the personal report of an injured employee. However, the culture needs to support reporting personal injuries, as well as discussing ways to prevent future incidents.

We should probably spend less time calculating summary injuries statistics and more time eliminating the barriers to personal reporting and analysis of safety-related incidents - from near hits and first-aid cases to lost-time injuries.

7.2. Recommendations of other Researchers

7.2.1. Definition and Identification of Major Hazard Installations

1.1 Competent authorities should make arrangements for existing and proposed new major hazard installations to be clearly defined by a list of hazardous substances or categories of substances and associated threshold quantities, which should include: (a) very toxic chemicals, (b) toxic chemicals, (c) flammable gases and liquids, and (d) explosive substances.

1.2 The definition and identification of major hazard installation by the competent authorities should be arranged in such a way that they allow priorities to be set for those installations requiring particular attention.

7.2.2. Information about the Installations

2.1 The works managements of all major hazard installations should notify details of their activities to the competent authorities.

2.2 For major hazard installations within the scope of the definition, a safety report should be prepared by the works management.

2.3 This information should be made available by the works management to all parties concerned in major hazard control system, including workers' representatives, competent authorities and local authorities where ever appropriate. These parties should respect the confidentiality of information obtained in the conduct of their duties, in accordance with national law and practice.

2.4 For works management the information should; (a) lead to an appropriate level of safety which should be maintained or updated on the basis of new data, (b) be used for communication with, and training of, workers, (c) be used as part of the license or permit application if such is required, and (d) be used for the preparation of an on-site and off-site (where appropriate) emergency plan.

2.5 This information should create awareness in workers at all levels to enable them to take appropriate safety precautions on site.

2.6 For the competent authorities the information should; (a) give insight into the plant and its hazards, (b) allow the evaluation of these hazards, (c) allow license or permit conditions to be determined where appropriate, (d) allow priorities to be set for the inspection of major hazard installations in their country or state, and (e) allow the preparation of off-site emergency plans (where appropriate).

2.7. The information should be systematically arranged in such a way that parts of the installation which are critical to its safety are clearly identified, possibly by the use of rapid ranking systems.

2.8. The information should represent the current activity within the installation. Works management should ensure that this information is updated regularly.

2.9. Relevant information in suitable form should be made available to public nearby.

7.2.3. Assessment of Major Hazards

3.1 Major hazard installations should be assessed by works management and, depending on local arrangements, by the competent authorities.

3.2 This assessment should identify uncontrolled events which could lead to a fire, an explosion or release of a toxic substance. This should be achieved in a systematic way, for example by means of a hazard and operability study or by check-lists, and should include normal operation, start-up and shut-down.

3.3 The consequences of a potential explosion, fire or toxic release should be assessed using appropriate techniques and data.

3-4 Particular attention should be paid to the potential for domino effects from one installation to another.

3.5 The assessment should consider the suitability of the safety measures taken for the hazards identified in order to ensure that they are sufficient.

3.6 The assessment of major hazards should take account of the likelihood of a major accident taking place, although not necessarily in the form of a full quantified risk analysis.

7.2.4. Control of the Causes of Major Industrial Accidents

4.1 Works management should control major hazard installations by sound engineering and management practices.

4.2 Works management should consider the possible causes of major accidents.

4.3 Works management should regularly evaluate these causes taking into account any changes in plant design and operation. In addition, further available information arising from accidents world-wide and technological developments should be included in this evaluation.

4.4 Works management should arrange for safety equipment and process-control instrumentation to be installed and maintained to a high standard consistent with their importance to the safety of the major hazard installation.

7.2.5. Safe Operation of Major Hazard Installations

5.1 The primary responsibility for operating and maintaining the installation safety should lie with works management.

5.2 Good operational instructions and sound procedures should be provided and enforced by works management.

5.3 Works management should ensure that workers operating the installation have been adequately trained in their duties.

5.4 Accidents and near misses should be investigated by works management.

7.2.6. Emergency Planning

6.1 Emergency planning should be regarded by works management and the competent authorities as an essential feature of a major hazard control system.

6.2 The responsibility for on-site emergency planning should lie with works management. Depending on local arrangements, the responsibility for off-site emergency planning should lie with local authorities and works management.

6.3 The objectives of emergency planning should be; (a) to localize any emergency that may arise and if possible contain them, and (b) to minimize the harmfül effects of an emergency on people, property and the environment.

6.4 Separate plants should be established for possible emergencies on site and off site. These should give details of appropriate technical and organizational procedures to reduce the effects and damage;(a) to people, property and environment, and (b) both inside and outside the installation.

6.5 The emergency plans should be clear and well defined, and available for use quickly and effectively in the event of a major accident. On-site and off-site plans should co-ordinate for maximum efficacy.

6.6 In industrial areas where available emergency equipment and manpower are limited, works management should attempt to make provisions for mutual assistance between the neighbouring industrial activities in the event of a major accident.

7.2.7. Sitting and Land-use Planning

7.1 Competent authorities should make reasonable attempts to ensure that there is appropriate separation between major hazard installations and (a) facilities such as airports and reservoirs, (b) neighboring major hazard installations, and (c) housing and other centres of population nearby.

7.2.8. Inspection of Major Hazard Installations

8.1 Major hazard installations should be regularly inspected in order to ensure that the installations are operated according to the appropriate level of safety. This inspection should be carried out both by a safety team which includes workers and workers' representatives and separately by inspectors from comment authorities. Both types of inspection may be carried out in appropriate order by ways.

8.2 Safety personnel from the installation within this safety team should be independent of production line management and should have direct access to works management.

8.3 Inspectors from competent authorities should have the right to free access all information available within the installation that is necessary in pursuit of their duties, and to consultation with workers' representatives.

7.2.9. Guidelines on Occupational Safety and Health

These guidelines should contribute to the protection of workers from hazards and the elimination of work-related injuries, ill health, diseases. incidents and deaths. The guidelines should:

1. **At National Level:** (a) be used to establish a national framework for management systems, preferably supported by national laws and regulations; (b) provide guidance form the development of voluntary arrangements to strengthen compliance with regulations and standards leading to continual improvement in performance; and (c) provide guidance on the development of both national and tailored guidelines on management systems to respond appropriately to the real needs of Organizations, according to their size and the nature of their activities.
2. **At the Level of the Organization:** (a) provide guidance regarding the integration of management system elements in the organization as a component of policy and management arrangements; and (b) motivate all members of organization, particularly employers, owners, managerial staff, workers and their representatives, in applying appropriate management principles and methods to continually improve performance.

7.2.10. The Occupational Safety and Health Management System in the Organization

Occupational safety and health compliance with the requirements pursuant to national law and regulations, are the responsibility and duty of the employer. The employer should show strong leadership and commitment to activities in the organization, and make appropriate arrangements for the establishment of management of policy, organizing, planning and implementation, evaluation and action for improvement.

7.2.11. Worker Participation

1. Worker participation is an essential element of the management system in the organization.
2. The employer should ensure that workers and their safety and health representatives are consulted, informed and trained on all aspects, including emergency arrangements, associated with their work.
3. The employer should make arrangements for workers and their safety and health representatives to have the time and resources to participate actively in the processes of organizing, planning and implementation, evaluation and action for improvement management system.
4. The employer should ensure, as appropriate, the establishment and efficient functioning of a safety and health committee and the recognition of workers' safety and health representatives, in accordance with national laws and practice.

7.2.12. Workers' Duties and Rights

It is increasingly recognized that the protection of life and health at work is workers' fundamental right. In other words, decent work implies safe work. Furthermore, workers have a duty to take care of their own safety, as well as the safety of anyone who might be affected by what they do or fail to do.

The cooperation of workers within the enterprise is vital for the prevention of occupational accidents and diseases. In particular, workers have a duty to:

1. take reasonable care for their own safety and that of others persons who may be affected by their acts or omissions.
2. comply with instructions given for their own safety and health, and those of others, and with safety and health procedures; and
3. use safety devices and protective equipment correctly (and not render them inoperative); report forthwith to immediate supervisor any situation which they have reason to believe could present a hazard and which they cannot themselves correct; and report any accident or injury to health which arises in the course of or in connection with work.

7.2.13. Employers' Responsibilities

The employer should have overall responsibility for the protection of workers' safety and health, and provide leadership for activities in the organization.

The enterprise policy should reflect the responsibility of employers to provide a safe and healthy working environment. The measures that need to be taken will vary depending on the branch of economic activity and the type of work performed. In general, however, employers should:

1. provide and maintain workplace, machinery and equipment, and use work methods, which are as safe and without risk to health as is reasonably practicable;
2. ensure that, so far as reasonably practicable, chemical, physical and biological substances and agents under their control are without risk to health when appropriate measures of protection are taken;
3. give the necessary instructions and training to managers and staff, taking account of the functions and capacities of different categories of workers;
4. provide adequate supervision of work, of practices and of the application and use of occupational health and safety measures;
5. institute organizational arrangements regarding occupational safety and health adapted to the size of the undertaking and nature of its activities;
6. provide adequate personal protective clothing and equipment without any cost to the worker;
7. ensure that work organization, particularly with respect to hours of work and rest breaks, does not adversely affect occupational safety and health;
8. take all reasonable and practicable measures to eliminate excessive physical and mental fatigue;
9. provide, where necessary, for measures to deal with emergencies and accidents, including adequate first-aid arrangements;
10. undertake studies and research or otherwise keep abreast of the scientific and technical knowledge necessary to comply with the obligations listed above; and
11. cooperate with other employers in improving occupational health and safety.

7.2.14. Action for Improvement

7.2.14.1. Preventive and Corrective action

1. Arrangements should be established and maintained for preventive and corrective action resulting from management system performance monitoring and measurement, management system audits and management reviews.
2. When the evaluation of the management system or other sources show that preventive and protective measures for hazards and risks are inadequate or likely to become inadequate, the measures should be addressed according to the recognized hierarchy of prevention and control measures, and completed and documented, as appropriate and in a timely manner.

7.2.14.2. Continual Improvement

1. Arrangements should be established and maintained for the continual improvement of the relevant elements of the management system and the system as a whole. These arrangements should take into account: (a) the objectives of the organization; (b) the results of hazard and risk identifications and assessments; (c) the results of performance monitoring and measurements; (d) the investigation of work-related injuries, diseases, ill health and incidents, and the results of recommendations of audits; (e) the outcomes of the management review; (f) the recommendations for improvement from all members of the organization, including the safety and health committee, where it exists; (g) changes in national laws and regulations, voluntary programmes and collective agreements; (h) new relevant information; and (i) the results of health protection and promotion programmes.
2. The safety and health processes and performance of the organization should be compared with others in order to improve health and safety performance.

7.2.15. Key Principles in Occupational Health and Safety

These Principles are all designed to achieve a vital objective and that is that work should, the place in a safe and healthy environment.

1. **All workers have right:** Workers, as employers and governments, must ensure that these rights are protected and foster decent conditions of labour. As the International Labour Conference stated in 1984: (a). work should take place in a safe healthy working

environment; (b) conditions of work should be consistent with workers' well-being and human dignity; and (c) work should offer real possibilities for personal achievement, self fulfillment and service to society.

2. Occupational health and safety policies must be established.
3. There is need for consultation with the social partners (that is, employers and workers) and other stakeholders.
4. Prevention and protection must be the aim of occupational health and safety programmes and policies.
5. Information is essential for the development and implementation of effective peogramms and policies.
6. Health promotion is a central element of occupational health practice.
7. Occupational health services covering all workers should be established.
8. Compensation, rehabilitation and curative services must be made available to workers who suffer occupational injuries, accidents and work-related diseases.
9. Education and training are vital components of safe, healthy working environments.
10. Worker, employers and competent authorities have certain responsibilities, duties and obligations.
11. Policies must be enforced.

Suggestions and Recommendations of the Present Research

The gold of this research was to identify causes of Industrial accident in NISOC. And to suggest suitable measures and recommendation for prevention of accidents. For this reason variables of each one of the three obtained major factors should be study carefully, and based on them give suggestions.

Lack of Attention to the Humanitarian Aspects in the Organization (NISOC), in Relation to Safety Aspects:

1. Friendly Relationship of Supervisors and Managers with their Personnel

In this research concerning responds to caused of Industrial accidents which have been mentioned by respondents, They mentioned that some of supervisors and managers behaviors, in their view area not proper and friendly , such as "Threatening of personnel by supervisors while working", "Forcefultion of supervisors instead of reformatory reminding", "Unfriendly relationship of supervisors with their personnel ", "Pointing to weakness of employees instead of strengthening their powerful points", and "lack of a friendly atmosphere situation in work area", concerned on these variable and employees mentioned, shows that the employees feels the organizations behaviors is not friendly and they have bad feeling about that. The results will take part of their metal power for the explanation, and their reaction to this type of behavior as mind-boggling. This action will not let them to concentrate on their duties and probably engaged them in accident involvement and will increase accidents. The suggestion is that supervisors and managers be friendly with respective honor behavior to their employees. For reaching this fact, firstly the supervisor and managers should have positive attitude to their employees and secondly put suitable rules and regulation for honor and friendly behavior with employees, and reject unsuitable behaviors.

2. Preparing Enough Actual Work Training for Different Personnel in Different Jobs and Duties

Some of employees as respondents of samples in this research, mentioned that lack/shortage of training, as causes of accident. And they mentioned following points; "Not giving information about accidents occurrence and their cases to employees ", "Non-use of experts' experiences, to exchange with others ", "Lack of actual work training during employment ", "Confusion because unclear of responsibilities", "Lack of constant training of managers and supervisors ", "Non-observance of expertise in professional work ", "Lack of skilled managers to execute organizations' programs ", "Non-consulting supervisors ", "Ignorance of employees of accidents related to their jobs ", base on those, suggestion is all personnel (Departmental as well as Contractual Employees) posted at installation/ work site should be imparted training (covering safety & skill aspects related to their assigned duties) before inducting them on the particular job. And organizations review " on-the- job training which means, first they needs of training with used of scientific methods, the base on that, design training programs.

3. Relieving personnel from fear Threats and Existence of Stress Problems in Work Areas

Some of employees as respondents of samples in this research, mentioned that existence of stress' problems in work area, as causes of accident. And they mentioned following points; "Existence of stress' problems in work area ", lack of expectation/argument between employees /colleagues in organization is one of factors which can reduce in organization. In such organization, employees instead using their energy on work to reach organization gold, they will use their energy on their argument. This type of problems will causes a damage to organization, indifferent manner. So those organization, find up such a problems, should used methods of problems /argument solving for peace of environment in work area.

4. Matching of Jobs' Physical Characteristics with Employees' Characteristics

Some of employees as respondents of samples in this research, mentioned that mismatch/unsuitability of employees characteristics with job characteristics, as causes of accident. And they mentioned following points; "Mismatch of employees' characteristics with the job", "Unsuitability of duties with moral values", "No interest of executives to obey rules and regulations", "Absence of motives to obey safety regulations ", "Lack of control by supervisors regarding to employee job", "Lack of sufficient of employee's liability ", "Lack of sufficient of employee's liability", "Giving responsibilities which are more than a personnel's ability ", "Giving responsibilities which are below personnel's ability", match of employees characteristics with job charteristics as different facts is important, such as and avoiding accidents. Job motivation/ satisfaction in organization as justices and, As example, if unsuitable employees be on the important job, the probably he will involved in accidents, and that will not be a supervised. The developed organisation for reach the gold. In one hand should use scientific matching method for matching employees charteristics with job charteristics during the hiring, replacing, position change of employees, and in other hand for matching employees with job requirement, they should use training in large scale. So the suggestion is in future hiring of employees in organization, base on scientific methods should do hiring, raises, and the job positions changing. Future the needs of training should be determined, then with use of scientific training methods, have training for employees.

5. Developing Safety Culture in the Work Place

Some of employees as respondents of samples in this research, mentioned that lack of safety culture in work area as causes of accident. And they mentioned following points; "Lack of responsible feeling of supervisors' projects, and factories regarding the health of employees", "Improper attention of supervisors to reports' of problems of tools, equipment and machines", "No interest of executives to obey rules and regulations", "Absence of safety culture in area ", "Forcing employees to do non secure work ", "Non existence of waive signals such as traffic signs and dangerous signals in area ", "Absence of audio-visual", "Unfamiliarity of people with danger signals related to gas and gasoline out of city". Since Safety culture organization is very important. In here this subject will be discussed more. We can say a Comprehension Safety culture constantly should be improve, the Comprehension Environment Safety culture should be base on employment satisfaction, occurrence team working, necessary education, training and suitable learning. This culture will give, priority, positive attitude to employees, and this will make them in different way and. The Safety culture will increase the philosophy of taking care of colleagues need of safety to employees. And this that safety is priority not, can be change with each. This expression in one hand will be as priority on theory of and in other hand will approve the explanation of scientific research of psychology (Geller 2001) in A Total Safety Culture :

- Everyone feels responsible for safety and does something about it on a daily basis.
- People go beyond the call of duty to identify unsafe conditions and at-risk behaviours, and they intervene to correct them.
- Safety work practices are supported intermittently with rewarding feedback from both peers and managers.
- people "actively care" continuously for the safety of themselves and others.
- Safety is no considered a priority that can be conveniently shifted depending on the demands of the situation; rather, safety is considered a value linked with every priority of a given situation.

This Total Safety Culture mission is much easier said then done, but it is achievable through a variety of safety rooted in the disciplines of engineering and psychology. Generally, a Total Safety Culture, requires contention to three domains.

1. **Environment factors** (including equipment, tools, physical layouts, procedures, standards, and temperatures).
2. **Person factors** (including people's attitudes, beliefs and personalities).
3. **Behaviour factors** (including safe and at-risk work practices, as well as going beyond the call of duty to intervene on behalf of another person's safety).

   This triangle safety-related factors has been termed "The Safety Triad" (Geller 1989, and et.ed Geller 1989) and is illustrated in Figure X.

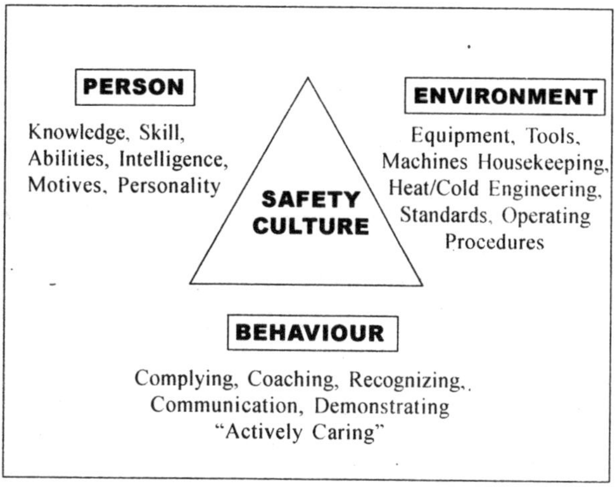

Figure: A Total Safety Culture requires continual attention to three type of contributing factors

These three factors are dynamic and interactive. Changes in one factor eventually impact the other two. For example, behaviours that reduce the probability of injury often involve environmental change and lead to attitudes consistent with safe behaviour. This is especially true the behaviours are viewed as voluntary. In other words, when people choose to act safety, they act themselves into safe thinking. These behaviours often result in some environmental change.

The behaviour and person factors represent the human dynamics of occupational safety the basic principle here is that behaviour-based and person-based factors need to be addressed in order to achieve a Total Safety Culture. These two divergent approaches to understanding and managing the human element represent the psychology of injury prevention.

Paying attention to only behaviour-based factors (the observable activities of people) or to only person-based factors (unobservable feeling states or attitudes of people) is like using to achieve a Total Safety Culture requires a comprehensive framework-a complete map of the relevant psychological territory.

6. Preparing Job Satisfaction and Motivation of Employees from Different Aspects of their Work

Some of employees as respondents of samples in this research, mentioned that lack of satisfaction in area of work and different duties, as causes of accident. And they mentioned following points; "Lack of job security", "Dissatisfaction with work environment condition", "Dissatisfaction of employees from their work", "Dissatisfaction of employees from their colleagues", "In justice in paying salaries and advantages", "Dissatisfaction of employees from their supervisors", "Dissatisfaction of employees from getting promoted" This variables are reflect employees attitudes to different of work and their work area. With regard to the relationship of attitude and behaviour involvement of dis-satisfied people on they jobs accidents are not very unlikely to happen, job satisfaction for many years have been under consideration of industrial/organizations/ experts and top managers of developed organization - BV considering deep dissatisfaction throught victims 'employees. The sugestions (recommendations) is that subject be study by separate researches, to find situation of employees Jobs attitutes in the organization, and the relationship, with same organizational variables. Then, base on obtained findings, develop and performs situation programmes to reduce dissatisfaction and increase employees satisfactions.

7. Offering Equal Opportunities to the Personnel

Some of employees as respondents of samples in this research, mentioned different points in related to discrimination and injustices of managers with their employees, as causes of accident. And they mentioned following points; "Unsuitable punishment for mistakes", "Imposition of Pressure of work on personnel's shoulders instead of the system", "Delays in changing shifts", "Long overtimes", "Lack of proportional assessment method", "Forcing employees to do non secure work ". This feeling of employees how think they have been discriminated and injustices can make them with boggling-mind, and probably will increase accident involvement. So organization executive should studied and if need, change rules and regulations, in case existence discrimination and injustices behaviour, and actually do approving. Preparing justice of supervisors and managers with employees, and not aloud them to discriminate against their personnel in the work area.

8. Preparing Suitable Human Pattern for the Personnel to follow Work Safety Regulations

Some of employees as respondents of samples in this research, mentioned that lack of suitable pattern for personnel to obey work safety regulations can be as causes of accident. And they mentioned following point; "Lack of suitable pattern for personnel to obey work safety regulation". This point is very important, because this is one of social learning discussions'. Theories related to social learning is very important in social-psychology and in their execution of social behaviour is very beneficial. If there be a pattern of social-environment to show the approach of special behaviour, many observers will follow that behaviour approach. If in one work area, subject of safety be under consideration as important fact, and the people in that area do safe behaviours. Many of other employees of that society will go toward/ develop safety behaviours. Of curse that subjects is true too. If in one work area, the people ias a pattern have risky behavior. Many of other employees will follow their behaviors. So suggestions is plan such a way that champion people in work area, as a pattern act/ do safe behavior and safety behavior of them be encourage and those who do at-risk behavior be punished.

9. Solving Personnel Problems in Relation with their Family Problems

Some of employees as respondents of samples in this research, mentioned that family problems and work problem' as causes of accident. And they mentioned following points; "Stress because of family sicknesses", "Anxiety because of family problems", "Sickness of personnel", "a long time for being far from family ". "Anxiety regarding their children's future", family problems and work problem' should be separated. But actually this is imposable. Usually work problems will go to the family and family problems' come to work. So in the result, organization should consider the families difficulties' and problems. They should have suitable way to solve problems of many employees.

10. Reducing Long Time Overtimes

Some of employees as respondents of samples in this research, mentioned that long time of overtime working, as causes of accident working as overtime for long time, probably will engaged employees in accident and it will increase accident involvement. Solution is the agreement with employees for overtime working, by consideration on their abilities.

11. Preparing Suggestions' Channels to Receive Employees' Suggestions

The suggestion system is one of regular god employees' shared in organizations' decisions. If this system be proper, can have effective results. The employees suggestion system should be under consideration and actually should be effect the organizations' decisions. Also suitable and encouragement should give to good suggestion will be effective By furnishing active suggestion system, organization and employees both will have benefit of that.

12. Preventing Fatigue from Work

This is clear that fatigutal employees in work will probably increase accident involvement. One method to prevent fatigue is short rest.

Suggestion is that every two hours, give 20 minutes break as rest to employees. Of course should do it in the ways that during the break time, other people should take care of system/duties, and not let the system be stopped.

Shortage of Technology

Mentioned following points; "Non attendant of safety and fire extinguishers' officials in accidents' place on time" the above points shows that fire extinguish service should be review and in case of problems' existence, should do something that fire extinguishers and their facilities be on the place on right time. Also the facilities should be enough for fire extinguishes.

1. **Attendant of Safety and Fire Extinguishing Officials in Accidents' Place on Time**

   Some of employees as respondents of samples in this research, mentioned that shortage of fire extinguishes' service as causes of accident. And they mentioned following points; "Non attendant of safety and fire extinguishers' officials in accidents' place on time", the above points shows that fire extinguish service should be review and in case of problems' existence, should do something that fire extinguishers and their facilities be on the place on right time. Also the facilities should be enough for fire extinguishes

2. **Offering Suitable Skill amd Safety Trainings Corresponding to the Work Conditions**

   Some of employees as respondents of samples in this research, mentioned that shortage of training, as causes of accident. And they mentioned following points; "Shortage of safety training corresponding to the work conditions" "Execution of work by people unfamiliar with the task ". "Absence of proper assessment of the employees" learning, after training to make sure, they had good training", "Lack of safety information". "Unsuitable safety training". As early suggestion, in second item of first factor, is all personnel (Departmental as well as Contractual Employees) posted at installation/ work site should be imparted training (covering safety & skill aspects related to their assigned duties) before inducting them on the particular job. Here the suggestion is base on scientific study, obtained , the need of training, and different needs of organizations training ,and the base on that, design training programs.

3. **Encouraging Employees to use Safety/Protective Facilities**
Some of employees as respondents of samples in this research, mentioned that non used of safety equipment by employees, as on-the-time service as causes of accident. And they mentioned following points; "Lack of suitable distance and space between machines", "Carelessness of inspectors while inspecting machines and equipment", "Lack of regular control & inspecting on machines, tools, equipment by responsible people", "Lack of regular service and maintenance of tools, machines, and equipment", "Use of non suitable place for working/operation", "Dirtiness of the work place (trash, grease and ...", "Incomplete-evacuation of gas before working". "Slipperiness of place", "Shortage of safety & protective equipments in machines and installations". On the time control and inspection of machine, tools, equipment, and on the time services and repairing is very important for prevention industrial accidents. Preventive / Periodic maintenance schedule of Safety Equipment / System to be chalked out and religiously followed to ensure their reliability. Working place need to be kept spick and span, free slippery substances such as oil, mud, and obstruction before commencement of work. Also the suggestion and solution ways on quality control of machines and equipment, services by inspectors, and review of that by expert people, and solving the shortage and problems, if there is one should be done.

4. **Preparing Suitable Needed Facilities to Extinguish Fire**
Some of employees as respondents of samples in this research, mentioned that shortage of fire extinguishs' facilities, as causes of accident. And they mentioned following points; "Shortage of suitable facilities like water, sand, extinguishers to extinguish fire etc.".the suggestion is after studying the subject by expert people, furnished the needs.

5. **Preparing standard parts, tools, equipment, machines and safety clothes and medical facilities**
Some of employees as respondents of samples in this research, mentioned that lack /non-standard of safety equipments and medical facilities, as causes of accident. And they mentioned following points; "Non-standard machines/equipment and tools"," Shortage of safety and protective tools and equipment". "Non-standard tools, clothes and safety equipment". "Shortage

of communication facilities in operation of regions", "Defects and wears of machines, parts, tools and equipments", "Shortage of parts,, tools and suitable equipment for the job", "Shortage of medical facilities while doing work/operation with accident risks", "Lack of developed technology in oil industries", "Non-suitable/ secure place for equipment, tools, and machines" By consideration to important of safety/ standard tools equipments and medical facilities, in relation to caused accident involvement. The suggestion is that *"Preparing medical facilities on site of work/operation with high accident risks."* And on the time inspection and control by responsible experts, and on-the-time service of equipment, tools, and machines is very important in accident prevention. So, this subject be study by expert people, to have good solution ways for prevention.

6. Regular Service and Maintenance, Control and Inspection of Machines, Tools, and Equipment by Responsible People on Work

Some of employees as respondents of samples in this research, mentioned that lack of on the time inspection and control by responsible experts, and on-the-time service as causes of accident. And they mentioned following points; "Lack of suitable distance and space between machines", "Carelessness of inspectors while inspecting machines and equipment", "Lack of regular control & inspecting on machines, tools, equipment by responsible people", "Lack of regular service and maintenance of tools, machines, and equipment", "Use of non suitable place for working/operation", "Dirtiness of the work place (trash, grease and ...", "Incomplete-evacuation of gas before working". "Slipperiness of place", "Shortage of safety and protective equipments in machines and installations". On the time control and inspection of machine, tools, equipment, and on the time services and repairing is very important for prevention industrial accidents. Preventive / Periodic maintenance schedule of Safety Equipment / System to be chalked out and religiously followed to ensure their reliability. Working place need to be kept spick and span, free slippery substances such as oil, mud, and obstruction before commencement of work. Also the suggestion and solution ways on quality control of machines and equipment, services by inspectors, and review of that by expert people, and solving the shortage and problems, if there is one should be done.

7. **Standard Transportation**

Some of employees as respondents of samples in this research, mentioned that problems in related with different transportation, as causes of accident. And they mentioned following points; "Lack of enough visibly while driving on the roads", "Un proportional load with capacity of machines", "Use of worn and retted off automobiles", "Non-standard roads use of for related work of oil industries", "Technical deficiency of automobile". The suggestion is properly trained, suitably experienced drivers (at least having five years driving experience in driving similar type of vehicles) should be engaged in NISOC as well as contract vehicles. Good condition of vehicle must be ensured. Art of defensive driving to be inculcated in drivers. Over exertion and fatigue leads to accident. So drivers must be given proper rest in intervals during continuous driving. The driver of a particular vehicle should not be changed frequently because it takes time for the new driver to get accustomed and familiar with the vehicle. *"Standardizing roads used of for related work of oil industries"*. Also, since this points are complete technical, the subject should be study by expert people, and in case of existence problems, solve problems.

8. **Replacing worn of transferring pipes of gas and gasoline**

Some of employees as respondents of samples in this research, mentioned that worn transferring pipe of gas and gasoline, as causes of accident. And they mentioned following points; "Weariness of transferring pipes of gas and gasoline. The suggestion is, the subject be study by expert people, and in case of existence problems, solve problems.

9. **Different problems**

Some of employees as respondents of samples in this research, mentioned that different points as basic problems which may causes of accident. Such as following points "Executive request of doing rapidly work without attention to their risks". *"Execution of high risk tasks without haste on irrational speed. (Preparing non- Irrational haste and rapidly work without attention to their risks"*. "Carelessness on the job", "Irrational haste while working", "Problem of addiction","Problem of addiction." Shortage of suitable time table for doing work". The suggestion is, *"Preparing suitable standard distance and space between machines and equipment.", Better harmony, co-ordination and communication during work particularly in case of accident-prone area like Derrick floor, Pipe rack area* etc. must be maintained. And the other problems should be study by expert peoples and in case of existence problems, solve them.

Carelessness from Management Side Towards General Personnel's Problems

1. **Solving Problems of the Personnel Dwellings and Financial problems**

   Some of employees as respondents of samples in this research, mentioned that the finical and dwelling problems, as causes of accident. And they mentioned following points; "Financial problems of personnel." "Problem of personnel's dwellings", So organizational managers should consider the finical and dwelling problems of their employees, and try their best to solve them.

2. **Removal of Discrimination and Unbiased Assessment in the Organisation, such as giving Advantages, Financial Benefits, Raises, etc.**

   Some of employees as respondents of samples in this research, mentioned that discrimination in organization, as causes of accident. And they mentioned following points; "Lack of unbiased assessment by supervisors regarding personnel's job", "Injustice in dividing/giving welfare facilities", "Discrimination in the work area ( ) and giving unjustified advantages ", "Lack of fair rules and regulation for employees' promotions", "Random decision making of supervisor in important works". Existence of discrimination and injustice in organization can do damage to the organisation. If employees feel injustices and discrimination. They efficient of their work will reduce and involved them in accident occurrence. And unconsciously, they will do reaction in work area. Also the mind-boggling which will causes accident, can be happened employees by injustices and discrimination, unconsciously. So the suggestion is management of organisation choose a suitable method to not have any root to discrimination and injustices in organization.

3. **Use of Shared Management**

   Some of employees as respondents of samples in this research, mentioned that lack of employees sharing in organisation decision in relative to their as causes of accident. And they mentioned following points; "Improper treatment of personnel by supervisors", "Carelessness of supervisors to their personnel's problems and try to solve them ","Lack of executive authority for doing responsible jobs". One of management methods base on theories and scientific behavior research to make good developed organisation, with concerned to different problems and different area is sheared management. Share management can be perform different approaches and different size. The suggestion is that organization management furnished employment share in organisations' decisions as their possibility.

4. **Preparing a Suitable System of Encouragement and Punishment**
Some of employees as respondents of samples in this research, mentioned that lack of suitable system for encouragement and punishment, as causes of accident. And they mentioned following points; "Supervisors' lack of attention to personnel's suggestions." "Lack of a system of encouragement and punishment to do the jobs".
Encouragement and punishment system can effect the efficiency of employees work unconsciously in relation with different suggestion for jobs. If there be suitable encouragement with good behavior to the organization gold's and suitable punishment to bad behavior, many of organization problems will be over. This subject in relation with accident involvement is ture. So the suggestion is that, Personnel should be encouraged and motivated by Installation / Site Incharge / Concerned officer to report "near-miss". And the organization management review this system in their organization, and in case of necessary action base on scientific behavior and finding, do changing.

5. **More Considration and Care of Managers and Supervisors for their Personnel Problems, Suggestions, and Talents of Employees and Taking proper Steps toward them**
Some of victim employees as respondents of samples in relation to causes of accident, mentioned some points as; "Ignorance of talents of employees for doing work", "Carelessness of supervisors to their personnel's problems and try to solve them", "Supervisors' lack of attention to personnel's suggestions". Organization it will be related to work efficient of employees. If organization employees does not have serious problems, and they be able to mention problems to organizational executives for finding solution. If organization consider to employees suggestion and affect actual performance on the good suggest ,

and used them in organization. Organization will increase. The suggestion is that Safety Suggestion Scheme may be used as an avenue to receive suggestions from workers and safety Committee should give them serious consideration.Accepted Suggestions with Committee's suggestion must be forwarded to Management for final decision. A communication should also be sent to the originator explaining reason for rejection, modification or acceptance. Once the suggestion has been accepted, the originator must be rewarded suitably. Strict compliance of recommendations suggested by safety officers etc. during Internal/External Safety Audit of Installation. Case studies with remedial measures to prevent such accidents in future (related to their assigned duties) should be discussed in the safety meetings as well as on the job. Any operational abnormality observed should be brought to the knowledge of the Installation/site Incharge and to be rectified on top priority. Every morning, before commencement of work, safety meetings should be held, chaired by Installation In charge /Site In charge to review potential safety problems and action plan to solve them. The details of safety meetings need to be recorded in hardbound register for record, reference and follow up. So, organizational management study this subject deeply and use and perform the effective suggestion in organization.

Conclusion

While supporting the above mentioned views of Geller for developing 'Safety Culture' to avoid most of the accidents and improve the working environment of the installations, I have further investigated the causes of accidents through my research already mentioned in the previous chapters in detail. The findings reveal the new aspects related to the causes of the accidents and on the basis of these findings some more measurers have been suggested to further reduce the agony of accidental hazards.

It is important to mention here that as a result of this study and analysis two aspects (factors), such as *"Lack of attention to the humanitarian aspects in the organization (NISOC), in relation to safety aspects"* and *"Carelessness from management side towards general personnel's problems"*, have came to light which are responsible to a large extent to cause an accident. These aspects have been discussed and analyzed in detail in chapter 6. So to prevent accidents we should prepare standard safety equipment and tools, besides training and concentrating on human aspects of organizations.

Further, it has been found that maximum number of accidents take place at Derrick Floor and at Drilling Rigs due to non-usage of Personal Protective Equipment (PPE)/Improper usage of PPE. So, we should be more careful and particular about the effective and proper usage of PPE by the workers.

The other aspect which has come to light is that the maximum number of accidents occurred during the day time (from 10:00 AM to 4:00 PM). The Managers, Supervisors and all the workers need to more careful and vigilant during these hours. Also, most of the accidents were caused due to slip, fall and striking against or by objects. Moreover, the maximum number of accidents along the non-mine area including fatal accidents occurred on roads. So, we need to improve the working environment and surroundings to avoid such occurrences.

To sum up, the following recommendations have been put forth to prevent occurrence of accidents as far as Mines are concerned:

1. All personnel (Department as well as Contractual Employees) posted at installations/work sites should be imparted training (covering safety aspects related to their assigned duties) before inducting them on the particular job.
2. Strict compliance of recommendations suggested by safety officers etc. during Internal/External Safety Audit of Installation.
3. Case studies with remedial measures to prevent such accidents in future (related to their assigned duties) should be discussed in the safety meetings as well as on the job.
4. Any operational abnormality observed should be brought to the knowledge of the Installation Incharge/Site Incharge and to be rectified on top priority.
5. Personnel should be encouraged and motivated by Installation/ Site Incharge/ concerned Officer to report every "near-miss"
6. Proper use of safety kit as safety shoes, hand gloves, helmets etc. must be ensured while working.
7. Preventive/Periodic maintenance schedule of Safety Equipment/ System to be chalked out and religiously followed to ensure their reliability.
8. Working place need to be kept spick and span, free of slippery substances such as oil, mud and obstruction before commencement of work.
9. Better harmony, co-ordination and communication during work particularly in case of accident-prone area like Derrick Floor, Pipe Rack area etc. must be maintained.

10. Properly trained, suitably experienced drivers (at least having five years driving experience in driving similar type of vehicles) should be engaged in NISOC and ONGC as well as contract vehicles. Good condition of vehicle must be ensured. Art of defensive driving to be inculcated in drivers. Over exertion and fatigue leads to accidents. So drivers must be given proper rest in intervals during continuous driving. The driver of a particular vehicle should not be changed frequently because it takes time for the new driver to get accustomed and familiar with the vehicle.
11. Every morning, before commencement of work, safety meetings should be held, chaired by Installation Incharge/Site Incharge to review potential safety problems and action plan to solve them. The details of safety meetings need to be recorded in hardbound register for record, reference and follow up.
12. Safety Suggestion Scheme may be used as an avenue to receive suggestions from workers and safety Committee should give them serious consideration. Accepted Suggestions with Committee's suggestion must be forwarded to Management for final decision. A communication should also be sent o the originator explaining reason for rejection, modification or acceptance. Once the suggestion has been accepted, the originator must be rewarded suitably.

If the aforesaid measures are effectively implemented, I not only hope but am sure that it will further reduce hazardous as well as minor accidents in the industrial installations.

Terminology

All accidents are incidents. All incidents are not accidents. All injuries result from accidents. All accidents do not result in injury. An accident is an unexpected, unplanned event in a sequence of events, that occurs through a combination of causes; it results in physical harm (injury or disease) to an individual, damage to property, a near-miss, a loss or any combination of these effects. (Ridley, 1995: (L. Banlor)

Ability Test: A test that measures the extent to which a person is capable of performing a certain task or occupation, such capability being the product of heredity and experience. (Aiken,1979:301)

Age Norms: The average score an aptitude or achievement test made by children of a given chronological age. (Aiken,1979:302)

Accident: An accident is an incident which occurs as the effect of a string factors; or an accident is an incident which invariably results from a completed sequence of factors culminating in the accident itself. Accident; is a casualty or unforeseen event, usually characterized by suddenness and external force or violence. Or it is applied most frequently to an unfortunate happening that causes death or personal injury or damage to or loss of property, or an accident is an occurrence that could not have been prevented by the exercise of ordinary care. (Encyclopaedia Americana 1993 : 80)

Generally, we say that an accident is an undetermined and an unexpected casual event, which happens on the job within the working time. It results in human and financial damages. (Mohseni Parsa,1362:4) Or an accident is an occurrence, which can be caused by a number of variables and different factors causing such an accident errors in operator-machine design, work conditions, worker behavior etc. These factors can be divided into two categories, human or environmental factors. Also accident is, an UN-intended occurrence arising out of and in the course of employment of a person resulting in bodily fatal, serious or minor injuries.

Fatal Accident: An accident causing loss of life immediately or subsequent death of a person.

Serious Accident: An injury which involves or in all probability will involve the permanent loss of any part or the use of any part or section of body or the permanent loss of or injury to the sight or hearing or any permanent physical capacity in or the fracture of any bone or one or more joints or bones or any phalanges of hand or foot.

Minor Accident: Accidents, which do not fall in the category of serious or fatal accidents and are usually sever in nature, are called minor accidents. Such accident involves the enforced absence of person from work for a period of 72 hrs. or more.

Mine Accident: Accident occurred during the operations in the mine or during other supporting operations relating to mine in the mine area.

Major Accident: An unexpected, sudden occurrence including, in particular, a major emission, fire or explosion, resulting from abnormal developments in the course of an industrial activity, leading to a serious danger to workers, the public or the environment, whether immediate or delayed, inside or outside the installation and involving one or more hazardous substances.

Non-mine Accident: Accident occurred in places other than mines like road, residential colony, office premises, workshops, etc.

Biserial Correlation Coefficient: A measure of the correlation between two variables, such as the relationship between scores on a single test item (1 or 0) and scores on the test as a whole, in which one variable is dichotomized (i.e., has only two possible scores). It is assumed that scores on dichotomized variable would be normally distributed if the variable were measured more precisely. (Aiken,1979:303)

Correlation: The degree of relationship or association between two variables, such as a test and a criterion measure. (Aiken, 1979: 4)

Cross-Validation: Read ministering a test (or group of test items) that has been found to be a valid predictor of a criterion for one group of examinees to a second group to determine whether the test is also valid for that group.

Dangerous Occurrence: An accident which threatens the life of any person in connection with oil field operation but does not result in any injury to a person.

Direct Factor are those, which cause an accident visibly 26 these also, include incidents which cause visible injuries. These factors may be prevented by the use of proper safety rules and regulations of each job as well as by proper training and control.

Employee means an individual who works under contract of employment. (Ridley, 1995: (Simpson)

Emergency Plan: A formal written plan which, on the basis of identified potential accidents at the installation together with their consequences, describes how such accidents and their consequences should be handled either on site or off site.

Emergency Services: External bodies which are available to handle major accidents and their consequences both on site and off site, e.g., fire authorities, police, health services.

Examinee: Examinees' standings on a test may be evaluated by referring their raw scores to the norm table appropriate for their particular group. In this way norms serve as a frame of reference for interpreting raw scores. They indicate an examinee's standing on the test relative to the distribution of scores obtained by other people of the same age group, sex and so on (Aiken,1979:51). There is almost always some shrinkage of the validity coefficient obtained with the first group of examinees. (Aiken,1979:305)

Environmental Factors: Environmental factors are place-related, and include physical and chemical factors such as light, noise, heat, wave radiation, vibrations, temperature changes, humidity, various pressures, the existence of gasses, radioactivities, harmful vapours and particles, which can be the main factors in the occurrence of accidents in occupational environments.

Factor: A dimension, trait or characteristic of intellect or personality on a number of tests. (Aiken,1979: p. 306)

Factor Analysis: A mathematical procedure for analyzing a table of inter correlation among tests to determine the minimum number of factors or dimensions needed to explain the inter correlation. (Aiken, 1979: p.306)

Hazard: A physical situation with a potential for human injury, damage to property, damage to the environment or some combination of these. The hazard presented by a substance is its potential to cause harm. Hazard is associated with the degrees of danger, and is quantifiable. (Ridley,1995: L.Banlor)

According to Wechsler, (1975), Definitions of Intelligence; In the years since Bineett's early work, many new tests of intelligence have been developed, and much research and theorizing on the nature of intelligence has taken place. Intelligence has been viewed by educators as the ability to learn, by biologists as the ability to adopt, by psychologists as the ability to deduce relationships, and by computer scientists as the facility to process information. (Aiken,1979:107)

Hazard Analysis: The identification of undesired events that lead to the materialisation of the hazard, the analysis of the mechanisms by which those undesired events could occur and usually the estimation of the extent, magnitude and relative likelihood of any harmful effects.

Hazard and Operability Study (HAZOP): A study carried out by application of guide words to identify all deviations from design intent having undesirable effects on safety or operability, with the aim of identifying potential hazards.

Hazardous Substance: A substance which by virtue of its chemical, physical or toxicological properties constitutes a hazard.

Hot Work: An activity involving a source of ignition such as welding, brazing or spark-producing operations.

Human Factors: An accident is a human problem. Human factor is often recognized to be responsible for the occurrence of certain accidents inflicting harm upon one self and others.

Indirect Factors, which include the human factors, are the invisible causes of accidents, despite the fact that other factors appear to be the cause.

Individual Test: A test administered to only one examinee at a time by the examiner. (Aiken,1979: 307)

Job Analysis: A general term for procedures used to determine the factors or tasks that make up a job. Job analysis is usually considered a prerequisite to the construction of a test for predicting success on a job. (Aiken,1979: 308)

Norms: A list of scores and the corresponding percentile ranks, standard scores, or other, transformed scores of a group of examinees on which a test was standardized (Aiken,1979:309). But in this research Safety Norms stands for all technological aspects of safety such as personel protecting equipment, tools, machines, building environment and safety rules and regulation, training, education, etc.

Occupational Health: Occupational health should aim at the promotion and maintenance of the high degree of physical, mental and social well-being of workers in all occupations; the prevention amongst workers of departures from health caused by their working conditions; the protection of workers in their employment from risks resulting from factors adverse to health; the placing and maintenance of the worker in an occupational environment adapted to his physiological and psychological capahis job. The main focus in occupational health is on three different objectives: (i) the maintenance and promotion of workers' health and working capacity; (ii) the improvement of working environment and work to become conductive to safety and health and (iii) development of work organizations and working cultures in a direction which supports health and safety at work and in doing so also promotes a positive social climate and smooth operation and may enhance productivity of the undertakings. The concept of working culture is intended in this context to mean a reflection of the essential value systems adopted by the undertaking concerned. Such a culture is reflected in practice in the managerial systems, personnel policy, principles for participation, training policies and quality management of the undertaking. (Stellman, 1998: p.19.19)

Oil Mines: All borings, bore holes, petroleum wells and accessory petroleum conditioning plants including pipe conveying petroleum with an area duly demarcated by the owner or agent shall be deemed to constitute one mine.

Operational Safety Concept: Strategy for process control, incorporating a hierarchy of monitoring and controlling process parameters of protective action to be taken.

Preliminary Hazard Analysis: A procedure for identifying hazard early in the design phase of a project before the final design has been established. Its purpose is to identify opportunities for design modifications which would reduce or eliminate hazards, mitigate the consequences of accidents, or both.

Personality: The sum total of all those qualities, traits, and behaviours that characterize a person's individuality and by which, together with physical attributes, the person is recognized as a unique individual. (Aiken,1979:310) To be useful, psychological and educational tests, like other measuring instruments must be fairly consistent or reliable in what they measure. (Aiken,1979: 58)

Prospective Ergonomics: Means searching for alternatives in work design which prevent fatigue and exhaustion on the part of the working subject in order to promote human productivity ("...for the benefit of ourselves and others"). This comprehensive approach of Prospective Ergonomics includes workplace and equipment design as well as the design of working conditions determined by an increasing amount of information processing and a changing work organization. (Stellman, 1998: p. 29.2-5)

Risk: The likelihood of an undesired event with specified consequences occurring within a specified period or in specified circumstances. It may be expressed either as a Frequency (the number of specified events in unit time) or as a Probability (the probability of a specified event following as prior event), depending on the circumstances. The risk from a substance is the likelihood that it will cause harm in the actual circumstances of use risk expresses the likelihood that the harm from a particular hazard realized. (Ridley, 1995: Banlor)

Regression Equation: A linear equation for predicting criterion scores on one or more predictor variables, a procedure often employed in selection programmes involving the use of test scores. (Aiken, 1979: 312)

Risk Management: The whole of actions taken to achieve, maintain or improve the safety of an installation and is operation.

Safety: Safety means accident and injury prevention, which saves human investment, itself being the largest national asset in every country. In other words, safety is a factor concerned with influencing an employee's mind, resulting in a proper attitude to govern his behaviour at work. Safety is the condition of being free from the danger of harm. Or as a legal concept, it implies a state of relative security from accidental injury or death due to measures designed to guard accident.(Encyclopedia Americana 19 93:87). Or safety provides tranquility and security of worker which is based on national interests and economic of the country.

Safety Report: The written presentation of the technical, management and operation information covering the hazards of a major hazard installation and their control in support of a justification for the safety of the installation.

Safety Audit: A methodical in-depth examination of all or part of a total operating system with relevance to safety.

Safety Team: A group which may be established by the works management for specific safety purpose, e.g., inspections or emergency planning. The team should include workers, their representatives where appropriate, and other persons with expertise relevant to the tasks.

Types of Norms among the most popular types of norms, *Percentile norms* are easy to compute and to understand and, therefore they are quite common in published tests. Tables of percentile norms within grades, ages, sex, occupations, and other groups are reported for many cognitive and affective tests; *Standard scores Norms,* which are converted scores having any desired mean and standard deviation; *Normalized standard scores* (Aiken,1979:52).When standardizing a test for the purpose of determining norms, careful attention is given to the characteristics of the population for whom the test is intended (Aiken,1979:52). On the other hand, stratified random sampling involves stratifying, or classifying the population of interest on certain variable (age, grade, sex, etc.) and then selecting an appropriate proportion of people at random from each stratum. Because there is less chance of selecting an atypical sample with the stratified procedure, the resulting norms serve as a sounder basis for interpreting scores on the test than those obtained from simple random sampling. (Aiken,1979: 52).

Trait is "a generalized and focalized neuropsychic system (peculiar to the individual), with the capacity to render many stimuli functionally equivalent, and to initiate and guide consistent (equivalent) forms of adaptive and expressive behavior". (Aiken, 1979: 227).

Work: Means an activity a person is engaged in whether as an employee or as a self-employed person. (Ridley, 1995: (Simpson), p.72).

Workers: All employed persons.

Works Management: Employers and persons at works level having the responsibility and the authority delegated by the employer for taking decisions relevant to the safety of major hazard installations. When appropriate, the definition also includes persons at corporate level having such authority. (ILO, 1998:).

Summary

The study "The Relationship of Human Factors and Safety Norms with Involvement in Industrial Accidents" examines the industrial safety as key conceptual variables, which directly indirectly influence the process of formulation and implementation of strategies in an industrial organization.

Since the last few decades while the industry is amazingly prospering towards modern technology, it entailed complicated production techniques inherently associated with many dangers. In the event of an accident the tragedy may cause serious major irrevocable damage. It has been observed that industrialization and complexity of industrial activities have raised the serious problems of occupational accidents in the form of industrial hazards or ailments.

Such hazards have caused detrimental health impacts, ranging from catastrophic direct effects like the recent cholera epidemic in Latin America and the chemical poisoning outbreak in Bhopal, India (Bhopal, India 1985, had Environmental Hazard in Methylisocyanate, as Acute Lung Disease, which caused 2,000 deaths and 200,000 poisoned), to chronic effects (like Love Canal tragedy in USA). Environmental health impacts thus include the indirect effects of industrial disruption of adequate food and housing, as well as the degradation of the global systems on the health of the planet depends.

I this study the main emphasis is on the occurrence of accidental hazards because when they occur, they cause disaster howsoever big or small it may be. The significant fact, which is a matter of great concern, is that the disaster affects every country of the world, but it is the poorest countries where people most frequently lose their lives.

Above all, to evaluate the magnitude of the problems, it is revealing to learn that in today's world accidents cause more death than any single illness. Really the losses due to industrial accidents are phenomenal and call for immediate attention of the scientists, engineers, doctors, psychologists, social thinkers, industrialists, managers, etc. to address the situation for the salvation of human sufferings.

Despite this worrying situation, international awareness of the magnitude of the problem remains surpassingly modest. The inadequate dissemination of knowledge and information hampers action, especially in developing countries. It also limits the capacity to design and implement effective policies and programmes. To reduce the human suffering and financial loss associated with these risks, there is a need for increased and sustained action to protect occupational health and safety, and the environment.

In the past various studies were made to identify the causes of accidents. Ways to minimize these causes were implemented. And, this practice has positive results. The identification of work process and operations, raw materials and chemicals used or generated. Also a variety of workplace hazards, such as noise, unfavourable climatic conditions, unfavourable lighting conditions, vibrations and combinations of these, can sometimes give birth to an accident occurrence due to working in three-shift systems, irregular systems and night-shift systems in two-shift systems.

However, an understanding of the 'cause and effect' relation of the accident-causing factors is required before continuous improvement of safety processes can be undertaken.

In this research, factors responsible for the occurrence of accidents have been divided into two categories; (1) *Technological Factors* (Direct Factors) such as safety norms, (2) *Human Factors* (Indirect Factors) such as Employee's Age, Job Experience and UMD.

The researcher's aim is to study some of the related compilation of these characteristics with accident involvement on NIOC's employees. Because it is believed that these factors have relationship with accident involvement in NIOC's employees.

For investigation, the primary data for analysis was generated through structured questionnaires at different levels of education for workers and managers. It was further substantiated by personal interviews of selected organizations in Iran. Secondary data (case studies, research papers and book, reports etc.) was also used to reinforce the analysis.

This study was made to determine the dimensions of the industrial accidents and safety measures in the Oil Industry, to identify the major variables related to the occurrence of accidents and to identify the relationship among industrial accidents, safety norms and human factors including Individual Characteristics such as Employees' Age and Job Experience and Cognitive Ability (Understanding of Mechanical Dynamics, UMD), specifically of the employees of NISOC. One of the biggest and pioneer oil industry of Iran.

It is important to mention here that during the course of study two new aspects (factors), that is,"

Bibliography

Books:

1. Aiken, Levisr, "Psychological Testing and Assessment", 1979, Boston: Allyn & Bacon.
2. Alli, Benjamin O., "International Labour Organization", 2001, ILO, Geneva.
3. Bamber, L., (Principles of the Management of Risk), in "Safety at Work", John Ridley, (1995), 4th Edition, Butterworth-Heineman Ltd.
4. Bamber, L., (Risk Management: Techniques and practices), in "Safety at Work", John Ridley, (1995), 4th Edition, Butterworth-Heineman Ltd.
5. Blalke, Aronald p. (1948),"Industrial Safety,IInd edition, Fifty Avenue, Prentice, Hall Inc., New York, 1970.
6. Cattell, R.B., (1957), Personality and Motivation Structure and Measurement. London, Harrage & Co., Ltd.
7. Eysenck, H.J. (1970), The Stricture of Human Personality, London.
8. Golmohammadi, Hassan (1363), The Aspects of Safety, Hygiene and Fire in Shops and Plants, Tajresh Press, Iran.
9. Geller, Scott, E., "The Psychology of Safety Handbook", 2001, Imprint of CRC Press LLC, Lewis Publishers, Boca Raton, London, New York, Washington, D.C.
10. Ghiselli, E.E., and Brown,C.W., (1955), Personnel and Industrial Psychology (2nd ed.) New York: Mc-Grow-Hill.
11. Gorden, J.B.; Akman, A. and Brook, M., (1971), Industrial Accident Static: Are-examination, New York Praeger.
12. Hale, A.R., (The Individual), in "Safety at Work", John Ridley, (1995), 4th Edition, Butterworth-Heineman Ltd.
13. Handbook of Industrial Safety Standards (1954), Accident Prevention Dept., Association of Casualty Security Company, 60 John Street, New York 38.
14. ILO, (1998). Prevention of Major Industrial Accidents, International Labour Organization, Geneva.

15. ILO, (2001). Guidelines on Occupational Safety and Health Management System, International Labour Organization, Geneva.
16. Kantowitz, B.H. and Sorkin, R.D. (1983). Human factors: Understanding people- system relationships, New York: Wiley.
17. Kohar , George M., Hayhurst, Emergy R., (19), "Industrial Health", P. Blackiston Son & Co., Philadelphia.
18. Landy, F.J. and Trumbo,D.A., (1980), Psychology of Work Behavior (Rev. ed.) Homewood, IL; Dorsey Press.
19. Mackeven, J.A., (1995), Work Conditions and the Work Environment, Human Resource Coordinator.
20. Maslow, A.H., (1970), Motivation and Personality, (2nd. Ed.), New York: Harper & Row.
21. Meister, D., (1987), Behavioral Analysis and measurement Methods, New York: Willey.
22. Mohseni Parsa, M., (1962), Statistical Study of Work Accidents, School of Safety & Work Heighen,Teharan.
23. Muchinsky, Paul M., (1990), Psychology Applied To Work: An Introduction to Industrial and Organizational Psychology, Third Edition, Brooks/Cole Publishing Company Pacific Grove, California.
24. Rajabi, Abrahim (1962), Safety in Industrial, Tehran Press, Iran.
25. Ridley, John (1995), Safety At Work, Fourth Edition, Butterworth-Heineman Ltd.
26. Ridley, J., (1995), (The Management of Risk), in "Safety at Work", 4th Edition, Butterworth-Heineman Ltd.
27. Ridley, J., (1995), (Employer's obligation for safety), in "Safety at Work", 4th Edition, Butterworth- Heineman Ltd.
28. Ridley, J., (1995), (Safe Use of Machinery), in "Safety at Work", 4th Edition, Butterworth-Heineman, Ltd.
29. Riggo, Ronale, (1990), Introduction Industrial/ Organizational Psychology, Scott, Foreman and Company, USA.
30. Sanders M.S. and McCormick, E.J. (1993). Human factors engineering and design (7th ed.) New York McGraw Hill.
31. Saxena, A.N. (1978), Training Manual 4 "Industrial Safety", National Productivity Council, Printed at HIND Union Press, New Delhi.
32. Sheehy, Noel P. and Antony J. Chapman (1987), "Industrial Accidents", Department of Psychology, University of Leeds, UK, International Review of Industrial and Organisational Psychology, Edited by C.L. Cooper and I.T.Robertson, John Wiley & Sons Ltd.

33. Show, L., and Sichel, H.S., (1971) Accident Proneness. Oxford: Pergamon Press.
34. Simpson, S., (Principal Health and Safety), in "Safety at Work" by John Ridley, (1995), 4th Edition, Butterworth-Heineman Ltd.
35. Simpson, S., (Subordinate safety legislation), in "Safety at Work" by John Ridley, (1995), 4th Edition, Butterworth-Heineman Ltd.
36. Skelletty, E.J. (Civil Liability), in "Safety at Work" by John Ridley, (1995), 4th Edition, Butterworth-Heineman Ltd.
37. Spearman, C., (1927), The Abilities of Man. London: Macmillan.
38. Stellman, Jeanne Mager, (1998). Encyclopaedia of Health and Safety, 4th Edition, International Labour Organization (ILO), Geneva.
39. Stellman, J.M., (1998), ("Disaster and Major Accidents" by Bertazzi, Pier Alberto), in "Encyclopaedia of Health and Safety", 4th Edition, (ILO), Geneva.
40. Stellman, J.M., (1998), (Electricity-Physiological Effects by Folliot, Dominique), in "Encyclopaedia of Health and Safety", 4th Edition, (ILO), Geneva, p. 40.3.
41. Stellman, J.M., (1998), ("Prevention and Standards" By Comini, Renzo), in "Encyclopaedia of Health and Safety", 4th Edition, (ILO), Geneva, pp. 40.10-11.
42. Stellman, J.M., (1998), ("Stress and Burnout and Their Environment" By Freudenberger, Herbert J.),in "Encyclopaedia of Health and Safety", 4th Edition, (ILO), Geneva, pp. 5.15-16.
43. Stellman, J.M., (1998), ("Cognitive Disorders" By Heaney, Catherine A.), in "Encyclopaedia of Health and Safety", 4th Edition, (ILO), Geneva, p. 5.18.
44. Stellman, J.M., (1998), ("Role of the Employee Health Service in Preventive Programmes By Cowell, John W.F.), in "Encyclopaedia of Health and Safety", 4th Edition, (ILO), Geneva," p.15.17.
45. Stellman, J.M., (1998), (" Health Improvement Programmes at Maclaren Industries, Inc. : A Case Study By Arnold, Ian M.F. and Louis Damphousse), in "Encyclopaedia of Health and Safety", 4th Edition, (ILO), Geneva, pp. 15.20-21.
46. Stellman, J.M., (1998), (" Corporate Occupational Health Services in the United State: Services Provided Internally" By Burn, Wiliam B. and Robert J. McCumey),in "Encyclopaedia of Health and Safety", 4th Edition, (ILO), Geneva, p. 16.35.
47. Stellman, J.M., (1998), ("Introduction and Overview By Hecker, Steven), in "Encyclopaedia of Health and Safety", 4th Edition, (ILO), Geneva, pp. 18.2-5.

48. Stellman, J.M., (1998), ("Principles of Training" By Atherley, Gordon and Dilys Robertson), in "Encyclopaedia of Health and Safety", 4th Edition, (ILO), Geneva, p.18.5.
49. Stellman, J.M., (1998), ("Summary of Generic Prevention and Control Strategies By Cooper, Cary L. and Sue Cartwright), in "Encyclopaedia of Health and Safety", 4th Edition, (ILO), Geneva, p. 34.65.
50. Stellman, J.M., (1998), ("Sources of Fire Hazards" By Banlry, Tamas), in "Encyclopaedia of Health and Safety", 4th Edition, (ILO), Geneva, p. 41.8.
51. Stellman, J.M., (1998), ("Prevention of Heat Stress" By Nurneley, Sarah A.),in "Encyclopaedia of Health and Safety", 4th Edition, (ILO), Geneva, p. 42.10.
52. Stellman, J.M., (1998), ("Hours of Work" By Knauth, Peter), in "Encyclopaedia of Health and Safety", 4th Edition, (ILO), Geneva, p. 43.2.
53. Stellman, J.M., (1998), ("The Nature and Effects of Noise" By Suter, Alice H.), in "Encyclopaedia of Health and Safety", 4th Edition, (ILO), Geneva, pp. 47.2-4.2.
54. Stellman, J.M., (1998), ("Linkages Between Environmental and Occupational Health" By Yassi, Arnalee and Tord Hjellstrom), in "Encyclopaedia of Health and Safety", 4th Edition, (ILO), Geneva p. 53.2.
55. Stellman, J.M., (1998), ("Introduction" By Saari, Jorma), in "Encyclopaedia of Health and Safety", 4th Edition, (ILO), Geneva p. 56.2.
56. Stellman, J.M., (1998), ("Concepts of Accident Analysis" By Jorgensen, Kirsten), in "Encyclopaedia of Health and Safety", 4th Edition, (ILO), Geneva, pp. 56.3-4.
57. Stellman, J.M., (1998), ("Cold Environments and Cold Work" Holmer, Inguar, Pre-Ola Granberg and Goran Dahlstram), in "Encyclopaedia of Health and Safety", 4th Edition, (ILO), Geneva, p. 42.29 .
58. Stellman, J.M., (1998), ("Theory of Accident Causes" By Raouf, Abdul), in "Encyclopaedia of Health and Safety", 4th Edition, (ILO), Geneva, pp. 56.6-7.
59. Stellman, J.M., (1998), ("Human Factors in Accident Modelling" By Ane-Marie By Feyer and Ann M. Williamson), in "Encyclopaedia of Health and Safety", 4th Edition, (ILO), Geneva, pp. 56.8-9 .

60. Stellman, J.M., (1998), ("Theoretical Principles of Job Safety" By Skiba, Renald), in "Encyclopaedia of Health and Safety", 4th Edition, (ILO), Geneva, pp. 56.30-31.
61. Stellman, J.M., (1998), ("Occupational Safety Research: An Overview" By Herbert I. Linn and Alfred A. Amendola), in "Encyclopaedia of Health and Safety", 4th Edition, (ILO), Geneva, pp. 60.2-3.
62. Stellman, J.M., (1998), (" Vibration" By Michael Griffin), in "Encyclopaedia of Health and Safety", 4th Edition, (ILO), Geneva, p. 50.2.
63. Stellman, J.M., (1998), ("Goals, Definitions and General Information" By Berrenice I. Ferrari Goelzer), in "Encyclopaedia of Health and Safety", 4th Edition, (ILO), Geneva, pp. 30.2-3.
64. Stellman, J.M., (1998), ("Health Protection and Promotion in the Workplace: An Overview" By Leon J. Warshaw and Jacqueline Messite), in "Encyclopaedia of Health and Safety", 4th Edition, (ILO), Geneva, pp. 15.2.
65. Stellman, J.M., (1998), ("Foot and Leg Protection" By Toyahiko Miura), in "Encyclopaedia of Health and Safety", 4th Edition, (ILO), Geneva, p. 31.6-7.
66. Stellman, J.M., (1998), ("Hearing Protection" By John R. Franks and Elliott H. Berger), in "Encyclopaedia of Health and Safety", 4th Edition, (ILO), Geneva, p. 31.11.
67. Stellman, J.M., (1998), ("Work-Related Diseases and Occupational Diseases: The ILO International List" By Michel Lesage), in "Encyclopaedia of Health and Safety", 4th Edition, (ILO), Geneva, p. 26.2.
68. Stellman, J.M., (1998), ("Protective Clothing" By S. Zack Manasdorf), in "Encyclopaedia of Health and Safety", 4th Edition, (ILO), Geneva, p. 31.16.
69. Stellman, J.M., (1998), ("Overview" By Wolfgang Laurig and Joachim Vedder), in "Encyclopaedia of Health and Safety", 4th Edition, (ILO), Geneva, pp. 29.2-5.
70. Stellman, J.M., (1998), ("Goals, Definitions and General Information" By Brenice I. Goelzer), in "Encyclopaedia of Health and Safety", 4th Edition, (ILO), Geneva, p. 30.4.
71. Stellman, J.M., (1998), ("Recognition of Hazards" By Linnea lillienberg), in "Encyclopaedia of Health and Safety", 4th Edition, (ILO), Geneva, p. 30.10.
72. Stellman, J.M., (1998), ("Occupational Disease Surveillance and

Reporting Systems" By Steven B. Markowitz), in "Encyclopaedia of Health and Safety", 4th Edition, (ILO), Geneva, p. 32.2.

73. Stellman, J.M., (1998), ("Overview and Philosophy of Personal Protection" By Robert F. Herrick), in "Encyclopaedia of Health and Safety", 4th Edition, (ILO), Geneva, p. 31.2-3.
74. Stellman, J.M., (1998), ("Eye and Face Protectors" By Kikuzi Kimuro), in "Encyclopaedia of Health and Safety", 4th Edition, (ILO), Geneva, p. 31.2.
75. Stellman, J.M., (1998), ("Head Protection" By Isabell Balty and Alain Mayer), in "Encyclopaedia of Health and Safety", 4th Edition, (ILO), Geneva, p. 31.11.
76. Stevenson, A. (1980). Planned Safety Management, London: Alan O Sborne.
77. Thorndike, R. (1963), Reliability Proceedings of the Invitational Conference on Testing Problems. Princeton, N.J., Educational Testing Service, 1964.
78. Vernon, H.M., (1936), Accidents and Their Prevention. Cambridge Univ. Press.
79. Viteles,M.S. (1932), Bingham and Slacombe, 1930, Industrial Psychology, W.W. Norton & Co. Inc. N.Y.
80. Watts, Brenda, (Explaining The Law), in John Ridley, "Safety at Work", (1995), 4th Edition, Butterworth-Heineman Ltd.
81. Werther, Jr., William B., Keith Davis (1982), Personnel Management and Human Relations, McGrow Hill, Tokyo.
82. William B. Werther, Jr. Keith Davis (1982), Personnel Management and Human Relations, McGrow Hill, Tokyo.
83. Wolman, B. (1976), The therapist's handbook, New York: Van nostrand Reinhold.
84. Zahedi, S.A.,(1369), Industrial Relation, Markaz Nasher Daneshhahi, Tehran, Iran.

Periodicals:

1. Adams, N.L., Barlow, A., and Hiddlestone, J. (1981). Obtaining ergonomics information about industrial accidents: A five-year analysis. Applied Ergonomics, 12, 71-81.
2. Adelstein, A.M., (1951), Unpublished Doctoral Dissertation on the Accident Rates of Railway Operatives, Univ. of Witwatersrand S.A.
3. Adelstein, (1952), in Brown, C.E., and Ghiselli, E.E. (1955), Accident Proneness among streetcar motor men and coach operators, Journal of Applied Psychology, 33, 20-25.

4. Alexander, W.P., (1953), Intelligence, concrete and abstract. Brit.J., Psycholo. Mongor. Suppl., 19.177.
5. Allodi, F., and Montgomery, R. (1979). Psychosocial aspects of occupational injury. Social Psychiatry, 14, 25-29.
6. Arbous, A.G., and Kerrich, J.E. (1951) Accident Statistics The Concept of accident proneness, Biometric, 7,340-430.
7. Asanga, Peter Masinga (1980), "Availability and safety Study of an Oil Refinery: The Availability and Safety Behavior since Commissioning in 1980 of The KADUNA Refinery is Study in Depth." Particular attention being given to the importance and effects of Human Factors (Nigeria), University of Brantford.
8. Balakumaran, W.A. (1994), Safety and Health of People at Work in Manufacturing Industries, Bull Madras Devel Seminar, Series 24 (12) De., 94, 511-17.
9. Biesheuvel, S. & White, M., (1949), The Human Factor in Flying Accidents. S.A.A.F. Journal 1, 2.
10. Bingham, W.V., (1928), Personality and Public Accident- The Study of Accident-Prone Drivers, Transactions Seventeenth Annual Safety Congress, N.Y.
11. Boden, L.I., Hall, J.A., Levenstein, C., And Punnett, L., (1984). The impact of health and safety committees, Journal of Occupational Medicine, 26, 824-834.
12. Brewin, (1982), in Foreman, E.H., Ellis,D., and Beavan D. (1983). Mea culpa? A study of the relationships among personality traits, life-events and ascribed accident causation, British Journal of Clinical Psychology, 22, 223-234.
13. Brown,C.W. and Ghiselli,E.E. (1948). Factors Related to the proficiency of motor coach operators, Journal of Applied Psychology 31, 477-480.
14. Brown, C.E., and Ghiselli, E.E, (1955), Accident Proneness among streetcar motor men and coach operators, Journal of Applied Psychology, 33, 20-25.
15. Brown, I.D. (1980). Error correction probability as a determinant of drivers subjective risk. In D.J. Oborne and J.A. Levis (eds.). Human Factors in Transport Research, Vol. 2, and User Factors: Comfort, the Environment and Behaviour. London: Academic Press. Bull, J.P. (1985). Disabilities caused by road traffic accidents and their relation to severity scores. Accident Analysis and Prevention, 17, 389-397.
16. Brown, S.H. (1981), Validity Generalization and Situational

Moderation in the Life Insurance Industry, Journal of Applied Psychology, 66, 664-670.

17. Brown, C. W. and E.E. Ghiselli (1984). Accident proneness among streetcar motormen and motor coach operators, Journal of Applied Psychology, 33, 20-28.
18. Broadbent, (1982) in Foreman, E.H., Ellis, D., and Beavan D. (1983). Mea culpa? A study of the relationships among personality traits, life-events and ascribed accident causation, British Journal of Clinical Psychology, 22, 223-234.
19. Bull, J.P. (1985). Disabilities caused by road traffic accidents and their relation to severity scores. Accident Analysis and Prevention, 17, 389-397.
20. Bulter, M.C. & Jones A.P. (1979) Perceived leader behaviour. Industrial Characteristics and injury occurrence in hazardous work environments, Journal of Applied Psychology, 84, 299-304.
21. Bureau of the Census (1981), Statistical Abstract of the United States, National Data Book and Guide to Sources, by U.S. Department of Commerce.
22. Cartwright, (1957), in Craske, S.(1968), A Study of the relation between personality and accident history, British Journal of Medical Psychology 41, 399-404.
23. Cardwell, (1948), in Crawford, P.L. (1965). Accident prevention through scientific selection, Personnel Journal, 44, 560-571.
24. Case and Stewart, (1957), in Crawford, P.L. (1965). Accident prevention through scientific selection, Personnel Journal, 44, 560-571.
25. Cellier, J.M. (1980) Workload and Safety in a task of handling. Travail Humain, 43, 3-16.
26. Cleland, (1971), in Smith, D.I., and Kirkham, R.W. (1981). Relationship between some personality characteristics and driving record, British Journal of Social Psychology, 20, 299-211.
27. Cliff, K.S. (1984). Accidents : Causes, Prevention and Services. London Croom Helm.
28. Cooke, W.N., and Gautschi, F.H. (1981). OHSA, plant safety programs, and injury reduction.
29. Cooke, W.N. and Blumenstock, M.W. (1979). The determinates of occupational injury severity: The case of Maine sawmitls, Journal of Safety Research, 11 (3), 59-67.
30. Cohen, A. (1977). Fuctures in successful safety programs. Journal of Safety Research, 9, 168-178.

31. Crawford, P.L. (1965). Accident prevention through scientific selection, Personnel Journal, 44, 560-571.
32. Craske, S.(1968), A Study of the relation between personality and accident history, British Journal of Medical Psychology 41, 399-404.
33. Denning, D.L., (1983), Correlates of employee safety performance, paper presented at the southeaster I/O Psychological Association Meeting, Atlanta, Georgia.
34. Dunbar, F., (1943); Rowson, 1944, English & Pearson, 1945, Psychosomatic Diagnosis. Paul B. Hoeber Incs-Medical Book. Dept. of Harper & Bros., N.Y. and London.
35. Edin, Math, Journa, (1925-26), Arbous, A.G., and Kerrich, J.E. (1951). Accident Statistics The Concept of accident proneness, Biometric, 7, 340-430.
36. Eduards, M.(198). The design of an accident investigation procedure. Applied Ergonomics, 12,111-115.
37. Embrey, D. E. (1979). Approaches to training for industrial inspection: Applied Ergonomics, 10,139-144.
38. Eyseneck and Eyseneck, (1962), The Personality of Drivers and Pedestrians. Medicine, Science, and the Law, 3, 416-423.
39. Eyseneck and Eyseneck, (1963), Craske, S. (1968), A Study of the relation between personality and accident history, British Journal of Medical Psychology 41, 399-404.
40. Eyseneck and Eyseneck, (1964), Craske, S. (1968), A Study of the relation between personality and accident history, British Journal of Medical Psychology 41, 399-404.
41. Farmer, E. and Chambers, E.G. (1926), A Psychological Study of Individual Differences in Accident Rates, I.H.R.B. Report No. 88.
42. Farmer, E. and Chambers, E.G. (1929), A Study of Personal Qualities in Accident Proneness and Proficiency, I.H.R.B.Report No. 55.
43. Farmer, E. and Chambers, E.G. (1933), Tests for Accident Proneness, I.H.R.B.Report No. 68.
44. Farmer, E. and Chambers, E.G. (1936), The Prognostic Value of some Psychological Tests.., I.H.R.B. Report No. 74.
45. Farmer, E. and Chambers, E.G. (1939), A Study of Accident Proneness Among Motor Drivers.., I.H.R.B. Report No. 84.
46. Foreman, E.H., Ellis, D., and Beavan D. (1983). Mea culpa? A study of the relationships among personality traits, life-events and ascribed accident causation, British Journal of Clinical Psychology, 22, 223-234.

47. Feggetter, (1982), in Foreman, E.H., Ellis, D., and Beavan D. (1983). Mea culpa? A study of the relationships among personality traits, life-events and ascribed accident causation, British Journal of Clinical Psychology, 22, 223-234.
48. Fine, (1963), in Smith, D.I., and Kirkham, R.W. (1981). Relationship between some personality characteristics and driving record, British Journal of Social Psychology, 20, 299-211.
49. Griffiths, D.K. (1985). Safety attitudes of management. Ergonomics, 28, 61-67.
50. Goldstein, (1962), in Crawford, P.L. (1965). Accident prevention through scientific selection, Personnel Journal, 44, 560-571.
51. Greenlund, Kurt Joseph,(1993), " Workers' Health and Safety in The United States: The Effects of Economic Segmentation and Social class".
52. Greenwood, M., and Woods, M. (1919). The incidence of industrial accidents upon individuals with special reference to multiple accidents. Industrial Fatigue Research Board, Report Number 4. London: HMSO.
53. Hakkinen,1958; Tiffin & McCormick,1958; Shaw, 1965, in Tillman, W.A. & Hobles, G.R. (1949) ; Keehm, 1961; Eysenck, 1965, The accident-prone automobile driver: A study of the psychiatric and social background. American Journal of Psychiatry, 106, 321-331.
54. Hale, A.R. (1960), In Craske, S. (1968), A Study of the relation between personality and accident history, British Journal of Medical Psychology 41, 399-404.
55. Hall,(1984), Is safety training worthwhile? Journal of Occupational Accidents, 6, 17-33.
56. Home Woel, ILO (1956), and Model Code of International Safety, Home Woel, ILO Irwin Inc., Illinois.
57. Hansen, C.P. (1988), Personality Characteristics of the accident involved employee, Journal of Business and Psychology, 2, 346-365.
58. Hansen, C.P. (1989), A causal Model of the relationship among accidents, Biodatam, Personality, and Cognitive factors, Journal of Applied Psychology, 74, 81-90.
59. Hart, S. A., and Bartolussi, M.R. (1984). Pilot errors as a source of workload, Human Factors, 26, 545-556.
60. Hoiberg, A. (1980). Sex and occupation deferences in hospitalization rates among navy enlisted personnel. Journal of Occupational Medicine, 22, 685-690.

61. Irwin, J.O. (1941), Comments on Paper by Chambers, E.G. and Yule, G.U., Theory and Observation in the Investigation of Accident Causation, J. Roy. Statics. Soc. (Supplement) VII, 2.
62. Janzen, J.M. (1983), A study of the relationship of locus of control, age, and work experience variables use to discriminate individuals susceptible to industrial in the Sawmill industry, Dissertation.
63. Jimenez, P.P. (1977). Aggressiveness as a cause of accidents. Revistade-Psicologia-General-V-Applicada, 32, 573-579.
64. Jones, 1933; Menninger, (1936), in Craske, S.(1968), A Study of the relation between personality and accident history, British Journal of Medical Psychology 41, 399-404.
65. Jorekog, K.G. and Sorbom D, (1979), Advances in factor analysis and structural equations models. Cambridge, Ma: Abt Books.
66. Jorekog and Sorbom, (1984), LISEL VI. Chicago: International Educational Services.
67. King and Lee, (1976), in Smith, D.I., and Kirkham, R.W. (1981). Relationship between some personality characteristics and driving record, British Journal of Social Psychology, 20, 299-211.
68. Knowles & Kreitman, (1965), in Craske, S. (1968), A Study of the relation between personality and accident history, British Journal of Medical Psychology 41, 399-404.
69. Kjellen, U. and Baneryd, K. (1982). Changing the local safety and health practices at work within the explosives industry. Ergonomics, 26, 863-877.
70. Kjellen, U. (1984). The deviation concept in occupational accident control-1. Accident Analysis and Prevention, 16, 289-306.
71. Krejcie, R.V. and Morgan, D.W. (1979), Determining sample size for research activities, Texas A and M. University.
72. Levin, Oler, and Whiteside, J.P. (1985). Injury incidence in paint company. Accident Analysis and Prevention, 17, 67-73.
73. Levenson, H. (1980). Industrial accidents and recent life events. Journal of Occupational Medicine, 22, 53-57.
74. Lick, Henry Benedict,(1990) "The Effects of Organizational and Environmental Climate Factors on A Joint Union-Management Safety Training".
75. Malcolm S.A. (1995), Social Safety Net: A Review, diseshiah Southern Econ. 33 (19) 1 Feb., 95.
76. Mansuso, J. S. J, (ed.,) m (1983), Occupational clinical psychology, New York: Praeger.
77. Maritz, J.S. (1950), On the Validity of Inferences drawn from the

Fitting if Poisson and Negative Binomial Distribution of Observed Accident Data, Psycho. Bulletin' 47, 5.

78. Mayer, H.E. (1981). On the relationship between an industrial worker's qualitative performance on porteus Maze Tests and reported incidence of industrial accidents. Dissertation Abstracts International, 41, 12-B, 4445.
79. McKenna, S.P. (1978). The effects of first aid training on safety: A field study of approaches and methods. Ph.D. thesis, University of Aston, Birmingham.
80. McKenna, and Hale, A.R. (1982). Changing behavior toward danger: The effect of first aid training. Journal of Occupational Accidents, 4, 47-60.
81. McKenna, F.P. (1983). Accident Proneness: A conceptual analysis. Accident Analysis and Prevention, 15, 65-71.
82. Mcfarland, R.A. (1957), Psychological and Psychiatric aspects of highway Safety, Journal of the American Medical Association, 163, 233-237.
83. Metts, A. (1982). The relationship between work injury and smoking habits among a group of cotton textile workers. Dissertation Abstracts International, 42, 11-b, 4373.
84. Mintz, A. and Blum, M.L., (1949), Are-examination of the Accident-Proneness Concept. Jour. of Appl. Psycho. 33.3.
85. Moffie, D.J. (1952), Relation between psychological tests and driver performance (Highway Research Bulletin.
86. Moffie, (1955), in Crawford, P.L. (1965). Accident prevention through scientific selection, Personnel Journal, 44, 560-571.
87. Naatanen, R. and Summala, H. (1975). A simple method for simulating danger-related aspects of behavior in hazardous activities. Accident Analysis and Prevention, 7, 63-70.
88. Nation Safety Council (1941), Teaching Safety to New Employees, Safe Practices Pamphlet, Nation Safety Council, No. 54, Chicago.
89. National Safety Council, of USA 1978:24-6.
90. Newbold, E.M.(1926), Contribution to the Study of Human Factor in the Causation of Accidents. I.H.R.B. Report No. 34.
91. Newbold, E.M., (1927), Practical Applications to the Statistics and Repeated Events, Particularly of Industrial Accidents. J. Rev. Statis. Soc. 90, 487.
92. Newbold, Farmer and Chamber. (1926), in Arbous, A.G., & Kerrich, J.E. (1951) Accident Statistics The Concept of accident proneness, Biometric, 7, 340-430.

93. Rasmussen, J. (1982). Human error. A taxonomy for describing human malfunction in industrial installations. Journal of Occupational Accidents, 4, 311-333.
94. Reason, J.T. (1985). Slips and mistakes: Two distinct classes of human error? In D.J. Oborne, (ed.), Contemporary Ergonomics 1985. London: Taylor & Fracis.
95. Reber, R.A. and Wallin, J.A., (1983). Validation of a behavioural measure of occupational safety. Journal of Organizational Behaviour Management, S, 69-77.
96. Ruch, Kenneth Elmer(1994), " Factors Influencing Performance in Manufacturing Work Systems: An Examination of Causal Relationships of Organizational Structure and Situations Work place Variables on Proactive Management Behaviour".
97. Saari, J., and Lathela, J. (1981). Work conditions and accidents in three industries. Scandinavian Journal of Environmental Health, 7, 97-105.
98. Sarace, (1978), in Foreman, E.H., Ellis,D., and Beavan D. (1983). Mea culpa? A study of the relationships among personality traits, life-events and ascribed accident causation, British Journal of Clinical Psychology, 22, 223-234.
99. Schelegel, J. (1979). New contributions of psychology to accident prevention. Bulletin de Psychologie, 33, 241-247.
100. Schenk, J., and Rausche, A. (1979). The personality of accident-prone deicers, Psychologie Und Praxis, 23,179-186.
101. Sheehy, Noel P. and Antony J. Chapman, (1987), "Industrial Accidents", International Review of Industrial and Organizational Psychology, Edited by C.L. Cooper and I.T. Robertson, John Wiley & Sons Ltd.
102. Smith, D.I., and Kirkham, R.W. (1981). Relationship between some personality characteristics and driving record, British Journal of Social Psychology, 20, 299-211.
103. Stuart, J.C., and Brown, B.M. (1981). The relationship of stress and coping ability to the incidence of diseases and accidents. Journal of Psychosomatic Research, 25, 255-260.
104. U.S. Dept. of Labour Bureau of Labour Standards (1953) Safety Subject, Bulletin No. 67 (Revised).
105. Taylor, D.H. (1981). The hermeneutics of accidents and safety. Ergonomics, 24, 287-495.
106. Tiffin, 1952, Lawsche, 1952, Schaeffer, 1941, in Crawford, P.L. (1965). Accident prevention through scientific selection, Personnel Journal, 44, 560-571.

107. Tiffin, Parker, and Habersat, 1949, in Crawford, P.L. (1965). Accident prevention through scientific selection, Personnel Journal, 44, 560-571.

108. Tillman, W.A. & Hobles, G.R. (1949) ; Keehm, 1961; Eysenck, 1965, The accident-prone automobile driver: A study of the psychiatric and social background. American Journal of Psychiatry, 106, 321-331.

109. U.S. Department of Commerce Bureau of the Census (1981), Statistical Abstract of the United Sates. National States. National Data Book & Guide to Sources.

110. U.S. Department of Labour Occupational Safety and Health Administration, 1981.

111. Whereas, (1939), in Arbous, A.G., & Kerrich, J.E. (1951) Accident Statistics The Concept of accident proneness, Biometric, 7,340-430.

112. Whitfield, R.A., Zador, P., and Fife (1985). Projected mortality from injuries. Accident Analysis and Prevention, 17, 67-73.

113. Woel, Home, ILO (1956), and Model Code of International Safety, Home Woel, ILO Irwin Inc., Illinois.

114. Wyatt, S., (1947) A Study of Certified Sickness Absence Among Women in Industry. I.H.R.B. Report No. 86.

115. Zohar, D. (1980). Safety climate in industrial organizations. Theoretical and applied implications. Journal of Applied Psychology, 65, 96-102.

Index

D

E

F

J

K

L

M

N

Q

R

S

T

U

V

W

Y

Z